D1236748

✝ CORONADO'S QUEST ✝

CORONADO'S QUEST

The Discovery of the Southwestern States

BY A. GROVE DAY

Berkeley and Los Angeles · 1964

UNIVERSITY OF CALIFORNIA PRESS

92
V393d

UNIVERSITY OF CALIFORNIA PRESS
BERKELEY AND LOS ANGELES
CALIFORNIA

CAMBRIDGE UNIVERSITY PRESS
LONDON, ENGLAND

MANUFACTURED IN THE UNITED STATES OF AMERICA

TO
VIRGINIA

Contents

[vii]

Illustrations

Introduction

THE AMERICAN SOUTHWEST, *that region of sunlit mesas and deep-shadowed canyons, of snow-topped continental rooftrees of rock, of sandy flats and high piny parks, is a land that has never been conquered. It is called the Coronado Country.*

Ten thousand years ago, the Asiatic ancestors of the American Indians began drifting down in swelling waves of migration to make this part of the New World a range for the human species. Four hundred years ago, white men clothed in metal and carrying metal weapons disturbed the Stone Age somnolence of the native tribes to gaze for the first time on the virginal grandeur of this land.

They came, they saw, they thought they conquered. From their base in Mexico, no longer the domain of proud Montezuma, the iron men of Iberia struggled northward by sea and by land. Into the lap of Mother Spain, then mistress of the world's mightiest empire, they showered parchment documents giving claim to a quarter of a continent and the adjacent seas. Spanish

navigators sailed the vermilion waters of the Gulf of
California; Spanish expeditionary forces gazed in won-
derment and awe across the Grand Canyon of the Colorado. The Spanish war cry of "St. James!" mingled with
the whoops of embattled pueblo dwellers in the "new"
Mexico. Centuries before the time of Carson, Pike,
or Frémont, sturdy Andalusian chargers pursued the
thundering buffalo along the banks of the Arkansas.
The banner of Charles V, emperor of the Holy Roman
Empire, floated over an immensity of empty American
prairie. A lifetime before English was spoken in any
home between the Arctic Pole and Cape Horn, the conquistadores under the leadership of young Francisco
Vásquez Coronado, their golden-helmed general, dwelt
in the walled stone towns of the American Southwest.

It was not yet called the Southwest in the days when
the spirit of the conqueror burned fervidly in the heart
of every Spanish youth. Nor was the first invasion of
our country beyond the Mississippi a "westward movement"; it was a northward movement.

The first act in the unfolding drama of Spanish occupation of this continent began when the voyages of
Columbus opened the way for the colonization of the
West Indian islands and the east coast of Central America. The second act was the conquest of the Mexican
plateau by Fernando Cortés and the founding of magnificent imperial colonies southward to the Isthmus.
The third act opened in the year 1540 when Francisco
Vásquez Coronado led northward from Mexico the
most notable and far-reaching exploring expedition

ever to set foot on the soil of what is now the United States of America.

At the close of the conquest of Mexico, mystery still blanketed most of the North American continent. Almost every mile of ground north of the twentieth parallel was terra incognita. No one in the civilized world could with assurance sketch even the crudest map delineating the shape of that quarter of the globe. Mexico might be a part of a great island-continent barring the direct east–west sea road to the spiceries of the Orient. It was more likely, the wiseacres thought, a southern extension of the Asian mainland, a great peninsula of India Superior. Or ocean might cover the north, and those blank spaces on the maps could be filled by sketches of dolphins and sea monsters and caravels under full sail.

The dark blanket had been lifted, it is true, along a few hundred leagues of coast line on the Atlantic. John Cabot and his son Sebastian, Venetian mariners in the service of England, as early as 1497 sailed down from the codfish banks of Newfoundland for an indeterminate distance south, and for bringing this seaboard under England's claim were rewarded by a free gift of ten pounds. In 1513, in the flowery Easter season, Juan Ponce de León touched the "island" of Florida and gave it its name, and by 1519 Alonso Alvárez Pineda had charted the Gulf of Mexico from Florida to the river of Pánuco, a point which Juan de Grijalva had reached coming northward around Yucatán in the previous year. The region between the mouth of the Pánuco, near

modern Tampico, and the Río de Palmas to the north of
it was the scene of an attempted settlement by Francisco
de Garay in 1523. In 1521, when Ponce de León was making a second attempt to settle the Land of Youth, Lucas
Vásquez de Ayllón touched near the Cape Fear River
on the Carolina coast, and five years later he returned
to set up at the mouth of the Savannah River the ill-
fated colony of San Miguel de Gualdape. And in 1528
Pánfilo de Narváez, thinking he had arrived at the
mouth of the Río de Palmas where he had permission
to set up a colony, landed in Florida at Tampa Bay and
began his disastrous march inland, on the first exploration of the interior of our southern states.

Efforts at discovery on the Mexican mainland resulted in equally meager accomplishment. Immediately after the fall of the Aztec capital, Fernando Cortés,
first and greatest of the conquistadores, sent out his
lieutenants, Sandoval, Olid, and Pedro de Alvarado, to
explore the surrounding country, but, with the exception of the establishment in 1522 of the town of San
Esteban del Puerto at the mouth of the Pánuco to forestall the claims of Garay, all these efforts were directed
to the west, where settlements were made along the Pacific, and to the south, joining up the explored mainland with newly discovered areas spreading out from
Balboa's Isthmus of Darien. By 1525 the imperial province of New Spain, forged by Cortés, reached its greatest extent, stretching from Colima to El Salvador on
the west and from Pánuco to Honduras on the east. It
was only then that the great conqueror began to turn

his attention to the northern lands. But there the way was blocked to him for years, and even as late as 1530 the town of Colima, due west of Mexico City, remained the northern Spanish outpost in the region bordering on the South Sea.

Cortés, like Coronado after him, was led on by native tales and by extravagant legends. Travelers' tales as often as not were the inspiration that drew the early explorers over many a weary league of emerald jungle or sandy waste. Legend was fed not only by legend, but by reality. It is no marvel that these straying Iberians should have found marvels, for the New World was bursting with rare sights. Eldorado had been found time and again. Nothing in the pages of any of the popular romances of chivalry could have prepared the conquerors for the sight of the empires of Montezuma or Atahualpa. What reason, then, to doubt that beyond the next summit might be found another Tenochtitlán, another Cuzco? Or even the New Jerusalem, the palace of the Grand Cham, the city of Prester John? Monsters and wonders they had seen in plenty. Gold there was, gold to be poured out on dicing tables, gold for the captain, gold—a fifth of all the gold—for the king. On, then, in pursuit of the dream, the new-old legend!

Cortés, chasing a legend, spent the latter years of his active life in attempting to wrest the secret of the north from darkness, but not even his imaginative brain could give him an inkling of the magnificent territories that lay beyond his reach. Past the borders of the known was a wild and grand expanse which still challenges the

*imagination. But as far as ran the knowledge of civil-
ized men, that land might as well have lain on the dark
side of the moon. Horrors might hover over every mile.
The venturesome discoverer would at least expect to
find impassable mountains, enormous lakes, intermi-
nable deserts, raging rivers. He might be engulfed in
chasms, or be shriveled in the blasts from titanic vol-
canoes. If men could live anywhere there, they might
be savage demons, the Devil's own helpers, or they
might be resplendent kings and superhuman sages, for-
got by the world since the Golden Age.*

*Coronado and his companions were to change all
that, to bring light from the darkness, to widen the girdle of the known. They were to find the mountains and
the rivers, to cross the deserts and descend the chasms,
and to mark on their crude maps the ways thither. They
were to find many a savage and a few wiser natives, and
one malignant man who in their eyes was certainly tu-
tored at the throne of hell. The marvels that they met
were brought back with them, ensnared in words, to
dazzle the eyes of their monarch and his councilors; and
a brave new world was opened to the wonder, the enterprise, the avarice, and the benevolence of the white
race.*

*The story of Coronado's quest for Cíbola and Qui-
vira, "on the backe side of Florida," is the old story of
the discoverer soul. The plot is the struggle of men
against space and time, the conflict of men and men,
the conquest of the unknown. The modern history of
the Southwest begins with the penetration of that im-*

mense territory by the Spaniards under Coronado's command. His is the gallant figure that must typify the adventure of exploration in that part of the New World.

To the Spanish Crown, Coronado brought in tribute his claim to the magnificent domain stretching from Kansas to California. Under his leadership, white men first grappled with the roughhewn mysteries of those lands, and stamped the brand of Spain upon a fourth of the area of the United States. His luck and his un-luck were both so great that it is only now, four centuries after his gallant dash into the heart of America, that we may venture to appraise either the man or his acts—Francisco Vásquez Coronado, governor of New Galicia, soldier of Spain, crusader, gold-hunter, legend-chaser, the last of the great conquistadores.

In preparing this the first biography of Francisco Vásquez Coronado, the writer has felt a keen obligation to the highest historical accuracy. This book is based primarily upon a study, covering some years, of all the extant original documents dealing with Coronado and his period and with the discovery of the Southwest. This study of originals has been supplemented by a scrutiny of all the important secondary works and research papers—archaeological and ethnological, as well as purely historical—which treat these subjects. Finally, much of the territory covered by the Coronado expedition has been retraced, in Mexico as well as among the plains and mountains of the southwestern United States. Documentary evidence may be quoted for virtually every detail in the pages that follow. It is hoped that the Bibliography and the Chronology will be especially useful to students of the period.

Celebration of the Coronado Cuarto Centennial throughout the southwestern states makes 1940 the most appropriate year for the publication of this biography of the discoverer. The story of Coronado's journey in our Southwest exactly four hundred years ago may be read for its own worth as a brave adventure with which every American should be familiar. But to a great extent, this section of the United States, which was explored many years before the English colonies on the Atlantic seaboard were planted, is still a frontier. One can best understand the present and future development of the Southwest by comprehending its beginnings, when the forces that are making its destiny first germinated. The modern history of the American Southwest opens with the epic of Francisco Vásquez Coronado.

A. G. D.

STANFORD UNIVERSITY, CALIFORNIA
May, 1940

CORONADO'S QUEST

The Northern Mystery
Summer, 1536

FERNANDO CORTÉS, first and greatest conqueror of the New World, stared gloomily from the terrace of his new palace in Cuernavaca. He stood in his old defiant pose, jutting out his fox-brush of a beard, fast graying in these days.

Unseeing, he gazed over the palm-dotted valley, where lay the fields of sugar cane he had planted. His eyes swept beyond, to the horizon, where the misty snows atop sleeping Popocatepetl seemed to hang suspended.

Cuernavaca, the most charming valley in the world for a man wishing to spend his latter days in peace. But Fernando Cortés had never been a peaceful man. Now, fifteen years after the conquest of Montezuma's empire, Fernando Cortés was by royal patent Marquis of the Valley of Oaxaca and Captain General of New Spain and the Coasts of the South Sea. A thumping title; but to its owner it gave no more real power than had once

been wielded by the bold young soldier who had kid-
naped Montezuma from his own palace. Yonder, toward
Popo, lay the capital city of Mexico, which Cortés and
his men had wrested from the Aztec lords; and in that
city sat a new ruler of Mexico, a viceroy sent by suspicious Spain to check the latest designs of the Marquis
Cortés.

Yes, and beyond this narrow valley of Cuernavaca lay
all the great province of New Spain, which Fernando
Cortés and his men had brought as a loyal gift into the
empire of Charles V. A domain several times the size of
Old Spain, it extended from the Tropic of Cancer south
to the Isthmus of Darien. And the man who had found
and welded that wide kingdom of terra firma was now
exiled from the capital city that he had built on the
ruins of Aztec palaces!

Those new rulers of New Spain, the viceroy and
the rest, could not long hope to keep the eagle spirit
penned in a narrow valley. Cortés, shut out of partici-
pation in the civil administration of the province, his
advice no longer sought even on military affairs, still
held the royal license to explore, conquer, and settle
any new islands found in the South Sea, as well as
any part of the mainland coast not already discovered.
Cortés had found Mexico; now, to retrieve fortune, he
must find another Mexico. Northward, up the coasts
bordering on the great South Sea, the new Mexico must
lie. It must be found. By St. James, it would be found!

This time, no futile searching for Amazons. It was
brave young Gonzalo Sandoval who had heard, years

ago on the coast of Colima, of a northern island where lived no men, but only women who were warriors and who wore pearls and plates of gold.[1] That old tale was captivating enough to inspire the greed of a Nuño de Guzmán. But Fernando Cortés would seek other things quite as rich—the spiceries of the Orient.

Those riches were there. Nine years ago, one of two ships sent westward by Cortés had reached the fragrant Moluccas. There must be a shorter way, a way along the coasts, a route not haunted by the specter of scurvy, a safe way from Spain to the Grand China. All explorations to the south of Mexico had revealed no clue to a strait cutting through the New World. The secret must lie, then, to the north.

If, as many geographers thought, Mexico was part of the continent of Asia, the Cathay of Marco Polo, then by cruising northward along the coasts a mariner might come at last to India.[2] If, however, America were a separate continent, by cruising northward a mariner could find the place where the land gave way to ocean, thus affording an outlet eastward to the Atlantic. That would be a discovery! A northwest passage,[3] a short route from Spain to India, by way of New Spain! It was inconceivable that America Septentrional could extend to the regions of the pole.

True, all the efforts of Cortés to find that passage had so far been futile. "The nuts were not worth the noise," another might have said. Three fine expeditions, gone to disaster on that savage northern coast.

---

[1] For notes to the Prologue, see pp. 325–327.

Balor R.

Oceano Septen trional

Tierra del Laborador

Tangut R.

Tierm del Bacalaos

India Superior

Catayo R

Mangi R

India

La florida

Zagatai

La china

Nueva hispania

pegu

merico

Malucho

nombre de dio

hispagnola

gilolo.

mar del Sur

Cafnlla del oro

Soma tra

liaua

El Brasil

El Peru

Oceano meridional

Strecho de Fernande magalhaes

Tierra del Fuego

THE NEW WORLD AS MAPPED IN 1548

This misconception of the New World as an extension of Asia was current at about the time Cortés began exploring the northern Pacific coast. (From map of world in Ptolemy atlas, Venice, 1548.)

Two good ships lost with Cousin Diego Hurtado de Mendoza in 1532. A year later, two more ships sent with Cousin Diego de Becerra up the great gulf washing between the west coast of New Spain and the other shore where lay the Amazonian island of Santa Cruz.[4] The Gulf of Cortés.[5] The island of Santa Cruz, where that Basque pilot Jiménez, the mutineer who had killed Becerra, his captain, had in turn been killed by Indians. Bloody Santa Cruz, called California!

And then the third cast of the die, the expedition of last year to colonize the mainland at Santa Cruz. It had been a great mustering, with Marquis Cortés himself to lead it. His name had been enough to attract three or four hundred men, good men, not only soldiers, but blacksmiths, carpenters, surgeons. The shipload of negro slaves—that had been a mistake. Cortés, whose memories of Santa Cruz were still tender, felt in recollection the sharp pangs of the belly. It had all been mistake after mistake, the lack of provisions the worst. Cortés remembered ruefully the voyage he had made to the mainland to gather food in the west-coast domains of Guzmán. The return trip, when Cortés himself had had to take the wheel from the pilot, who was killed by a falling yard, and the ship had been driven far out of her course. The day when they had stumbled at last upon the mouth of Santa Cruz; and how half the colonists who had not died before of hunger now died of overeating.

Yet Cortés would not have given up Santa Cruz, called California, had it not been for the prayers of his wife and friends, combined with the threat personified in the new viceroy, Mendoza. And so here he was, back in New Spain and penned in the old narrow valley.

California.⁶ That had been an ironical name enough. Everybody knew the passage in that storybook, *The Exploits of Esplandián:*⁷ "Know that on the right hand of the Indies there is an island called California, very close to the side of the Terrestrial Paradise; and it was peopled by black women, without any man among them, for they lived in the fashion of Amazons. Their island was the strongest in all the world, with its steep cliffs and rocky shores. Their arms were all of gold, and so was the harness of the wild beasts which they tamed to ride; for in the whole island there was no metal but gold."

The island of fabled Queen Calafía. Well, Santa Cruz had certainly been no terrestrial paradise! A fool's paradise, rather. Perhaps there were gold and pearls; there were certainly steep cliffs and rocky shores.

But what lay beyond California? The Northwest Passage, perhaps. It must be found. There was only one way to find it. Another fleet must somehow be built, and money for the search must be raised. Cortés would pawn his wife's jewels, if need be. Beyond California must lie the new Mexico that was ripe for the hand of a conqueror. The shipyards of Tehuántepec and Zacatula would be busy again, building a fleet for Cortés to send to the new lands.

Again the dark look of conquest came to the face of Fernando Cortés. He turned with new decision to give the first orders. The viceroy yonder in Mexico would stop him if he could. The world was filled with the enemies of Fernando Cortés. But the final cast of fortune must be made if he was to win again to power. It might be necessary for Cortés to journey to Spain to get his rights. He had done it once before. He, Cortés the Marquis, had given Charles V more provinces than the emperor's ancestors had left him cities! Surely he would not be cast aside now, like a worn-out blade. . . .

Cortés, standing there on the terrace overlooking his sunny vale of peace, guessed that he might have to go to Spain. He could not guess that he would stay in Spain until he died, and nevermore look upon the New Spain he had conquered. In Spain he would die; Fernando Cortés was never to see the new lands that lay beyond California.

Nuño de Guzmán, governor of New Galicia, stood on the balcony of his house in his tiny capital town of Compostela, near the coast of the great South Sea. He scratched his chin and looked after the little cavalcade that was vanishing down the road to the east, on its way to Mexico. Those four wandering men would have a pretty tale to tell the viceroy, but it could not be helped.

There, under escort, went Cabeza de Vaca and his three companions—the shipwrecked Spaniards who had walked for a thousand weary leagues, from the Northern Sea of Florida all the way across a great unknown interior country, to come out near the Southern Sea at

Guzmán's town of Culiacán. Cabeza de Vaca—"Cow's Head."[8] A strange sobriquet; and Cabeza de Vaca was a strange man enough. If Cabeza de Vaca's story were true, then Nuño de Guzmán would have to go conquering again.

Guzmán had come far since the days when, as a bustling young lawyer, he had got himself made president of the province of Pánuco. After that it had been easy to get himself made president of the first *audiencia* of New Spain. Then had followed a riotous year of unchecked power. He had been a little king for the while. The pickings had been good; but Guzmán and his friends had stirred up too many hornet's nests, and excommunication by an irate Church was nothing to sneer at. And so the only thing to do was to play the conqueror. Cortés had been in Spain; it was a good time to steal his thunder and set off to find that island of Amazons, with its pearls and gold.

They should have succeeded. Guzmán's army of conquest had been strong—two hundred good Spanish horsemen and three hundred foot soldiers, not counting the eight thousand Indians drafted into the service. They had made a good march to the north in the spring of 1530 and discovered two provinces, Jalisco and Sinaloa, to add to the Crown of Spain. But they had found neither gold nor pearls; and conquests must be paid for. Of course it was against the law to take slaves unless the tribes were hostile; but it was easy enough to make a tribe rebellious, and burning their villages was a sure way. As for anybody appealing to the law—well,

in those fine days Guzmán had been the only law recognized in Mexico![9]

And then, after a full year of marching, two hundred
leagues[10] north of Colima, they had come to Ciguatán,
the country of the Amazons. They had discovered the
bitter truth of the oft-repeated fable. The villages on
the river of Ciguatán were inhabited only by women
and children. Their men had been warned of the approach of the warring Spaniards, and had departed to
hide in the hills. No gold, no pearls were to be found
anywhere.

Then had begun the wearisome efforts to push beyond, grappling with the terrible mountains of the interior, toward Topira, where the warriors were said to
wear armor of gold. Hopeless, the assaults on that great
mountain barrier! Then the building of the town of
San Miguel de Culiacán,[11] still the outpost of Guzmán's
province of New Galicia. A fine province. What a pity
that he now had to take orders in most things from the
busy viceroy in Mexico!

Had Guzmán not fallen ill five years ago, he told
himself, he and his men might have found the path
northward that this Cabeza de Vaca had recently followed southward to Culiacán.[12] Guzmán would have
learned the secrets of the hardy tribes that had turned
back the expeditions which he had sent out from Culiacán. He might have gone beyond and found a new
Mexico in the north. There were rich cities there. Did
not Cabeza de Vaca say he had heard from the Indians
that to the north were pueblos with many inhabitants

and very large houses of stone, four and five stories high? And in the village that Cabeza de Vaca called Hearts[13] the Indians had presented him with turquoises and five arrows tipped with emeralds![14]

Yes, Guzmán might have found those pueblos, had he not fallen ill. And then Cortés had returned from Spain, with new honors—a marquis, no less!—and with a royal license to explore by sea. Cortés was the great enemy; the conqueror had never forgotten how Guzmán had helped to press the charges against him during the trial of 1526.[15] Well, Guzmán had done what he could to thwart the sea expeditions of Cortés. But Guzmán nowadays had plenty to do to keep his hands on his province of New Galicia, to which he had been banished. There had been talk of a trial. And now this licentiate Diego de la Torre would soon be arriving in Compostela to hold a formal inquiry upon Guzmán's acts.

It would be impossible to get away to the north until De la Torre was disposed of somehow. A curse on the meddlesome viceroy in Mexico City! Cabeza de Vaca would go straight to him with his wonderful story, of course; and Mendoza was a man who could understand a nod, a man who well knew how to lick his own fingers. Mendoza would not let another royal officer push ahead of him if it came to discovering cities of great wealth in the north.

Those pueblos that Cabeza de Vaca reported were the Seven Cities of the Bishops. Guzmán was sure of it. He recalled once more the old tale. After the invading

Moors captured Mérida in Spain, eight hundred years
ago, the fugitive Christians fled to the seacoast, and
there took ship under the guidance of the archbishop
of Oporto and six other holy bishops. They wished to
find haven in the Fortunate Isles, but their fleet was
blown far out into the Western Ocean; and reaching
the great island of Antilia, they burned their ships and
built seven cities. A Portuguese mariner asserted that
he had seen this paradise, where even the sands of the
beach were one-third pure gold. But Columbus in all
his voyaging had not found Antilia, and now some
knowing mapmakers thought that the cities of the
bishops, *Septem Civitates,* were to be searched for on
the New World mainland to the north of Florida.[16]
What if the rumored pueblos of Cabeza de Vaca were
the golden Seven Cities?

Now Guzmán remembered the tale of Tejo. He had
always believed that story. Tejo,[17] an Indian of the valley of Oxitipar, had come into his service when Guzmán had been governor of Pánuco, in which province
the valley lay. Tejo had maintained that when he was
a small boy he had accompanied his father, a trader
long dead, into the back country north of Pánuco to
exchange parrot feathers for the plentiful gold to be
found there. Tejo had gone with his father more than
once, and had seen seven very large towns, like the
towns about Mexico, with streets filled with the shops
of silversmiths. To get to these cities, said Tejo, one had
to travel northward from Pánuco, between the two seas,
for forty days through a desert where nothing grew ex-

cept grass of less than a hand-span in height.[18] Could the cities visited by Tejo be the Seven Cities of the old legend?

Again, everyone in Mexico knew the tale about Aztlán. The Aztec priests asserted that the birthplace of their nation was to be found at Aztlán or the "place of herons"—seven great caves to the northwest, from which the seven Nahua tribes had migrated in the old time.[19] These seven "caves" might well be the seven cities of which Cabeza de Vaca had heard!

Guzmán had tried to worm all the information he could from this Cabeza de Vaca fellow. The man had been royal treasurer with the expedition of headstrong Pánfilo de Narváez, which had vanished into Florida in 1528. A horrible tale, that was, of shipwreck and starvation and plague and even cannibalism. Of all that great force, only Cabeza de Vaca and his three companions were now alive, and they had existed for six years in vile slavery to the Indians of the regions north of Pánuco. Then Cabeza de Vaca and Castillo Maldonado and Dorantes, along with Esteban, the negro slave, had escaped and begun their year's march toward the setting sun. Guzmán had gathered that the travelers had held themselves up before the Indians as white workers of magic and healers of the flesh; it was certain that when Guzmán's man Diego de Alcaraz had stumbled upon the tattered wanderers, north of Culiacán, Cabeza de Vaca was being followed by six hundred stout Indians from Corazones, who worshiped him as a god, a Child of the Sun.

When Guzmán had received them at Compostela, Cabeza de Vaca and his three companions, even after their six weeks of rest at Culiacán, looked still like men who had spent six years in slavery. They were mightily bearded, burnt black by the sun, emaciated as skeletons from eating desert herbs and even stewed ants. Guzmán had given the four peregrines some of his own garments to wear—after all, it might pay to appear friendly to them. But Cabeza de Vaca had confessed in Spanish rusty from disuse that these clothes were worse than a horsehair shirt of penance to one who for years had gone in naught but a breechclout. Nor could they find rest on the soft beds Guzmán had showed them—so long had the wanderers slept on the ground they could find ease nowhere else.

Cabeza de Vaca had been wrathful much of the time, too, all because of the trick that Diego de Alcaraz had tried to play in the matter of those six hundred Indians. Alcaraz, naturally, had snared and chained the Indians to use as slaves, which were very scarce nowadays in New Galicia; but Cabeza de Vaca, perhaps because he had been a slave himself, had made such an outcry before Melchor Díaz, mayor of Culiacán, that the Indians had been freed and had been allowed to settle at Bamoa. Those Indians would make good interpreters, if an expedition could be formed by Guzmán to march north and find the Seven Cities.

Guzmán mopped his brow, and retreated into the shade of his house, away from the July sun. That was the great question now—how to get an expedition together. Tejo had died on the return from Culiacán; he could not lead the party—but other guides might be found. If any expedition were to be sent, surely Nuño de Guzmán should command it! He was conqueror of New Galicia and governor, and had formally claimed for the Crown all lands lying northward of it. His men at Culiacán were close to the new land. Any expedition would have to pass through New Galicia and use Culiacán as a base. Of course, Cortés would be difficult, and Mendoza would oppose everybody. Nuño de Guzmán was not now, alas, the only law in Mexico! But once this troublesome De la Torre, with his royal order to hold an inquiry upon the deeds of Guzmán, was put out of the way, then—to the north! To the Seven Cities! ...

But Nuño de Guzmán, like his rival Cortés, was to go back to Spain—to die there in a common jail. Nuño de Guzmán was never to go upon any expedition to the pueblos north of New Galicia.

Antonio de Mendoza, first viceroy of New Spain, Count of Tendilla, Mendoza the Good, sat in his vice-regal chair in his audience room in the Casa de los Cabildos, overlooking the great plaza of Mexico City.

Knight of Santiago, cousin to the archbishop of Seville, and a relative of the royal house, he looked to be what in truth he was, an alert and gifted administrator. Black-bearded, ruffed, sharp-eyed, with a high forehead and a hawk's-beak nose, he was the most important personage in the New World. A skilled organizer, legal-minded, just, listening to the lowliest of his people but taking orders from none save his imperial master, he was more than able to deal with the lawless ferocity of a Guzmán, able to deal even with the stubborn desperation of an aging Cortés.

Four men had just left the chamber—Cabeza de Vaca and his companions. They had spoken briefly of their almost incredible odyssey through the deserts of the north; and now they had gone to repose themselves after the hard journey to Mexico and to enjoy the bountiful hospitality of Mexico's viceroy. Behind them they had left in Mendoza's brain the seed of a rich idea.

The viceroy had listened eagerly to the tale. Beyond those deserts lay great cities of emeralds, of gold, of South Sea pearls. An Indian had been seen who wore a copper bell figured with a carven face. In those lands, the natives wore sewn skins and planted maize. Beyond the desert lay a large land mass between the oceans, and this virginal country might extend even to the boreal circle, and be filled with multitudes of pagan souls. Here was an adventure in which the most powerful magistrate of the Crown in New Spain might find profit for the Crown, and employment for the long-sworded *caballeros* who had accompanied the new viceroy to the land of Montezuma. Gold—emeralds—heathen souls to be brought to God!

Of course, it might be some time before a great expedition could be organized to follow the clues brought by Cabeza de Vaca. Money must be raised, a royal commission must be won, and all other contenders for the right to discover—such as Fernando Cortés—must first be eliminated from the field. Mendoza had been in Mexico for less than a year, and, although many things had been put to rights, a myriad crowding needs still claimed his labor. Public safety must come first; he had no more than a thousand soldiers under his command in the city, and the supply of arms and powder was woefully low. What if an Indian rebellion should break out? Or a negro revolt? Already there were almost as many negro slaves in New Spain as there were Spaniards. Yes, it might be some time before Mendoza would be free to send explorers to look for an Eldorado to the north.

But such a discovery would be to the highest interests of the Crown. The viceroyalty was still on trial. The sure way to make the viceroy esteemed at home and abroad would be for him to add new lands to the empire of Spain—lands, in particular, that would contribute to the swelling flood of gold and jewels that must keep pouring into the coffers of conquering Charles V. Cortés, the Marquis of the Valley, had won everything he had by a single bold venture in discovery and conquest. Now, that same Cortés was feverishly hunting a second Mexico by sea. For all Mendoza knew, a third voyage to the country of Santa Cruz might end not in failure, but in the discovery of a treasure house in the north. Any sort of alliance with Cortés was out of the question; there was no room in Mexico for two viceroys. Anyone making partnership with Cortés might well share the fate of Diego Velásquez, former governor of Cuba, who, much to his loss, had been the earliest backer of the ambitious Cortés. No; if another Eldorado was to be found beyond New Spain, it should be found by a royal party sent out by the emperor's first officer in New Spain!

Trustworthy guides would be needed to find that northern country of high stone houses. Could Cabeza de Vaca be persuaded to return to the land of his torments? Mendoza thought not. Cabeza de Vaca was all on fire to go to Spain. The wanderer had eaten the bitter crust of slavery among an alien race. Now he dreamed of getting the emperor's ear and winning the right to colonize Florida, to make of it an earthly heaven where slavery would be unknown. Cabeza de Vaca, with such hopes glowing in his heart, would not long remain in Mexico.

Well, then, perhaps one or both of his Spanish companions—Castillo Maldonado and Dorantes—would guide an expedition. Or even the Moorish negro, Dorantes' man Esteban, would serve. The black man knew the trails, as well as the speech of the Indians in those lands. When the time came, Mendoza was sure that he could persuade one of these three peregrines to guide an exploring party. Meanwhile, he would do all he could to recompense Castillo Maldonado and Dorantes for their sufferings in the wilderness. Perhaps a wealthy marriage could be arranged for each of them.

It might be well to send some clever person through New Galicia with a small band of guides to verify some of the points of the Cabeza de Vaca journey, to spy out the land before any large army was got together to make a conquest. A person with all the proper qualifications might not be easy to find; but sooner or later the viceroy would find him.

Mendoza clapped his hands in sudden determination. "Ho, Francisco!"

From the next room appeared his personal secretary. "Your excellency, I am here."

"What do you think of the story we heard from these shipwrecked mariners? A new Mexico to be found beyond the deserts of the north, eh?"

"I think, your excellency, that much glory and gain could be won for the king in the discovery of those lands."

"So do I, young hidalgo. They have promised to make me a map, showing the way to this new country. I should like to lead an army there, if ever I am free to go. And when that time comes, you, of course, shall go with me, Francisco Vásquez Coronado!"

But Viceroy Mendoza was not fated to go to the new Mexico in the north.

Bearded, black-skinned Esteban, Dorantes' man Stephen, who had trodden the unknown *llanos* of the mysterious north, now walked the streets of a bustling city, swaggering and boasting among the many negro slaves of the capital. He who had lived on scrapings of hide and mesquite beans mixed with clay now gorged on rich foods that he had forgotten existed. Born in Azimur on the Atlantic coast of Morocco to a life of servitude, he had been a sharer in what was surely the greatest overland journey in all history. With relish he told over and over the tale of those wanderings, delighting at the astonishment of his hearers, who listened popeyed with wonder.

Yet these simple pleasures soon began to bore Esteban. Here in Mexico he was still a slave. More and more he looked back on the days when he had escaped with his white companions and made the great march toward the setting sun.

It has been a triumphal progress. At each village the inhabitants had heaped up all their possessions as gifts; and Cabeza de Vaca blessed the gifts and returned them to their owners. Always they were accompanied on their way by hordes of rejoicing Indians who shouted to the heavens of the holiness and miraculous healing skill of the white wizards.

In those days black Esteban had been in his glory. He was the one to march in advance of the procession, leading the Children of the Sun to the land of the sun. He it was who organized the reception at each new town on the route, gleaning information about the villages ahead, speaking with a thick-lipped drawl the dialects he had picked up, grinning at the shy Indian womenfolk. He had pranced ahead always, an ebon major-domo, beating a drum of hide and shaking a bright-feathered gourd rattle, gift of a medicine man of the plains. Esteban still had that rattle; he knew its power over the Indians. He had been himself a noted medicine man, a maker of magic. But here in Mexico he was again a slave.

Some day, Esteban promised himself, he would shake

off slavery and return to that land in the north. He knew the trails better than anyone. He was a famous figure among the Indians, could speak many of their tribal tongues, and was expert in the sign language of the prairie. A medicine man of his stature could grow rich by free gifts from the Indians. Yes, some day Esteban of Azimur would return to the north! . . .

He could not dream that in the north he would meet the strangest adventure of all. For this lowliest of wanderers, this humblest member of the company that had discovered Texas and the north Mexican states, was by a whim of destiny to become the undisputed discoverer, in his lone right, of the states of New Mexico and Arizona,[20] the black ambassador of the white race to the red men of the walled pueblos. He would live to prance arrogantly, plumed rattle in hand, into the Seven Cities, there to meet a curious doom that is still recounted beside tribal campfires in the heart of the American Southwest.

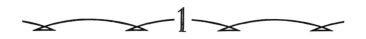

Fledgling Conquistador

1510–1539

A YOUNG MAN with a career before him was among the train of Don Antonio de Mendoza when the first viceroy of New Spain entered Mexico in 1535. He was a young hidalgo bearing the proud name of Francisco Vásquez Coronado.[1]

His forebears had come from France and were "descendants of the house and royal blood of France,"[2] bearing on their early escutcheon three silver fleurs-de-lis on a blue field. The Spanish branch was established by Vasco Rodríguez, Master of the Order of Santiago in 1324 and governor of Castile; his brother, Gonzalo Rodríguez, Great Commander of León; and their sister, Teresa Rodríguez de Balboa. The family first settled in the province of Galicia and took their surname of De Cornado, or Coronado, from the village of Cornado near Coruña, whence they spread to several other places in northern Spain, notably to Salamanca. The Salamanca branch took the name of Vásquez de Coro-

---

[1] For notes to chap. 1, see pp. 327–329.

nado, a name that soon grew illustrious in the bishopric. The arms of the Vásquez branch were a rampant golden lion, crowned (*coronado* in the Spanish tongue) with gold, all on a field of red with a golden bordure having eight blue fleurs-de-lis.

Francisco was born in Salamanca about 1510, second son of Juan Vásquez de Coronado, Lord of Coquilla, and Isabel de Luxán. When Francisco was a lad of ten, his father signed a paper that was to have its effect upon the future careers of his sons. Juan Vásquez had almost lost his own inheritance because of a lawsuit which had been brought against him by the children of his father's second wife. He therefore decided to guard his children from similar legal troubles by creating a *mayorazgo,* or entailed estate, passing from eldest son to eldest son.[3]

Through this document Gonzalo, the eldest of the four sons of Juan Vásquez, became the fortunate heir. Two daughters became nuns, and suitable endowments were made to their convents. Francisco and any younger brothers were to be given outright sums in return for relinquishing all claims upon the estate. With their expectations thus early cut off, the boys had to forge their own fortunes. They did so, with the result that Francisco's younger brothers are also known to history's pages. Juan Vásquez, who was born in 1523, landed in Mexico in 1540 and twenty years later became the first governor of Costa Rica. Pedro, the youngest, accompanied Philip II to England for the marriage in 1554 with Queen Mary, and later fought valiantly in the navy of Don Juan of Austria.

In the days when Francisco Vásquez Coronado was a youth, Spain was building the largest empire that the world has ever known. The proper field of endeavor for a well-born young man was therefore either at court or in the colonies. Francisco went to court, and there he met Don Antonio de Mendoza; when the new viceroy entered Mexico, Francisco was in his retinue, sword at side, and before him great hopes of taking a leading part in the discovery of new lands to add to Spain's colonial possessions in America.

Mendoza, from the start, was much impressed by the young man's abilities, and soon Coronado was working intimately at the viceroy's side as a sort of secretary and chamberlain. Through the cordial interest of Mendoza, the fledgling conqueror was shortly to gain both lands and an alliance with a powerful family of Mexico.

Before two years had passed, Coronado made a brilliant marriage with Beatriz de Estrada. She was a daughter of Alonso de Estrada, who before his death in 1530 had been royal treasurer of New Spain and a man of wealth and power. Estrada never made any secret of the fact that he was a son, on the wrong side of the blanket,* of his high majesty King Ferdinand, founder of the Spanish Empire; and thus the bride of Coronado was blood cousin to the reigning emperor, Charles V.

The Estrada family was among the most prominent in the capital. A sister of Beatriz had married Jorge de Alvarado, one of five brothers who had been captains under Cortés in the Conquest; Jorge had left the wars and was now succeeding his father-in-law as royal treasurer. A brother of Beatriz was in the Church, an author who as Fray Juan de Magdalena had translated from the Latin the *Escala Espiritual de San Juan Climaco*, which was published in 1536, the first book printed in the Western Hemisphere.[5]

The widowed mother of Beatriz, Doña María Gutiérrez Flores de la Caballería, who had often complained to the king of the difficulty of finding suitable young men to wed her daughters in outlandish Mexico, must have been pleased with her new son-in-law, for with his bride Coronado received as dowry a large estate, "the half of Tlapa,"[6] bringing an income of more than three thousand ducats.

At this time Coronado also obtained by royal grant[7] the estate of one Juan de Burgos, who had forfeited his rights by persistently refusing to leave the ranks of bachelordom. It was the desire of the emperor to encourage colonists who, like Coronado, would settle down and produce heirs, and a royal decree had forbidden the holding of land grants by unmarried men.

Coronado's marriage, although it made him a man of position and property, was also something of a love match. Doña Beatriz was a noble and comely lady, and Coronado was to show himself on at least one occasion to be fantastically jealous. The future leader of the northern expedition had already given hostages to fortune. There were to be many who would come to say afterward, as did the soldier-chronicler Pedro de Castañeda, that the members of that expedition "were unfortunate in having a captain who left in New Spain estates and a pretty wife, a noble and excellent lady, which were not the least causes for what was to happen."[8]

The long-feared negro uprising in New Spain gave Coronado a chance to win his spurs in command of a military force. The revolt of the black slaves against their Spanish masters, resulting from a widespread plot, came in September, 1536, but was stamped out after some bloodshed. An aftermath of this rebellion was the uprising early in 1537 in the mining region of Amatepeque, where the negroes had "elected a king." Coronado, with the title of *visitador*, or inspector, was sent to quell the revolt, and after some fighting, in which Indians of the district served as Spanish allies, the rebels were put down and several dozen ringleaders were hanged and quartered.

His ability to command and his levelheadedness in council were recognized in the following year, when Mendoza took an unusual step. Simply on Mendoza's nomination, Coronado was appointed a *regidor*, or member of the town council of Mexico City, at the meeting on June 14, 1538. He replaced Francisco de Santa Cruz, who had resigned. He took office without the usual appointment signed by the king, and was allowed a year and a half in which to obtain this royal sanction.[9] In the minutes of that meeting Coronado, recommended as "a gentleman of good lineage, outstanding ability, and high conscientiousness, who had come to those parts to serve His Majesty . . . and had settled with the intention of remaining in the country,"[10] was put down as a married man having more than one child.[11] He is also mentioned as being a citizen of Mexico, although no record has been found of any earlier claim to citizenship. At any rate, Coronado was soon to be legally recognized as a citizen, and a most prominent one.

Cabeza de Vaca had reached Spain in 1537 to tell the king of his hopeful project of colonizing Florida, only to find that he was too late; Hernando de Soto, wealthy governor of Cuba, has just been given that dubious privilege, and a great expedition was already being formed to penetrate the swamps and bayous along the Gulf coast. De Soto's representative in New Spain, Alvaro de Sanjurjo, was now busy serving notice on possible interlopers, and in August, 1538, he called Coronado as a witness to the formal notification of Fernando Cortés that Cortés was not to interfere with De Soto's royal right to conquer Florida. A month later Sanjurjo summoned Coronado to recognize the same royal order on his own account—not as a mere citizen, but "as governor, as the said Sanjurjo declared him to be," of New Galicia!

Coronado, who had still to reach the age of thirty, was climbing up in the world. He replied to Sanjurjo's demand by respectfully promising obedience to all the commands of his emperor, but observed that there was no call for him to be served with this *proceso,* "since he was not governor, nor did he know that His Majesty desired to have him serve in such a position; and if His Majesty should desire his services in that position, he would obey and submit to the royal provision for him whenever he was called on, and would do what was most serviceable to the royal interests."[12]

This answer did not satisfy Sanjurjo, who had apparently received some secret and well-founded notice of Mendoza's intention to appoint Coronado to the governorship of the province which Nuño de Guzmán had discovered. But Coronado rightly refused to act in the matter, since no definite steps had then been taken to replace the previous governor, Diego Pérez de la Torre, Guzmán's successor, who had been killed fighting Indians earlier in the year.

The affairs of the province of New Galicia were in a tangled state. Most of the natives were in open rebellion or hiding in the hills. Missionary work was at a standstill. The roads were dangerous for unarmed parties, and the few settlements were little more than frontier way stations. San Miguel de Culiacán, the northern outpost, was on the verge of abandonment.[13] An energetic governor was badly needed.

At the death of De la Torre, Cristóbal de Oñate, one of Guzmán's most able and honest captains, had been left in charge. Mendoza soon appointed Luis Galindo, chief justice, as temporary governor; but before the middle of October, 1538, the viceroy took the responsibility of again appointing Coronado to a vacant post in anticipation of royal confirmation. Coronado's salary as permanent governor was to be one thousand ducats a year from the royal treasury and fifteen hundred more from the revenues of the province—providing these revenues were not too poor to make up that sum.

After attending the meeting of the *regidores* on October 15, Coronado left Mexico for New Galicia, to administer affairs in his new province and to hold a court of review on the acts of his unfortunate predecessor. He was at Tonalá, or Guadalajara, on November 19, to approve the elections of judges and magistrates for that town as well as for the village of Compostela, and on December 15 wrote to the king from the province, giving an account of his labors in charge of the government by virtue of a royal writ issued by Mendoza.[14] Early in the spring of 1539, Coronado set out on his first expedition in search of a treasure house in the north.

Viceroy Mendoza had never forgotten, even in the press of other affairs, the plan he had conceived of discovering Cabeza de Vaca's white cities beyond the northern desert. The appointment of his friend and protégé Coronado as governor of New Galicia, with authority to push the exploration of its northern frontier, was part of that plan. And things would go forward rapidly now, for Mendoza had also found the man who would be sent ahead with the negro Esteban to spy out the land. The man he had chosen was a friar of the wandering Order of St. Francis, Fray Marcos de Niza ("Mark of Nice"), at present a guest in the house of the archbishop of Mexico.

Mendoza had already made one effort to follow up the news given him by Cabeza de Vaca. On December 10, 1537, more than a year after the arrival of the peregrines in Mexico, the viceroy wrote that he had proposed to one of the survivors, Andrés de Dorantes,[15] that he lead an expedition. Mendoza later stated in a letter to the emperor that he had planned to send Dorantes with a company of horsemen and some holy friars to seek the country they had heard about, and that he had spent a considerable amount of money in preparations, but "nothing came of it, I do not know why."[16]

Perhaps the reason was that Mendoza felt that such an expedition should be under the command of a man of more importance than Dorantes—one of his own officials, or even Mendoza himself, if he could be spared to leave the country. As will be seen, his final choice as leader was Francisco Vásquez Coronado. But first he deemed it wise to send ahead an advance party, guided by black Esteban, to reconnoiter the wilds. This peaceful penetration of the country would be a delicate task, and would require the services of a particular type of person. And then a brilliant scheme occurred to him. Why not merely send several priests on this ticklish errand?

In the guise of missionary activities, Mendoza's aims could be carried out under the auspices of the Church, although the friars would be responsible to the viceroy for taking possession, in the name of the king, of any lands discovered and for bringing back a careful survey of the country traversed. No expense to the Crown would be involved. With friars as agents, the unknown Indian country could be passed through without any need for fighting, for the holy men were well skilled in conciliating the natives of new lands. The more Mendoza thought about it, the more appealing his idea seemed to him. If there was failure, the loss would be small, and no odium would fall upon his administration. If any great discovery was made, it would be secretly and promptly reported to the viceroy, who could act upon the news before any of the other strong claimants to the right to explore—there were several possible rivals aside from Cortés—could interfere or make ready to supersede him.

Probably this clever plan of using missionaries as advance agents of conquest—an economical combination of spiritual and worldly aims which was in later years to become the chief method of extending Spanish dominion into unknown territories—did not come all at once to the viceroy's mind. But it was made feasible because of the peculiar character of the man he finally chose to carry out the plan. In the person of Fray Marcos de Niza he had at hand a perfect instrument for the great work.

The career of Fray Marcos, mystery man in the discovery of the American Southwest, is one big question mark. For some reason his contemporaries have little to say about him, and the early chroniclers of the Franciscan order even less. He may have been an Italian, for the town of Nice was then part of the Duchy of Savoy, but more probably he was French.[17] He made profession as a member of the Seraphic Order of St. Francis about 1531 and soon departed to take up labors in New Spain. However, it was several years before he reached there. In Santo Domingo he paused for a while, then changed his plans and went to the newly discovered province of Peru, which Pizarro and his brigand band were plundering with a right Christian will.

He may have made a trip from Peru to Guatemala, from there returning to Peru with the interloping army of Governor Pedro de Alvarado and witnessing various events of the Peruvian conquest. Later he asserted that he had been appointed to the important post of commissary of his order in the Peruvian "Province of the Twelve Apostles," although it is likely that he was merely a *custodio,* an elective officer. He testified that he had witnessed in Peru much cruel treatment of the Indians, and his statement was incorporated in one of the fiery appeals of the zealous Bartolomé de las Casas,[18] "Apostle to the Indies." During this time Marcos may have written some very scholarly works[19] on the Indians of Peru and various events of the conquest, but strangely not one of these writings has been preserved. It is fairly certain that he accompanied Pizarro on his march south and witnessed the capture of the Inca ruler, Atahualpa. He may have remained in Peru for some time, although more likely he soon returned to Guatemala with Alvarado.[20]

He was then invited to Mexico by Archbishop Juan de Zumárraga; in a letter[21] written on April 4, 1537, the bishop mentioned that Marcos was staying with him, and was "a great religious person, worthy of credit, of approved virtue and of much religion and zeal." Although he may then have done some missionary work

in Jalisco and might have talked with Fernando Cortés about going to California with the forthcoming sea
expedition, little more was heard of Marcos until October, 1538, when he was commissioned by Viceroy Mendoza—who probably acted on the recommendation of
Zumárraga[22]—to start out in company with the negro
Esteban and Francisco Vásquez Coronado in search of
golden territories to the north.

The viceroy could not, in his own opinion, have
chosen a better man to spy out the land toward the
Seven Cities. Marcos, now vice-commissary of the Franciscan order in New Spain, occupied a prominent position among the members of his confraternity. He had
labored among the Indians of Peru and Guatemala,
and was supposed to be skilled in cosmography and the
art of navigation. He had an inordinate curiosity, and
was an experienced traveler in rough country. Most
of all, he was ambitious and could be made to feel that
his interest lay in serving the viceroy to the utmost of
his ability. Hence, if need be, he might not be above
wording his report to meet the requirements of the occasion. How well the report that he finally presented
did meet those requirements will shortly be seen.

Marcos, the remarkable friar, accompanied Governor Francisco Vásquez Coronado to New Galicia, and
at Tonalá, or Guadalajara, on November 20, received
his marching orders from the viceroy, forwarded by
the father-provincial of the Franciscans, Antonio de
Ciudad-Rodrigo. These instructions[23] illustrate nicely

the explicit care with which the viceroy of New Spain prepared all his undertakings.

In these instructions Marcos was enjoined first of all, upon his arrival at Culiacán, to impress upon the citizens the viceroy's command that the Indians of the province, who had been subjected to brutal handling since the time of Nuño de Guzmán, should be well treated, and also to assure the Indians themselves that they should no longer be made slaves nor removed from their lands. The previous year, Pope Paul III had issued a brief declaring his decision that the Indians were to be considered as a part of the human race, and that anyone who should enslave them risked excommunication. But most of the Indians of New Galicia were still in hiding. This tardy admonition to the people of Culiacán was essential in preparing the way for a peaceful penetration into the northern wilds peopled by a hardy Indian race.

Marcos was also ordered to inform Mendoza regarding the efforts of Coronado to obtain the conversion and good treatment of the Indians near Culiacán. The priest, in other words, was to be an independent observer of the deeds of the secular officer of New Galicia. This situation, as Mendoza well knew, would tend to keep Coronado from becoming too friendly with Marcos. The viceroy was being careful. In those days, it was not wise to allow two powerful men to become hand in glove when they were acting, far from the central authority, in matters where treasure might be involved.

Furthermore, if Marcos found a way to enter the

country beyond Culiacán, he should take the negro Esteban with him as a guide, and also some of the Christianized Indians[24] who were then serving with Coronado as interpreters. The friar was told to travel circumspectly, giving the natives no cause for hostility.

The chief duty impressed upon Marcos was to spy out the land, to be a sort of one-man scientific expedition. "You shall take much care to observe the people that there are, whether they be many or few, and if they are scattered or live close together. Note the quality and fertility of the soil, the climate of the country, the trees and plants and domestic and wild animals which there may be, the nature of the ground, whether rugged or level, the rivers, whether great or small, and the stones and metals which there are in the country. Send or carry back samples of such things as it is possible to do so, to the end that His Majesty may be advised of everything. Always endeavor to obtain information about the seacoast, that of the north as well as that of the south, because the land may narrow and in the country beyond some arm of the sea may enter."[25] Mendoza, like Cortés, was looking for the elusive Northwest Passage.

Marcos was instructed, if he came to the coast, to leave letters under crosses erected on headlands, so that they might be found if ships were sent up the Gulf of California; and in any event he was to send frequent messages back by Indian runners. If any large town was found, "where it may seem to you that there is a good situation to establish a monastery," he should send word swiftly and secretly.

Finally, strangest command of all, the barefoot friar was ordered to take possession of the new country for the Spanish Crown, in the name of the viceroy, erecting the signs and performing the ritual customary for this act.

Early in the year 1539, following these orders, Marcos and a companion friar, Honorato, were at Culiacán with their black guide, who had been lent by his master Dorantes to aid in the viceroy's great work of exploration.[26] Governor Coronado was also at Culiacán with an armed force and, with Marcos to help, at once set about carrying out Mendoza's plans.

The scheme of pacifying the Indians of the frontier was set afoot without great difficulty. The Christianized Pimas from Bamoa were sent into the back country to notify the people of the friendly intentions of the whites. After about twenty days, four hundred of the hill Indians were brought before Coronado. They said that, on behalf of all their countrymen, they came to see and know the men who have given them the boon of allowing them to return to their homes and sow corn in security, "for through a space of many years they were driven to flee into the mountains, hiding themselves like wild beasts, for fear lest they should be made slaves."[27] Coronado answered them with reassuring words and gave them food and presents; Friars Marcos and Honorato taught them to make the sign of the cross.

Now that the danger of hostile Indians near Culiacán was removed, Marcos and Esteban set out to find

Topira,[28] the golden region to the east that Guzmán had sought to win. On February 7 they left Culiacán, and traveled for some distance into the rocky fastnesses of the Sierra de Durango.

On his return to Culiacán a few weeks later, Marcos gave an account of his discoveries in glowing words, although it is likely that he saw very little and understood only imperfectly what was told him. The Indians of Topira, he said, had come out to receive him joyously. "There are no great cities there, but the houses are built of stone and are very good, and in them they have a great store of gold, which is as it were lost, because they do not know what use to put it to."[29] The Durango Indians did have a quantity of placer gold which they used in trade with the coast, and it was probably this gold that had lured Guzmán to exhaust his forces in repeated attempts to penetrate the sierras in 1531. It is harder to find any shadow of foundation for the wonderful story of Marcos that "the people wear emeralds and other precious jewels upon their bodies; they are valiant, having very strong armor made of silver, fashioned after divers shapes of beasts." They were willing, after a little persuasion from Marcos, to become Christians and subjects of Spain, and to trade their gold for things more useful to them.

This report of Marcos—to which he added a hearsay account of the barbarous savages of the interior, and their temples of skulls and living sacrifices of men on burning pyres—was so promising that Coronado decided to conquer Topira.

Marcos, Honorato, and Esteban, the negro, left Culiacán on March 7 for the north, on a journey that was to be one of the most momentous in the history of the New World. The next day, Coronado sat down and wrote a letter to the secretary of his friend the viceroy.[30] With him at Culiacán the young governor had an imposing force of a hundred and fifty horsemen and two hundred foot soldiers, crossbowmen, and gunners, and was well provided with trade goods and herds of hogs and sheep. Why not, he pondered, use these to make a great conquest that would bring instant fame to the name of Coronado?

All that was lacking was a shipment of ammunition which was on the road and should reach him by April 10. On that date, he wrote, he would start out for Topira. He had heard that it was more than eighty leagues off, and that it lay between two rivers and held more than fifty inhabited towns. He expected to travel "many leagues over high mountains, which reach up to the skies, and over a river which at the present time is so big and swollen that it can in no place be waded over." Beyond Topira, the Indians said, lay another country, nameless but even more wonderful, where the people raised maize, beans, chili peppers, melons, and gourds, and "fowls of the country." These people wore on their bodies emeralds and other precious stones, and chains of gold; they ate from gold and silver plates, and even covered their houses with these metals!

"I assure your lordship," he vowed, "that I do not mean to return to Mexico until I am able to inform your honor more perfectly regarding the condition of the place; and if I find anything that we may do good in, I will stay there until I have advised your lordship, so that you may command what you wish to have done. If it turns out so unluckily that there be nothing of importance, I will seek to discover a hundred[m] leagues further, wherein I hope to God there will be something found in which your lordship may employ all these gentlemen and those that shall come hither hereafter."

Coronado planned to make a circuit toward the north and come out at the valley of Corazones, or Hearts, some hundred and twenty leagues above Culiacán on the Cabeza de Vaca trail, hoping there to make rendezvous with Fray Marcos when that worthy would be returning from his exploration of the north; but this was not to be. Like Guzmán before him, the eager young commander was soon to be turned back from the quest of Topira and its fabled emeralds.

In this maiden venture in search of an Indian Eldorado, Coronado was undoubtedly a trifle too willing to give full acceptance to stories told him by the natives—a trait that was to betray him more grievously in his later and greater journey of discovery. Mendoza, in his letter to the emperor, implied as much. He said, after stating that he had merely ordered Coronado to find some means of learning conditions in the Topira country, that "he, supposing this to be a matter of great moment, determined himself to go and search for it."[32] But Mendoza, of course, was writing after the event, when he had learned that Coronado had been forced to turn back because of the scarcity of provisions for his large force and because of the impassability of the mother range of Durango, at this point one of the most forbidding mountain barriers of the continent.

And so Coronado withdrew from the rugged northern frontier, to carry on his administrative duties. Late in the spring he was back in Guadalajara, making certain civic improvements that would justify the grant of title as a "royal city," with its own coat of arms.[33]

It was not until early in July that he heard again from Fray Marcos. The friar, returning posthaste and alone from his great adventure beyond the deserts, had appeared in Compostela. There he was promptly joined by Governor Coronado, who listened spellbound to the wonderful story that Marcos had to tell. The Seven Cities had been discovered!

2

Coronado's Forerunners

Summer, 1539

CORONADO, after writing a brief letter to the emperor[1] confirming the story that Marcos had found a new land that would rival the riches of Marco Polo's Cathay, set out in company with the friar for Mexico to relate the wonderful news to the viceroy.

By the middle of August they had reached the capital, and on the twenty-sixth of the month the report that Marcos had written in Compostela was attested by his superior, Fray Antonio de Ciudad-Rodrigo. This account of the discoveries of Marcos, which was to set New Spain and Europe agog and lead directly to a military exploration of wide expanses of the American Southwest,[2] was so astounding that, to quiet spreading doubts, the friar appeared on September 2 and swore under oath to the veracity of his statement—a most unusual proceeding.

Marcos worded his report in a way that might be calculated to meet Viceroy Mendoza's every need. Not too

---

[1] For notes to chap. 2, see pp. 329–333.

explicitly, he told of great wealth possessed by civilized Indians living in cities to the north. No definite dates, traveling times, or directions that would be useful to rival explorers were given. He stated that almost from the outset of his journey he had discovered new lands where Christians had been previously unknown, thus attempting to nullify the standing claims of Cortés and Nuño de Guzmán to lands north of Culiacán. Those who read the report might well have asked for some stronger confirmation of the friar's words, for the report is a highly dubious document that contains more than one thumping falsehood. The friar's story, which was to set Coronado and his army marching north within a few months, repays a somewhat careful scrutiny.

Marcos, in company with the Moor Esteban and the Franciscan lay brother, Fray Honorato (who like his companion friar may also have been a native of Savoy),[3] had departed from San Miguel de Culiacán on Friday, March 7. They were guided by a number of Christianized Indians from Bamoa and from near-by villages on the route. Carrying bales of trade goods, the party journeyed safely to the Río Petatlán, so called because the natives covered their huts with *petates,* or woven mats of grass. There Fray Honorato fell ill, and after a stay of three days Marcos decided to go on without him. Welcomed on every side by the rejoicing natives of the countryside, whose fears of enslavement had been so recently allayed, the white friar and his black henchman pushed on up the coast.[4]

After traveling for some days through the uninhabited littoral on the lower Río Fuerte, Marcos was welcomed by other Indians who, he said, "were astonished to see me, as they had no news of Christians."[5] These natives told the friar that in the regions farther inland, four or five days off, where the chains of mountains ended, there was an extensive and level open region filled with large towns inhabited by a people clothed in cotton garments. These Indians were supposed to have much gold, from which they made vessels, and decorations for their noses and ears, and little flat sweat-scrapers of gold.

Marcos decided to leave this rich section to be examined on his return journey, and after three more days on his northern way came to a town which he called Vacapa,[6] "forty leagues from the sea," where food was plentiful because the natives irrigated their lands.

It was now two days before Passion Sunday, and Marcos determined to remain at Vacapa until Easter, in order to send Indian messengers to the sea to bring back some island dwellers of the coast to speak with him. But Esteban would not linger; it was settled that he was to push ahead to the north for fifty or sixty leagues and scout the country.

Black Esteban had been growing more and more fractious as he retraced the trail he had followed southward with Cabeza de Vaca. He had shown a distressing tendency to revive the old custom of having the natives of each new village lavish all their possessions as tribute to the godlike travelers. He did not disdain to accept turquoises from the adoring Indians, and his flashing eyes and ivory grin attracted a number of their women to the growing escort that carried his possessions. He was restive under the slow progress of the party; if he could but once get away from the friar's reprimands, he might push on swiftly to the heart of the unknown country, and win for himself⁷ the glory of being the lone discoverer of the land of high white houses!

Yes, Esteban was embarrassing company for a man of God, but he might serve excellently to bear the brunt of first contact with the unknown savages ahead. Marcos instructed him to push forward at once and send back word of his findings. Since the black man was unable to write, messages would be carried orally by fleet Indian runners. It was agreed that if he had any news of an important settlement he should return in person or send a runner with a prearranged sign. If the country was of moderate importance, the messenger would bring a wooden cross of a hand's breadth; if it was of great importance, the cross would be twice as large; and if it was bigger and better than New Spain, a great cross should be sent.

Esteban, with a glorious feeling of freedom, departed from Vacapa on Passion Sunday, and thenceforward was never again seen by his white masters. He traveled in rare style, with a set of green Spanish dishes for the service of his dinner, and a brace of terrifying greyhounds at his heels. Once more he was major-domo to white magicians, shaking his plumed gourd rattle and living on the fat of the land, served by a worshiping harem of Indian women. Four days after his departure, messengers from him appeared before Fray Marcos in Vacapa, bearing a wooden cross as tall as a man.

Esteban, the messengers reported, said that Marcos should come immediately, for the black scout had received an account of "the greatest country in the world." One of these messengers, a very intelligent Indian, asserted that he had visited that land. He told Marcos that it was a thirty-day journey from where Esteban was staying to the first city of the new country, "which was named Cíbola." Thus for the first time this impelling, magical name was heard by a European.[8]

The informant went on to assert that "in the first province there were seven very great cities, all under one lord; that the houses, constructed of stone and lime, were large; that the smallest were of one story with a terrace above, that there were others of two and three stories, while that of the lord had four. . . . He said that the doorways of the principal houses were much ornamented with turquoises, of which there was a great abundance, and that the people of those cities went very well clothed." There were reputed to be other provinces beyond this, each one much bigger than that of the Seven Cities.

Marcos could hardly believe his ears. This news of seven cities in the wilderness aroused him to a fever pitch of anticipation. Could it be that his eyes were shortly to rest upon the earthly paradise established by the voyaging bishops? Was he chosen to find the rich cities of gold and silver of which Tejo had told Guzmán? The shoeless friar gave fervent thanks to God.

He curbed his impatience, awaiting the return of the messengers he had sent to the coast. On Easter Sunday they came to him, bringing people who wore pearl shells on their foreheads and carried large shields of "ox-hide, so hard that I think that a bullet would not pass through them."[9]

On the same day, from the east, came "three of those Indians known as Pintados, with their faces, chests, and arms all decorated" with tattoo marks. These three Painted Indians,[10] whose territories were said to border on those of the Seven Cities, were in the procession that departed with Marcos from Vacapa on April 8, the second day of the Easter festival. The friar now hastened to catch up with Esteban, who was more than a fortnight's travel ahead of him.

But it proved to be impossible to overtake Esteban. Contrary to orders, the negro had not waited but had pushed ahead, after sending back another large cross and a message that the country beyond was the greatest of which he had ever heard.

Marcos traveled slowly, talking to the natives along the way. The Pimas confirmed the tale of the houses of Cíbola, and stated that beyond that place there were other kingdoms named Marata, Acus, and Totonteac. These natives reported that they were accustomed to travel to Cíbola to get turquoises, "cowhides," and other goods in return for service as laborers.

Here in his narrative Marcos first used the word "pueblo" to describe the villages of which he heard. It is a word that soon became generally used—and is still used—to designate all the town-dwelling tribes of the American Southwest, of whose existence sure news had now come for the first time to the ears of a white man.

Somewhat in the same triumphal manner as Cabeza de Vaca had journeyed, Marcos now went forward, received on all sides as a holy one, a medicine man from the white heaven. "They brought me sick persons that I might cure them and they tried to touch my clothes; I recited the Gospel over them." Marcos was hot on the trail now, and had little time for conversions, baptisms, and other missionary labors; the explorer in him was foremost. The scent grew stronger. He was presented with a strange "cowhide" which seemed surely to have been tanned by some highly civilized worker. The next day he received a third great cross from his black forerunner, with a message urging him to hurry, hurry! Pausing only to take formal possession of this fresh country for the Spanish Crown, the friar eagerly pushed ahead toward the four kingdoms of rumor.

Marcos traveled for seven days through a green, well-watered country,[11] full of game and populated by Indians clothed in cotton and leather, with turquoise pendants at ear and neck. Marcos himself wore a habit of dark woolen kersey cloth of the kind called *saragossa,* which Governor Coronado had given him; and he was startled when the Indians asserted that the people of Cíbola wore clothing of the same fabric, made from the fur of some animal of the size of the Castilian greyhounds that Esteban had with him.[12]

Two days beyond this valley Marcos came upon a "re-

A NEW WORLD LANDSCAPE

Artist's idea of a northern Mexico landscape. (From Hernández, *Nova*

freshing" village.[18] The friendly, corn-growing inhabitants confirmed in all respects the earlier rumors of Cíbola, and described in detail the streets and tall houses of that place. "I asked them," wrote Marcos, "if the men of that country had wings to climb those stories; they laughed and explained to me a ladder, as well as I could do."

Then for four days the friar traversed barren hills between two rivers, where food and huts were prepared

WITH NATIVE WILD LIFE

Plantarum, Animalium et Mineralium Mexicanorum Historia, 1651.)

for his lodging in advance, and so came to another rich and cultivated valley.[14] He was now in the country that Cabeza de Vaca had reached toward the end of his great pilgrimage, not far from the town of Corazones, or Hearts; but Marcos, perhaps because he wished to pose as a pathfinder all the way, made no mention of Cabeza de Vaca or of Corazones. Instead, he made a statement in connection with this place that is simply incredible.

He said that, "as it was very important to know the direction of the coast, I wished to assure myself and so went to look out for it, and I saw clearly that in latitude thirty-five degrees it turns to the west."[15] The implication that he was then near the seacoast was later to lead Coronado and others into a dangerous pitfall. Perhaps Marcos saw a crude map drawn by the Indians, and imagined the rest.

The friar journeyed through the pleasant garden valley of the Sonora for five days. In one of the numerous villages he met an old man who said that he was a native of Cíbola. The old Indian admitted that he was a fugitive whom the ruler of Cíbola wished to catch and punish. He said that this great lord of all the province of the Seven Cities, the chief who appointed all the local chiefs, lived in the biggest and most important of the cities, which was called Ahacus. From there he was even now directing a war against the kingdom of Marata toward the southeast. There was also another kingdom called Totonteac, which the old man said was the biggest, most populous, and richest in the world. There was still another realm called Acus (a province not to be confused, he carefully explained, with the city of Ahacus where the lord of Cíbola dwelt).[16]

In this valley, Marcos asserted, he saw more than two thousand tanned "oxhides," and quantities of turquoise necklaces, all of which were said to have come from rich Cíbola. The natives spoke of this place and of the kingdoms of Marata, Acus, and Totonteac as regions as well known to them as the palms of their hands.[17]

Again the friar had word of Esteban, who was now leaving the last river village before crossing the final wilderness between him and Cíbola.[18] The negro, whose band of followers had grown to a small army of three hundred—all of them marching joyously to wealthy Cíbola in the hope that many rich gifts would be proffered the black medicine man's escort—stated that the accounts of the Indians all along were to be fully relied upon. Marcos was inclined to agree, for since entering the country of these Indians, in which he had traveled one hundred and twelve leagues after first hearing of Cíbola, he had found a strict agreement in all their accounts of that promised land.

Impatient at delays, Marcos with "thirty chiefs" and his own followers carrying a supply of food reached this last village and on May 9 started into the wilderness. For twelve days, the friar wrote, they followed what seemed to be the main trail to Cíbola, well traveled, marked by old shelter huts and the remains of many bivouac fires. They lived well on venison, hares, and partridges. Somewhere ahead, on this ancient trade route, lay Cíbola; but between them and their goal was some of the roughest country in the Southwest.[19]

"At this juncture," runs the account of Marcos, "I met an Indian, the son of one of the chiefs who were journeying with me, who had gone in company with the negro Esteban. This man showed fatigue in his countenance, had his body covered with sweat, and manifested the deepest sadness in his whole person." He had cause to be weary and sad. Esteban had been captured by the warlike natives of the Seven Cities, and he and everyone with him were held as prisoners.

This chief's son who brought the news had been confined with the others in huts outside the walls of the town, without food or drink. The next morning, he told, he had gone out to get a drink at a near-by stream; when he had been there a few moments, he looked up to see Esteban in flight, pursued by the warriors of the city. He then saw some of his fellow tribesmen slain by the men of Cíbola; and in terror he crept upstream and at last made his escape back along the desert road.

Dire tidings! The Indians who were with Marcos began to weep and mutter, and cast sidelong glances at him. It seemed that the magical cross of the white man was of no avail against the spears of Cíbola. The Indians set up a wailing for their dead.

Marcos de Niza, fearing that he was lost, drew aside to pray. In prayer came decision. He returned to the party, and distributed to them most of the contents of the bales of trade goods which he had brought. These gifts, and the bold declaration of Marcos that they had nothing to fear, at last persuaded them to go forward.

Then, only "a day's march from Cíbola," two other fugitives appeared, covered with bloody wounds. Their first words caused the party to set up such a crying that Marcos had to beg them to be silent so that he might learn what had happened.

"How can we be quiet," they replied, "when we know that our fathers, sons, and brothers who were with Esteban, to the number of more than three hundred men, are dead? And we no more dare go to Cíbola, as we have been accustomed." Marcos, hiding his own fear, calmed them at last, and heard the bitter news. Esteban was dead.

The friar was instinctively sure it was true. The vainglorious negro had found in the warriors of Cíbola a spirit of savage resistance. Weeping himself, Marcos withdrew from his wailing escort, and took counsel with himself once more, for an hour and a half.

When he returned to the group, a Christianized Indian from Mexico, a namesake of Marcos, whispered that the others were plotting to kill the white man as the person responsible for the calamity. At once the friar divided up all his remaining trinkets, and began to argue the point. He finally pacified the throng by pointing out astutely that, should they kill him, they would do him no real injury because he would go at once to his heavenly home, but that then other Christians would come to avenge him and kill all the Indians.

At first it was impossible, he wrote, to persuade any of the party to push ahead and obtain further news. But as he insisted that in any event he must see, if only from a distance, the place where Esteban had met his end, at last two chiefs were prevailed upon to accompany him. With these chiefs and his own Indian interpreters, the friar, according to his story, hastened forward to his dangerous goal.

He came, he said, to a hill from which he had sight of the first city of Cíbola—the place that he had heard of under the name of Ahacus, where the lord of the country lived. "It is situated on a level stretch on the brow of a roundish hill. It appears to be a very beautiful city, the best that I have seen in these parts. . . . The town is bigger than the city of Mexico. At times I was tempted to go to it, because I knew that I risked nothing but my life, which I had offered to God the day I commenced the journey; finally I feared to do so, considering my danger and that if I died, I would not be able to give an account of this country, which seems to me to be the greatest and best of the discoveries."

With the aid of the Indians, he made a heap of stones and on top placed a small, slender cross, "not having the materials to construct a bigger one." Then, in the names of viceroy and emperor, he laid claim to all the seven cities and the kingdoms of Totonteac and Acus and Marata, and christened this land the New Kingdom of St. Francis.

He then started back, "with much more fear than food," and in two days, hastening with his robes kilted to the knee, caught up with the retreating Indians, who still mourned for relatives believed to be lying dead at Cíbola. His speed was amazing, considering that he was traveling, under the brassy midsummer sun, over the wild peaks and deserts of eastern Arizona. "Without tarrying I hastened in fear from that people and that valley. The first day I went ten leagues, then I went eight and again ten leagues, without stopping till I had passed the second desert."

On his return journey Marcos had hoped to explore the open valley where the people were supposed to possess vessels and sweat-scrapers of solid gold; but now, realizing that this might be more safely left to the time when the Spaniards would come to colonize Cíbola, he did not risk it. "However, I saw from the mouth of the valley seven moderate-sized towns at some distance, and further a very fresh valley of very good land, whence rose much smoke." Taking possession of all this country from a safe distance, he hastened to San Miguel de Culiacán. There he hoped to meet Coronado; but not finding him, the friar went on to the town of Compostela, two hundred and fifty miles farther south. There he met Governor Coronado, and there he wrote the famed report which now, once more in Mexico, he delivered to his father-provincial and to the viceroy.

Why had Esteban been killed? A year later, among the pueblos, Coronado was to hear the details of his spectacular death. The negro had learned too late that the town dwellers were by temperament much more ferocious than the simple hill tribes who had kissed the garments of Cabeza de Vaca. And Esteban had been both presumptuous and greedy, as well as fatally careless.

Many leagues in advance of Marcos, the former slave pushed on into the unknown mountains. He was now free, and almost a monarch among the Indians, who gave him an imperial escort. Vaunting ambition burned in his black breast.

Within a day's march of the first of the cities of Cíbola he sent forward, to announce his coming, a messenger who carried as an orb of power the pebble-filled gourd with two plumes—one white, the other red—that Esteban had acquired in Texas. This symbol of wizardry had once been part of the outfit of the traditional medicine man of those plains. But the red and white plumes were like an enemy battle flag to the haughty chiefs of Cíbola; they recognized it as the emblem of a tribe with which they had long been at war. The magic rattle was bad medicine, and was cast disdainfully to the ground.

"When your people reach our village," the messenger was told, "you will find out what sort of people live here, and instead of entering our town, you will all be killed."

This threat did not at all daunt the negro. Everything would be all right when once he presented himself in all his imposing finery. He grinned happily and marched on, with bells tinkling at his elbows and ankles. At sunset, before the high gates of the town, he demanded audience with the chiefs.

"I come to tell you," he cried, "that you must prepare to receive two white-faced men, servants of a very great lord beyond the sunrise, who know all about the great things of heaven, and are coming to instruct you in these divine matters."[20]

The proud announcement was met with coldness. Esteban and his followers were ushered into guarded huts outside the walls, while the solemn elders of the town held council.

These cunning chiefs were not to be imposed upon by a likely story. The prisoner was black of skin. It was clearly a lie that he was sent as an ambassador of white men, if inded there were men who were white. He must be, rather, a spy or a guide from some black southern nation who might be led by him to conquer their happy mesa country. Better that he should never return to them! Moreover, this thick-lipped man was shining with greed. He had asked for turquoises and much food, and cast eyes at their modest women!

The next morning, "when the sun was about a lance high," having spent the night without food or drink, Esteban and some of his friends left their quarters. The watchful townspeople, fearing that the strangers were escaping, ran in pursuit, and Esteban fled. Transfixed with many arrows, he fell dead like a black Sebastian among the simple people he had led to Cíbola, there to become rich.

To all the chiefs of the seven pueblos—so the voyager Alarcón was told many months later—a portion of Esteban's body was sent so that they might truly know that the brethren of this black man would never be guided by him to conquer the citadels of their homeland. To the chief lord of all the cities fell the spoil, two fierce greyhounds and four green dinner plates.

Though black Esteban thus perished on the threshold of the silvery city he had discovered, he was to be bloodily avenged. His name was to live in the histories of his white masters, and his fame was not to be forgotten among his unlettered killers. Even today, the red men of Zuñi tell how an obnoxious black man with two dogs came among them with greed in his heart. At night

some wise men of the high secret order took him outside the pueblo and gave him such a powerful kick that
he sped through the air back to the south, whence he
had come!

About pueblo campfires they tell also how, a long
time ago, when the ladder rounds were still unbroken
in Kya-ki-me, the black Mexicans suddenly fell upon
the town. "When they said they would enter the covered way, it seems that our ancients looked not gently
at them. . . . Therefore, these our ancients, being always bad-tempered, and quick to anger, made fools of
themselves after their fashion, rushed into their town
and out of their town, shouting, skipping, and shooting
with slingstones and arrows and tossing their war-clubs.
Then the Indians of So-no-li [Sonora] set up a great
howl, and thus they and our ancients did much ill to
one another. Then and thus was killed by our ancients,
right where the stone stands down by the arroyo of Kya-
ki-me, one of the Black Mexicans, a large man, with
chili lips [lips swollen from eating chili peppers], and
some of the Indians they killed, catching others. Then
the rest ran away, chased by our grandfathers, and
went back toward their country in the Land of Ever-
lasting Summer. . . . By and by they came back, these
Black Mexicans, and with them many men of So-no-li.
They wore coats of iron, and war-bonnets of metal, and
carried for weapons short canes that spat fire and made
thunder, so said our ancients, but they were guns, you
know. They frightened our bad-tempered fathers so
badly that their hands hung down by their sides like

the hands of women. And this time these black, curl-bearded people drove our ancients about like slave-creatures."[21] Yes, Esteban was to have his revenge.

Fray Marcos, in his official report, painted a stirring picture in heroic colors. There he stands alone, risking death and the loss of his discovery to gain from a hilltop a Pisgah sight of Ahacus, merely one of the promised Seven Cities but bigger than the capital of Mexico. A wondrous picture, which has inspired many a pen and brush. It is really rather a pity that historians cannot leave it in the original glowing tints; but the plain fact is that it is now impossible to believe that Marcos ever got within many a day's journey of Cíbola. His tale of seeing the city, even from afar, is pure falsehood or pure extravaganza.[22]

A contrasting picture, truer than the self-portrait of Marcos, may be sketched on the basis of modern evidence. The friar is marching through the desert somewhere in southern Arizona, expecting within a few days to feast his eyes upon the city whose walls and door-ways, and the very clothing of whose inhabitants, have been repeatedly portrayed to him by Indians who had walked its streets. Then suddenly comes word of the massacre of Esteban, and disaster to his peaceful plans.

His men are mutinous; his life, if he pushes on, will be worth less than a tallow candle. If he turns back now, he can take the secret of the north safely to Mexico, and later return to the land and its great promises. The Indians of Cíbola are in a killing mood. Nothing save the strictest obedience to orders would now force him to go on to almost certain death. Like any prudent man in such circumstances, he turns regretfully back—and small blame to him.

But now, trudging homeward, conscience pricks him. His orders to see everything for himself and to claim the country are clear. There will be many to call him coward if he returns with a report at second hand. And what, in that event, will become of the rewards that he might expect were his religious superiors and the viceroy to have the sure news of the north that he had promised to bring them?

Then comes temptation. He is the only white man within hundreds of miles; none can controvert his word. From his many talks with the Indians it would be easy to build a convincing recital of the wonders of Cíbola. He had almost seen that city; surely it would be but a small sin to say that he had actually looked upon it, if by so doing a great mission church might later rise in this country for the propagation of the word of God! As he marches, the vision that he might have had of this wondrous rich land rises before his mind's eye. It is a beauteous dream. Before he reaches Culiacán, it is hard for him to understand that it is only a dream, and not sober reality.

And so Marcos spread abroad the tale of how he had seen the lofty towers of the Seven Cities. He became at once the most famous man in New Spain, and through the grateful viceroy's aid was swiftly elevated to the post of father-provincial of the Franciscan order.[23] Inspired by his report, Mendoza at once began gathering together a great army to explore the new country. Francisco Vásquez Coronado was to spend three years of his life in dangerous discovery, in pursuit of the substance of a lie.

Did Friar Mark of Nice knowingly deceive the world? Or was he, perhaps, making a good story better? The American Southwest, the fringes of which he reached, has always been a land of exaggeration. Distances and vistas are treacherous there; in the rarefied atmosphere, a molehill seems a mountain, a gypsum-washed hut seems a palace afar. It is the land of cloud-castles, mirages of wonder, unbelievable tints and shades. All things are magnified, and white and red men alike are skilled in the drawing of the long bow. If it is true that Marcos de Niza, jongleur of God, was tempted in that wilderness by the Father of Lies, was tempted and fell, then he should at least be remembered as the first of a great company, the Munchausens of America, the mighty tellers of the tall tale.

Coronado, Captain General

August, 1539 – February, 1540

FRAY MARCOS, when he appeared in the city of Mexico with Coronado, was at once hailed as a sort of land-voyaging Columbus who had not only found the Seven Cities but had also discovered a new route to the spiceries of India. The immediate effect of his tale was to cause the viceroy to set about the mustering of a great military force that would start for the north, under the command of Francisco Vásquez Coronado, as soon as the roads were open in the spring.

The story of the discovery of Cíbola set the Mexican capital to resounding with the clink of the armorer's hammer and the babble of gossips telling each other of the wonders to be seen and the wealth to be gained by those lucky enough soon to be marching to the sack of the seven silvery pueblos. The speculations of every-one swung to the north like so many compass needles.

The written report of the friar was full enough of marvels, but Marcos was even more enthusiastic in private conversations. As a result of his elevation to the

position of father-provincial, the pulpits of Mexico re-
verberated with accounts of the wonders of Cíbola and
sermons on the benefits that might accrue from the
discovery. Bishop Zumárraga, writing to a friend in
Spain, said: "There are partridges and cows which the
father says he saw, and he heard a story of camels and
dromedaries and of other cities larger than this one of
Mexico."[1] Another priest wrote to a friend in Burgos
that the people the friar saw in Cíbola "wear shoes and
buskins of leather and many wear silk clothing down
to their feet. Of the richness of this country I do not
write you because it is said to be so great that it does
not seem possible. The friar himself told me this, that
he saw a temple of their idols the walls of which, inside
and outside, were covered with precious stones; I think
he said they were emeralds. They also say that in the
country beyond there are camels and elephants."[2] Surely
the good Marcos had hit upon the road to Cathay!

Even the barber who shaved Marcos on his return
from the north had a story from the holy man's lips.
As the barber afterward repeated, Marcos had told him
that "many settlements were there, in cities and towns;
and that the cities were surrounded by walls, with their
gates guarded, and were very wealthy, having silversmiths; and that the women wore strings of gold beads
and the men girdles of gold and white woolen dresses;
and that they had sheep and cows and partridges and
slaughterhouses and iron forges."[3]

Whether Marcos did or did not embroider his tale

---

[1] For notes to chap. 3, see pp. 334–337.

with fancies while being shaved, the fact remains that the popular belief in Mexico at this time was that the friar had found the way to new realms of wonder, a terrestrial paradise that would, mayhap, eclipse the fame of the late-found empire of the Incas.

Viceroy Mendoza may not have been as credulous as others, but he believed enough to begin spending a round sum of money in enlisting and equipping a fine expedition to send to the Cíbola country.

He had some prudent doubts. He sent an order to Melchor Díaz, mayor of Culiacán, to take his lieutenant Juan de Zaldívar and fifteen horsemen and make a reconnaissance northward as far as possible to see if confirmation could be found for the friar's report. Then, although he could not expect to hear from Díaz until the winter rains had ceased, Mendoza set about the task of organizing the expedition that would be commanded by Coronado.

Cortés, Marquis of the Valley, as the most prominent promoter of northwestern exploration, was equally excited by the story of Marcos. At about the time of the friar's arrival in Compostela, Cortés had dispatched from Acapulco three ships commanded by Francisco de Ulloa with orders to sail to the head of the Gulf of California. In a letter from Cuernavaca on August 6, the conqueror thanked Mendoza for sending news of the discoveries of Marcos and expressed himself as politely willing to collaborate on any venture which might be undertaken as a result of these tidings. But Mendoza, who had decided to curb the ambitions of

Cortés in every way, was unresponsive to the suggestion. The marquis was not to be permitted to put himself forward in this promising new enterprise.

Cortés, persisting in his offers, sought to enlist Francisco Vásquez Coronado as his intermediary. Several times he asked Coronado to induce Mendoza to join forces with him, even promising to pay all expenses of an expedition. The viceroy replied that he would not enter into any such partnership without express instructions from the emperor in Spain. Mendoza was not accepting favors or obligations from anyone, least of all from Cortés. "You know very well, for you know me," Coronado reported the viceroy as saying to him, "that I am not going to accept anything from the marquis or from anybody else, except from His Majesty, nor is it right to accept it. . . . So I charge you not to speak to me about this again."[4]

The breach widened after this rebuff. On August 26, the very day when the report of Marcos was attested by his superior, Mendoza issued a proclamation, aimed at Cortés, forbidding anyone to leave the country without his permission.

On September 4 Cortés appeared before the *audiencia* to request license to send a ship and thirty or forty men to the aid of Ulloa. He was refused. In a statement of grievances[5] made later in Spain, whither he soon retired, Cortés complained that Mendoza had gone to the length of seizing six or seven vessels which had not been able to get off with Ulloa; moreover, that the viceroy had sent a force to prevent Ulloa from touching at any of the west-coast ports, and that, when one vessel took refuge at Guatulco, he had ordered the sailors imprisoned and persistently refused to return the ship to its owners.

Smarting under these affronts, Cortés left for Spain to institute proceedings before the Council for the Indies. No sooner had he arrived in Spain when the court was thrown into an uproar by the news of Marcos and his exploits. Soon the Council was besieged by claimants for the right to explore Cíbola. Cortés, Nuño de Guzmán, and the agent of Governor Pedro de Alvarado of Guatemala each filed numerous petitions, testimonies, appeals, acts of possession, and counter-charges in which each objected to rival claims so strenuously that Villalobos, attorney for the Council, was to give as a conclusive reason for rejecting all claims the fact that each party had clearly proved that none of the others had any right whatever to a license to explore the new land.

Curiously enough, the strongest argument made by any one of the contenders was presented on behalf of a man who at the time was far out of touch with any of the happenings in the civilized world. Although Hernando de Soto, governor of Cuba, was deep in the wilds of what is now the southern United States, his attorney in Spain persistently urged his principal's right to a free hand. De Soto had been given on April 20, 1537, the power to "conquer, pacify, and people" the territories from Florida west to the Río de las Palmas. His representative maintained that De Soto was the heir to the country claimed by Pánfilo de Narváez, and that Marcos had but followed up a clue given by Cabeza de Vaca and other survivors of the Narváez expedition. De Soto had spent a great deal to outfit his expedition and should be allowed first chance at the harvest. De Soto was already on the ground, and it would be unfair, not to say dangerous, to put a competitor in the field, as scandals like those in Peru might result unless all rivals were kept away.[6]

Mendoza had already realized the danger that De Soto might hear of the discoveries in the north and decide to begin his explorations in the westernmost parts of the territory granted to him. In an effort to keep from De Soto a secret that was known to everyone in New Spain, Mendoza clamped down an embargo on the news brought by Marcos;[7] the viceroy was unaware that De Soto had left Cuba, on his way to conquer Florida, as early as the preceding May.

Mendoza was in a hurry. The only sure means by which he could forestall all possible competitors was by putting an expedition into the field as soon as possible. Rivals might clamor in Spain; the ships of Ulloa might be steadily nearing the silver walls of Ahacus; but meanwhile the enrollment of venturesome cavaliers for the Cíbola expedition went on apace in Mexico.

Mendoza's position in sending out the expedition to the north was a risky one. He had repeatedly asked, since the beginning of his administration, for license to explore, but no specific privilege had been given. In sending off a small army to conquer Cíbola he would assume a grave responsibility which he might at any time have to justify, should the king send a special judge to review his executive acts.[8] Mendoza knew from the first that when he commissioned the expedition, by virtue of his authority as the king's representative in New Spain, he was taking a chance that could be condoned only through a successful outcome. It was a a chance that in his judgment had to be taken.

Even the viceroy dared not draw upon the royal treasury to bear any of the cost of the expedition. All expenditures were to be met by Mendoza personally, by his friends, and by the members of the expedition. Most of the party, even the men in the ranks, had to pay their own expenses and provide their own arms, horses, and servants. The enterprise was a pure speculation, in which those who participated ventured their capital or services on the chance of a large return. If there was no return, then everyone stood to lose his venture—all except the king.

The king had nothing to lose and everything to gain. As in all other Spanish conquests, such as the famous plundering expeditions of Cortés and Pizarro, the king would here be entitled to a clear fifth part of all precious metals and other loot. Charles V, head of the Holy Roman Empire as well as king of Spain, was a bold, astute, and energetic ruler who was making himself master of Europe and building the greatest royal domain in all history. In order to carry on his incessant wars, he needed gold, shipload after shipload of gold; and he had learned by now how to get men to find this gold for him. Always there were plenty of venturesome gentlemen to make His Christian Majesty's discoveries for him. Not the least venturesome were the men who shared the viceregal bounty of Antonio de Mendoza in the capital of New Spain.

The city of Mexico in the year 1539 was not the thronged, barbaric island-city of pyramids and mansions over which Montezuma had ruled in his glittering heyday.

The stone edifices of the Aztec lords had toppled one by one before the battering rams of the Christian besiegers, and much of the beautiful lakeside had been filled in with the debris of palaces. The capital was now a colonial town of not more than fifteen hundred houses, many of them built of wood. In the narrow streets clumsy two-wheeled oxcarts disputed the way with dashing *vaqueros* from the viceroy's stock farms; chattering negro slaves shouldered quiet native porters; countrymen from snug, small farms brought their wares to the great marketplace and rubbed elbows with grave citizens proudly exercising their prerogative of bearing arms; tailors and tavern keepers doffed their caps to swaggering young blades who strolled arrogantly about the capital looking for adventures.

Most troublesome of all the populace in Mexico at this time were the several hundred of these bold spirits, soldiers of fortune, younger sons come from a crowded Old World with a sword for sale, the best and the worst blood of Spain. They spent the days roistering, dicing, dueling, getting into scrapes with outraged husbands and the town guard, living on the bounty of the more prosperous citizens, "bobbing up and down like corks on the water," according to Mota Padilla, "without having anything to do or knowing what to busy themselves with,"[9] pestering Mendoza for estates and rich maidens to wed, yearning for other Mexicos to conquer and spoil. Their restless vigor was running to waste, their valor dulled for want of challenge.

Mendoza, whose hospitality was taxed heavily each day to provide for these idle cavaliers, welcomed with delight the possibility of putting to work their very real talents in exploring and conquering new country and opening the border for settlement. He set Francisco Vásquez Coronado to the task, and within a few months, while in Spain other contenders clamored vainly for title to explore Cíbola,[10] more than three hundred gentlemen of fortune and discontented landholders had enrolled in Mexico for service on the northern quest.

It was understood from the first that Coronado was to be in command of the great new expedition. Mendoza had chosen him, and Mendoza was a judge of men, not at all the sort to put a well-born nincompoop in command of a highly speculative venture in which the viceroy and his friends were investing heavily—a venture that Mendoza himself had once hoped to lead in person.

Coronado, as governor of New Galicia, had been the chief instigator and organizer of the expedition from the beginning. He had already shown himself, in the Amatepeque affair and in the excursion toward Topira, to be reliable in command of troops. During his travels he had gained the friendship of many of the men who were enlisting under his banner. Mendoza had made his choice, according to Castañeda, "because at this time Francisco Vásquez was his closest and most intimate friend, and because he considered him to be wise, capable, and intelligent, as well as a gentleman."[11] Coronado's commission as captain general[12] (a third instance of Mendoza's willingness to appoint the young man to an important post without awaiting royal approval) commended him as a person who would properly and faithfully carry out whatever might be entrusted to him, and gave him unlimited powers of government in the lands to be explored. There was no suggestion of foolish favoritism to cloud the appointment. A number of other well-tried officials, such as the veteran Cristóbal de Oñate, lieutenant governor of New Galicia, were available, and if Coronado was chosen over them it was because he was fully worthy, in Mendoza's opinion, of his highest trust.

Coronado did not apparently strive for appointment to the important post of captain general of the expedition. Indeed, from the start he was regretful at leaving his family and estates in Mexico. In accepting the command he must have been impelled as much by duty as by vaulting ambition. The judgment of Mendoza was to be vindicated by the loyalty which Coronado's captains and soldiers—all volunteers who were accustomed to follow only men of their choice—gave unswervingly in the troubled times to come.

The new captain general remained in the capital during the autumn, busily leading in the formation of the expedition. Funds were raised to cover the great costs of the venture. Mendoza contributed sixty thousand ducats, and Coronado raised fifty thousand more—perhaps by mortgaging his wife's marriage portion. Other citizens of Mexico were likewise willing to invest heavily in the promising enterprise. To Coronado was given the privilege of allotting towns and parcels of land to the adventurers who were to accompany him, as well as shares in the wealth that it was expected would come from the discovery of a "hill of silver" and other mining deposits near Cíbola.

Coronado saw to the delivery to the king's factor of large amounts of trade goods for future distribution to natives along the way, to ensure their friendship and aid. He was also charged with the duty of making advances of arms, horses, and money to needy volunteers, signing the vouchers through which these necessities were portioned out "according to the needs he noticed in each one of the soldiers who went in the said expedition."[13] The fortunate recruits were looked upon as made men; "they traded for the licenses which permitted them to go as soldiers," wrote a contemporary, "and people sold these as a favor, and whoever obtained one of these thought that it was as good as a title of nobility at the least."[14]

After the *cabildo* meeting of October 13, Coronado left the capital, little supposing that he would not attend another meeting until exactly three years later, to the day.[15] He journeyed to his province of New Galicia to arrange for the conduct of affairs while he was absent and to prepare for the reception of the army that was to muster near the coast of the South Sea in the early spring, ready for the northward march.

The rendezvous of the Coronado expedition had been named as Compostela, near the seacoast of New Galicia. Mendoza had wisely decided that the members of the force should not leave the capital in a body, because such an army marching through the settled regions west of Mexico would create a hardship on the settlers and Indians along the route.[16] Moreover, by having the rendezvous some distance away, the capital would be rid the sooner of its impatient warrior guests.

Even this forethought did not prevent some plundering here and there as small parties drifted westward into Michoacán during December and January. To Compostela, named for the Old World shrine of Spain's patron St. James, flocked the pilgrims of adventure, gleaming like grail-seekers in their coats of mail. The townsmen, who had been eager to be rid of these warriors, were now sorry to see them leave. Indeed, so empty did the capital seem that the citizens of Mexico began to fear that New Spain was being deserted by all its able-bodied men and would be left defenseless should an Indian uprising break out.

Coronado learned of this apprehension when he reached Compostela after attending to last-minute duties in Guadalajara.[17] He spoke of it to Viceroy Mendoza, who, after planning for the dispatch of a fleet up the Gulf of California to support the land forces, had spent New Year's Day of 1540 at Pátzcuaro and then had passed through Michoacán in a triumphal progress to review the troops that had assembled by Shrovetide at Compostela.

Coronado did not wish it said that he had emptied New Spain of soldiers to follow him on a far journey, leaving his province defenseless. He therefore urged that an official inquiry should be made in order to quiet these complaints. He declared that, contrary to popular belief, few of the solid citizenry of New Spain were going on the expedition, that all soldiers were going of their own free will without secret inducements, and that their presence in Mexico would not be missed. He requested[18] that Mendoza permit all the royal officials of New Galicia, as well as other qualified witnesses who knew the members of the expedition, to attend the grand review and observe for themselves the sort of men who were going with Coronado.

This was done, and on February 26, a few days after the army had left Compostela for the north, the witnesses were called to testify before the licentiate Maldonado, judge of the highest court of New Galicia.[19] The general concensus was that only two citizens of Mexico—aside from Coronado himself and the army-master Samaniego—were in the ranks: one Alonso Sánchez, formerly a shoemaker and now an unsuccessful traveling provision merchant, and one Domingo Martín, who also was away from Mexico most of the time. One of the magistrates of Mexico stated that after the force had left he had been in the city and had noticed that it was still full of people and that the population had not been appreciably diminished by the departure of the members of the Coronado forces. Cristóbal de Oñate, lieutenant governor of New Galicia, said that only two citizens of Guadalajara were going, and not a single one from Compostela. As for the young gentlemen who had joined the expedition, it seemed to him that their departure would be a benefit, as they were leading vicious lives and had nothing with which to support themselves. From all this it may be seen that almost the entire army was made up of those needy fortune hunters who had crowded the viceroy's palace, and that the general verdict in Mexico was "Good riddance!"

Yet much of the bluest blood of Iberia was represented at the grand review that was held on the green plateau of Compostela on the bright Sunday morning of February 22, 1540. Pedro de Castañeda de Nájera, a soldier who was later to chronicle the great adventure, boasted that for its size it was the most noble and distinguished assemblage which, up to that time, had ever gathered in the Indies to take part in any conquest.[20]

In the van, surrounded by his staff, rode the general-elect, Francisco Vásquez Coronado, gleaming in gilded armor that was later to single him out for many a hard knock before the walls of Cíbola. Then followed two hundred and twenty-five horsemen, all superbly mounted on the sturdy Andalusian breed of horses for which the viceroy's stock farms were famous.[21] Every man was, as became his title of *caballero,* a skilled horseman. A few of them wore shining full harness of mail, most of them a sort of armor of native buckskin;[22] and all the troop made a fine martial picture with lances erect, swords and bucklers at side, and bright saddle blankets and bards flowing to earth from the backs of their prancing mounts.

Behind the riders strode some sixty foot soldiers—pikemen in iron pot-helmets or vizored headpieces of horny bullhide, crossbowmen, and harquebusiers with their unwieldly firearms over their shoulders.[23] Then came a crowd of Indian servants and negro slaves driving the baggage animals and proudly pulling half a dozen *pedreros,* or light fieldpieces of bronze. Behind these thronged, in brilliant headdresses of parrot feathers and with flesh daubed with war paint of black and ochre, a thousand Indian allies,[24] brandishing bows, slings, and flint-edged wooden maces.

Banners waving, the army was drawn up in companies before the viceroy and other royal officials. Mass was celebrated by the Franciscan father Antonio Victoria, and then Mendoza made "a very eloquent short speech."[25] He began by saying that, seeing the noble company that was here gathered together and knowing the good will and high worth of each of them, he would have liked to make every one a captain of an army. Although he could not do this, he knew that they would show their fidelity to their general, Francisco Vásquez Coronado. He then pointed out clearly the benefits that this expedition might win, through the conversion of unknown Indian tribes, through the profit that would accrue to the men as conquerors of new lands, and through the claim that they would have on His Majesty's favor and aid as a result of bringing a great country under the dominion of the Crown. The venture, he made clear, was not to be merely a gold raid, but a crusade as well.

Then each soldier swore obedience, upon the Gospels in a missal, to his captains and to Coronado, who was now proclaimed and sworn as captain general of His Majesty's newest army of occupation.

A gallant gentleman, Lope de Samaniego, a Guzmán veteran, *cabildo* member, and recently warden of one of the king's fortresses in Mexico, was made provost or army-master—a position he was not to live long to occupy. Pedro de Tovar, a younger son of the lord high steward and guardian of the demented Spanish queen mother Juana, was appointed ensign general. The captains were Tristán de Luna y Arellano, destined later to be another of the unsuccessful *adelantados* of Florida;[28] Diego de Guevara,[27] a nephew of the Count of Oñate; García López de Cárdenas, like his commander a younger son of a well-to-do family; Rodrigo Maldonado, brother-in-law of the Duque del Infantado; Diego López, a former alderman of Seville; and Diego Gutiérrez, leading the cavalry arm. Captain of the infantry was the adventurous Pablo de Melgosa of Burgos, and commanding the artillery was Hernando de Alvarado, scion of one of the leading families of Santander, "the mountain province." Alvarado, a relative of Pedro, the *adelantado* of Guatemala, had been in

New Spain since 1530 and had served under Cortés in 1536. The artillery was to prove of little value, and he was soon left free to become, as he did, one of the leading spirits in exploration.

Those on the personal staff of the general—some of whom later became captains—included Francisco de Barrionuevo of Granada, Francisco de Ovando, and Juan Gallego. Two other captains, Melchor Díaz and Juan de Zaldívar (nephew of Cristóbal de Oñate), were not present at the review; they were then returning from a winter scouting trip to the north, but were soon to join the army on the road. It was Díaz who, as mayor of Culiacán, had welcomed Cabeza de Vaca four years before, and he still held that post; he was a man, wrote Castañeda, "who, although not a gentleman, merited the position he held."[28]

Other outstanding members of the party were Alonso Manrique de Lara of Valladolid, an experienced soldier who had served at the conquests of Buenos Aires, Tabasco, and Yucatán; the knightly Lope de Urrea of Aragón; Juan de Céspedes, an ensign who had served the king at the siege of Oran in North Africa; Juan Jaramillo, veteran of wars in Italy and Tunis, who was to become a captain and write a valuable description of Coronado's exploits;[29] Juan Paniagua, a pious warrior who had served at Cartagena; Andrés de Campo, a Portuguese with a long journey ahead of him; Francisco de Santillana, a blacksmith and veterinarian who owned one of the two mares of the expedition; Cristóbal de Quesada, who was going to Cíbola by order of the gov- .

ernment "to paint the things of the country";[30] and the king's factor, Antonio de Rivero de Espinosa, in charge of a cargo of beads, hawk bells, and other trinkets to barter for food from the Indians along the way.

Among the gaudy gentry of war was conspicuously absent the plain-robed Fray Marcos de Niza, guide and inspiring genius of this brave expedition. With his characteristic impatience he had pushed on ahead in company with an escort of soldiers[31] and four fellow Franciscans, apostles of this new crusade. These were the lay brothers Fray Daniel and Fray Juan de la Cruz; Fray Luis de Escalona (or De Ubeda), former companion of the bishop of Mexico; and fiery Fray Juan de Padilla of Andalusia, who had been Nuño de Guzmán's chaplain at the conquest of Michoacán and a soldier in his youth. As they trudged along, upon the faces of the last three of these ardent Gray Robes might have hovered some joyful foreknowledge of the glorious martyrdoms they were to win in the savage wastes that now lay before them.

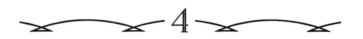

Misadventures of the Road

February–April, 1540

THE LITTLE ARMY of Coronado, although it had a sprinkling of veterans, was for the most part an army of young men. Their commander was himself barely turned thirty, and some of his officers were lads who today would still be at their lessons. But they were all men of Spain, and therefore quick to learn the trade of conquest.

To be a Spanish gentleman in 1540 was to be a warrior bred. Within a few generations the Spanish provinces, from a group of feudal baronies racked by centuries of war with the common Moorish foe, had become a united free nation, the champion of Christendom, foremost power in Europe, and almost sole proprietor of a virgin hemisphere. The young Spaniard, born among harsh mountains, bred in a barren country where the weakling perished, inheritor of a thousand skirmishes with the national enemy, was hardy, ascetic, alert, active, and courageous. He was inured to hardship and willing to risk the chances of war, although contemptuous of physical labor; wealth, to his mind, was to be won through freebooting, gambling, or the acquisition of large holdings worked by slaves. Against a knightly foe he could reveal a streak of lofty chivalry; his reputation for cruelty sprang from a hardened insensibility to suffering either in himself or in others. He was imbued with the crusading spirit, felt himself to be a favored warrior of Christ and the saints, and aimed at a piety that was superstitious observance of the forms of faith rather than its moral creed. He had an inordinate pride of race, of nationality, and of orthodoxy. He came to the New World not only to seek fame and wealth, but to find on the frontier a freedom of action that was steadily denied him by a growing absolutism at home. Physically, the sixteenth-century conquistador was tough, athletic, and of good stature, able to bear easily the heavy burden of armor in which he went to the wars.

The opponents of this little army on its northern foray were to be red men, Indians of a hundred different tribes whose customs were as strange as any described in the book of Marco Polo. On the dangerous road ahead lived the Huichol and Cora of Nayarit, the Totoram and Tepehuan of southern Sinaloa, the gentle Tahu and Guasave of the coastal plain, the wild Xixime of the river headwaters, the cannibal Acaxee of the mountains, the warlike Cahita of the Yaqui and Mayo valleys, the hard-working Pima of northern Sonora, the Colorado River tribes of Cocopa and Yuma, the semi-civilized town dwellers—Zuñi, Hopi, Tehua, Tigua,

Queres, Piro—of a hundred plateau pueblos, and, finally, the Apache and Caddo rovers of the Texas plains and the Wichita and Pawnee of the Missouri basin.

These native groups, whose origin, in the minds of some Spaniards, was still associated with the lost tribes of Israel, were of many levels of intelligence and achievement, and some of the best were well able to resist an invading force of the white race. Like the Spaniard, the Indian of highest type was strong, hardy, ascetic, and capable of great feats of action and endurance; he too was proud, deeply religious, and bred to the dangers of warfare. Moreover, his love of personal freedom was so great that he could not, even for the defense of his home place, long endure the discipline needed to create an organization that would transcend the ties of family or village.

In another and most important regard, the Indians were less than a match for a trained European force. They had taken only the first steps toward a material civilization such as had developed in the crowded continent of Europe. All these tribes were living in the Stone Age of culture. They had no horses, no plows; they did not even know the use of the wheel. The northern tribes had not a scrap of metal except a few beads of crude copper. There was not a gun or a flask of gunpowder on the entire continent north of the twentieth parallel. The natives had never heard of a sailing vessel, a printed book, a standing army, a pope, a factory, a tavern, or a House of Lords. However, the bare rumor that they did have one thing—gold—had been enough to set

European heads to plotting and the men of war to gathering. A land said to be full of yellow metal and bright stones, and inhabited by souls not yet converted to the Spanish idea of God, was enough to draw to it the most adventurous hearts among the young inheritors of *Orbe Novo*.

Now, at last, Coronado was on the march to Cíbola.

On Monday, February 23, 1540, the day after the grand review, leaving behind them in Compostela Lieutenant Governor Oñate in charge of Coronado's province of New Galicia, the army, with banners flying, took the "much used" trail northward from the town. The pathway, piercing through the overarching scrub thickets of the coastal plain, was an ancient one, the prehistoric trade route on which turquoises and hides had come down from the north to be exchanged for parrot feathers of the *tierra caliente*, a trail centuries old when Nuño de Guzmán's men followed it and studded it with little way-station settlements.

For several days Viceroy Mendoza accompanied the army, and turned back only regretfully, wishing that he might have been free to march with these bold young men to what all expected would be the conquest of an empire as mighty as that of Montezuma. Affectionately he bade farewell to his friend and, with his official attendants, retraced his steps toward Colima, leaving Francisco Vásquez Coronado to lead his men forward up the flood plain of Nayarit.

Their progress in those first days was discouragingly

slow. The horses, of which there were less than six hundred, were heavily laden with the baggage and other possessions of the novice conquerors. "As each one was obliged to transport his own baggage," wrote Pedro de Castañeda, "and all did not know how to fasten the packs, and as the horses started off fat and lazy, they had a good deal of difficulty and labor during the first few days, and many left many valuable things, giving them to anyone who wanted them, in order to get rid of carrying them. In the end necessity, which knows no law, made them skillful, so that one could see many gentlemen become muleteers, and anybody who despised this work was not considered a man."[1]

The soldiers were obliged to transport their gear themselves because Mendoza had issued strict orders against impressment of the native volunteers as burden bearers. The Indians were to be considered as free warriors, taking part in the expedition of their own accord; and if at any time some of them wished to turn back, they were to be allowed to depart freely and be given an armed escort. They were treated as allies rather than servants, were given goods from the stores of the royal factor to trade with the Indians met along the way, were taken care of during sickness, and were not pressed into service as carriers.[2] On this journey, as the general was to testify later, he saw soldiers of high rank marching on foot because they carried their food and other belongings on their horses. Other soldiers trudged along carrying corn for their mounts, and

---

[1] For notes to chap. 4, see p. 338.

Coronado himself "had many a time dismounted so the soldiers who were thus traveling laden would withstand the hardships with greater fortitude."[3]

Large herds of cattle, sheep, and swine—provisions on the hoof—were driven by Indians behind the main body.[4] These animals could not be hurried, and several days were lost at the Río Grande de Santiago, where the sheep had to be put over one at a time. The country was broken and hilly, with the volcanic peaks of Sanganguey and Ceboruco marking the grim eastern skyline. Beyond the Santiago the way narrowed to a corridor of coastal plain between the Pacific and the escarpment of the Sierra Madre, a plain cut crosswise before the advancing soldiers by the alluvial valleys of short, mountain-fed rivers whose plunging waters soon foundered in the sand-choked lagoons and marshes—the San Pedro, the Acaponeta, the Cañas (now marking the Sinaloa border), the Baluarte. The soldiers stumbled through swamps, slapping at the mosquitoes that rose about them in swarming clouds.

At the village of Aztatlán, on the lower Acaponeta River, the men of Coronado's army viewed the site of the great summer flood which had almost wiped out the army of Guzmán ten years before. Indeed, Guzmán's men were saved only because they had hastened to take refuge among houses built on some great mounds of earth made by hand, which the provident Indians of the region had constructed for such watery emergencies.

This valley, in Guzmán's time, had been densely populated by a people of fairly high culture, who lived in flat-roofed adobe houses, made excellent brick-red pottery, and were bountifully provided with the fruits of the soil. Guzmán's force had gathered enough food there to have lasted them for two years, had it not all been lost in the flood. The natives had many dogs, raised thousands of fowls, and even domesticated bees for honey and wax. Once proud and powerful, these people first had been harassed by the pillaging Guzmán and then had suffered plagues and attacks from the hill tribes, so that now the busy coastal towns which the first explorers had found were almost completely deserted.

When, in mid-March, Coronado's army reached Chametla on the Río Presidio, a town that had been settled and named Espíritu Santo by Guzmán, they found that it had been abandoned by the Spanish colonists, most of whom had gone to Peru. Situated upstream from the present-day city of Mazatlán, this fertile region, which only a few years before had supported twenty-two pueblos subject to the Indian lord of Chametla, was now inhabited by a poor furtive remnant who were openly antagonistic to the white invaders. The land was so barren of food that it became necessary for the army-master, Samaniego—who, as a former captain under Guzmán, knew the country—to lead a foraging party into the hills.

As the foragers penetrated the thick *monte,* or thorny bush, one of the harquebusiers, who had become separated from the others, was waylaid and captured by the lurking natives. He uttered a great shout, which came to the ears of the vigilant Samaniego and brought him to the rescue. The Indians fled at this attack, and the army-master, thinking everything was safe, raised the visor of his helmet just at the moment when an arrow came flying from a near-by thicket. The arrow entered one eye and pierced the brain—and thus died on active service Coronado's second in command. He was the first casualty of the Cíbola expedition, and a tragic loss it was, for his wise counsel was to be sorely missed.

Five or six other soldiers were injured by arrows before Captain Diego López could rally the men over the body of their fallen leader. They withdrew, bearing his body, which was buried in a little chapel in the deserted town of Espíritu Santo; his bones were afterward taken to Compostela. Samaniego, brave and skillful, had been beloved by all, and his loss was taken as an evil omen. The devoted soldiery relieved their feelings by capturing some of the rebel Indians of the neighborhood, and any who seemed to belong to the district where Samaniego had been slain were left swinging to trees as a warning to killers.

The recruits of the army had been blooded in a brush with hostile Indians—a skirmish that was portentous of much grim fighting to come. Cíbola was far away; death, it seemed, lay on every side. But those golden cities, they consoled themselves, might be worth many a hard knock.

As the army was on the point of leaving the town where Samaniego's body lay, an even more serious blow threatened their high hopes. Into camp galloped two captains fresh from the north, with news of the north.

The previous autumn, Melchor Díaz and Juan de Zaldívar had been sent out from Culiacán with fifteen horsemen to explore northward into the country that Fray Marcos had penetrated. Now, returning from this journey, they had met up with Coronado's army marching toward that same country. The news that they brought was not heartening to the commander.

Díaz told Coronado the tale. They had set out from Culiacán on November 17, 1539. Beyond the Río Petatlán, in spite of a bad harvest, Díaz had been provided with food by the Indians, who received with due reverence the wooden cross that he sent ahead to announce his peaceful coming. After journeying thus for a hundred leagues, he found the midwinter weather becoming frosty and increasingly cold; but he pushed on as far as the place called Chichilticalli, situated somewhere on or south of the great Arizona stream now called the Gila. Here he halted. Some of the Indians with him had been frozen to death; it was clear that he could not attempt to cross the wilderness already deep with snows; and he knew the time had come to return and tell what he had seen and heard.

The Indians of Chichilticalli had spoken to Díaz freely. Some of them declared that they had lived in Cíbola for fifteen and twenty years; and all separately confirmed many of the things that Marcos had described concerning the seven towns beyond the wilderness. The houses of Cíbola were made of stone with mud plaster, of three and four stories, with loopholes to defend the outer walls. When the town dwellers went out to fight, said the Chichilticalli Indians, they carried shields and wore colored leather jackets of cowhide, and in peaceful days they passed the time in singing and dancing and playing the flute.[5]

Much of this agreed with what Marcos had already reported. But the most alluring part of the friar's story could not be confirmed. The Indians which Díaz had met maintained that there was no gold or other metal to be found in the pueblos. It was true that turquoises were to be found there, although not a great many. Moreover, the tribes south of Chichilticalli had received the strange horsemen with sour faces and grim glances that were a portent of the welcome the white men might expect were they to push into the pueblo country. Orders had been sent out from Cíbola that if Christians came they should be killed like beasts, for they were mortal creatures, as could be proved by the bones of one of them—the unfortunate Esteban—who had been put to death by the men of Cíbola. If the men of Sonora did not dare to start this killing, they should send word to Cíbola, so that those fighting men could come south and do it for them.

Díaz now joined the company that had been assigned to him, while Zaldívar carried the report to Viceroy Mendoza.[6] The story of the expedition to Chichilticalli was by Coronado's order to be kept from the soldiery so that they would not be disheartened on the march before them.

But bad news has a way of leaking out, and before long the men were whispering that Díaz had heard of no great treasure land, that the Indians of Cíbola were warlike and well prepared to resist invasion, and that nothing had been found which could give substance to the golden visions of Fray Marcos. So great were the mutterings that Marcos himself, now acting as spiritual adviser to the army on the road, felt called upon to quiet these doubts. He "cleared away the clouds" by preaching an inspiriting sermon in which he told the men in plain terms that they were on the way to a good country where their hands would be filled; and for the time being the malcontents were quieted.

Thus encouraged, the army marched across the flat and wearisome plains along the road to Culiacán, foraging on the way. They crossed the Piaxtla and the shallow Elota. The limit of New Galicia was now not far off, and they pushed forward impatiently. Because of the heavily laden baggage train and the plodding cattle their progress had been painfully slow; in fact, this first leg of their long journey had consumed a full month when at last they came in sight of Culiacán, eighty leagues from their starting point of Compostela. On the eve of Easter, March 28, the army reached the town of San Miguel, on the banks of the Río de Ciguatán where Guzmán had thought to find the Amazonian women of legendary fame.

They were met by a delegation of citizens who had come out to welcome the young general and to ask a small favor. Would the army refrain from entering the town until the day after Easter? A few preparations must be made for a suitable reception of the king's brave soldiers. There were winks and hints. What about staging a sham battle that would display the prowess of the tiny militia force that held this frontier outpost of New Spain?

Such a martial demonstration appealed to everybody. "When," wrote Castañeda, "the day after Easter came, the army started in the morning to go to the town and, as they approached, the inhabitants came out in a cleared field with foot and horse drawn up in ranks as if for a battle, and having their seven bronze pieces of artillery in position, making a show of defending their town. Some of our soldiers were with them. Our army drew up in the same way and began a skirmish with them, and after the artillery on both sides had been fired they were driven back, just as if the town had been taken by force of arms, which was a pleasant demonstration of welcome, except for one artilleryman who lost a hand by a shot, from having ordered them to fire before he had finished drawing out the ramrod."

Thus, to the sound of gunfire and patriotic yells, subdued somewhat by a prophetic bit of bloodletting, the royal force under Governor Francisco Vásquez Coronado was welcomed into His Majesty's loyal town of Culiacán, there to be the guests of honor at the most lavish fiestas that the hospitable inhabitants could stage for them.

The generous welcome accorded to Coronado's army by the villagers of San Miguel de Culiacán must have inspired many an apprentice conqueror to dust off his martial finery and preen himself, thinking a month of marching well requited by such a gala reception. Although a camp was laid out for the soldiery on the outskirts of the village, the townsfolk opened their houses to all persons of quality in the army, and invited many to lodge with them. The year was bringing a bountiful harvest, so that there was more than enough for all to eat; moreover, supplies were so plentiful that when the army made ready to depart, a few weeks later, enough provisions were given them to load six hundred pack animals.

This hospitality was well repaid. Since food would be unobtainable in the country ahead, the expedition perforce had to carry all its supplies, leaving little place for personal belongings. Consequently, all the fine clothing and accouterments remaining to the soldiers must be left behind, and in this wise the townspeople fell heir to much discarded gear.

During the winter months, Mendoza had made arrangements for a sea expedition to act in concert with the land forces, his plan being for the ships to carry the army baggage. A small vessel, the "San Gabriel," which was to be part of the fleet, was now at the Culiacán roadstead, loaded with baggage and with a quantity of supplies for the sailors. However, the other ships of the fleet were just leaving Acapulco and could not arrive before the army left Culiacán. Many of the soldiers, therefore, preferred to bestow their possessions upon their hosts rather than entrust them to the deep. In this they probably were wise, for as it turned out the fleet was unable to make contact with the land forces at any time, and so all this gear was lost—"or, rather," as Castañeda euphemistically put it, "those who owned it lost it." Other articles which were sent by those at home in Mexico to the men of the army were entrusted to the ships coming from the south; nor did any of these reach their consignees in the army. Among this lading there were undoubtedly a few comforts sent by Doña Beatriz to her husband, the captain general.

The affection that Coronado held for his Beatriz was a subject for gossip throughout the country; and Castañeda has related, "for what it may be worth," a tale of how this jealous devotion was played upon by a soldier with more cunning than courage.

During the stay at Culiacán a young private named Trujillo[8] asserted that while he was bathing in the river a spirit appeared to him in a vision. Brought before the general, the young man confessed that the spirit was the Devil in person, who had told him that if he would kill Coronado he would be able to marry Doña Beatriz and thus win great wealth and an elevated position among his fellows.

This story was seized upon by the alert Fray Marcos, who proceeded to preach several fine sermons demonstrating that the Devil, infuriated at the good works which the expedition must inevitably perform, sought to disrupt the army by this attempt to have the commander killed. The other friars in the army reported the episode to their friends, so that shortly the pulpits of Mexico were buzzing with the tale. The upshot was that Coronado ordered Trujillo to remain behind in

Culiacán and forbade him to take further part in the expedition—which, judging from all the circumstances, was exactly what the fainthearted rascal had hoped to gain by inventing his story.

Fray Marcos de Niza was here, there, and everywhere in the camp, uttering sonorous heartening words. From now forward, he would be the guide to lead the army to the golden lands, of whose wealth he could not say enough. The vision of a great mission of God in the northern towns rose daily before him.

He was impatient at the delay caused by the late harvest at San Miguel. Often he was seen scurrying to Coronado's lodging, padding barefoot through the dust with his gray robe kilted up about his middle. Could nothing be done to hasten the army's departure?

Coronado considered. It would be impossible for the army to live off the country on the trail ahead. It might be bad policy to divide his force. But a smaller party, well equipped and riding light, could push ahead on the way, to scout the country. Coronado was fully as impatient as Marcos was to see the towers of Cíbola. Perhaps a flying squadron could be formed to carry the banner of Castile into the wilderness that lay ahead. Then came the decision—Coronado himself would lead a dash to the north.

The Hungry Journey

April 22 – July 7, 1540

THE SPRING SEASON was waning; and the progress of the
army so far, hampered as it had been by the necessity of
carrying all its provisions, had been disturbingly slow.
General Coronado began to assemble the flying column that he himself would lead to Cíbola.

He chose a force of some seventy horsemen, including personal friends such as Alvarado, Díaz, Tovar, Pablo de Melgosa, and García López de Cárdenas, who
had replaced the slain Samaniego as army-master. These
were supported by twenty-five or thirty foot soldiers
armed with harquebuses or crossbows, a few of the ar-
tillerymen with the six bronze swivel guns, and most
of the Indian allies. This advance party, it was planned,
would travel as lightly equipped as possible. Personal
effects were reduced to a pound for each man, since the
horses had to carry the weapons and the food—consist-
ing mainly of corn bread, for the new harvest had not
yet ripened.

Coronado ordered that in the absence of Melchor

Díaz, mayor of Culiacán, the town should be left in control of Don Hernando de Saavedra, uncle of that count of Castellar who had formerly been mayor of Seville. The main body of soldiers was to rest a while longer, then follow in a fortnight, after the harvest had been gathered, under the command of Captain Tristán de Arellano.

Francisco Vásquez Coronado, who later was several times to follow this same prudent plan of sending light scouting parties far in advance of the main body, set off with his picked men on April 22. So great was the zeal of the priests to enter the new field of unredeemed souls that not one of them would be left behind, even though their going meant leaving the army without spiritual counsel. An accident, fortunate for the rank and file, who would otherwise have gone priestless, befell Fray Antonio Victoria, a full-fledged cleric who could serve the Mass, when three days after the army's departure he broke his leg and had to be sent back to camp at Culiacán. The consolation that he could give, even when temporarily disabled, was to be gratefully received.[1]

The advance party found everything peaceful in the country which they crossed. The Indians recognized Fray Marcos and Melchor Díaz from their previous trips. The first way station beyond Culiacán was the settlement on the Río Sebastián de Ebora,[2] named for a Portuguese colonist who had been given a grant of land there. About eighty miles out from their starting

---

[1] For notes to chap. 5, see pp. 338–340.

point, the flying squadron came to the Indian settlements of Petatlán, the "place of mats."

The Cahitas of this valley, who in earlier times had lived in villages thickly crowded from mountains to sea, had suffered much from raiders and slavers working out of Culiacán. The Indians had learned to anticipate the wishes of their grim white neighbors, and now quickly offered food and lodging to Coronado.

At Petatlán the moist coastal plain gave way to typical desert, and the travelers swung farther away from the sea. "From this point on," wrote Castañeda, "there are no trees without spines, nor are there any fruits except a few tunas, mesquites, and pitahayas."[3] The cactus country opened out before them, sandy red soil dotted with clumps of thorn-armored mesquite, the pulpy green pads of the tuna or prickly pear, the ribbed column of the saguaro, the dusty gray sage. Heat shimmered from the shields and corselets of the cavalry; sword hilts were scorching to the touch. Eyes grew red-rimmed from sun and dust. Horses stumbled in the washing sands of gashed arroyos.

Three days after leaving Petatlán they crossed the Río Cinaloa,[4] a good-sized stream draining down from the lofty sierras. Thirty leagues beyond this crossing, Coronado calculated, was the place where they should start looking for the golden valley which Marcos had not dared to enter. He sent ahead a party of a dozen horsemen under Díaz with orders to make double marches and explore the country to the right of the trail, later making rendezvous at the junction of the

Río Mayo with the Arroyo de los Cedros which entered it from the north.[5]

The Díaz party traveled up the Mayo through very rough mountainous country for four days, but found no food nor any trace of gold—nothing, in truth, except an infertile terrain and a few poor villages with twenty or thirty huts apiece. No one knew anything of the earrings and sweat-scrapers of pure gold that Marcos had written about; and all said that naught was to be found upstream but uninhabited wastes and increasingly rugged mountains.

When Coronado's men were given this information, brought by the scouts to the meeting place at the Cedros junction, their disappointment was keen. Friar Marcos had to tax his inventive powers to escape from the tight position in which the news placed him. "The whole company felt disturbed at this," Coronado later wrote to the viceroy, "that a thing so much praised, and about which the father had said so much, should be found so very different; and they began to think that all the rest would be likewise. When I noticed this, I tried to encourage them as well as I could, telling them that Your Lordship had always thought that this part of the trip would be a waste of effort, and that we ought to devote our attention to those Seven Cities and the other provinces about which we had information."[6]

The squadron now started up the Cedros, along a trail becoming increasingly difficult—another grievance against the friar, who had claimed that the way would be plain and good, and that there would be only one small hill of "about half a league." The truth was that this stretch of three days' travel between the Mayo and the Yaqui (or Yaquimi) had many places where, as Coronado said, "it was impossible to pass without making a new road or repairing the one that was there. . . . There are mountains which, however well the path might be fixed, could not be crossed without great danger of the horses falling over the edge." The beasts which hauled the field guns undoubtedly found this stretch the most difficult going of any yet encountered.

By way of the Cedros headwaters and the deep and rushing Río Chico the party came to the banks of the Río Yaqui. On the lower reaches of this stream, Diego de Guzmán, exploring in 1533, had parleyed with a band of Yaqui Indians, who had brazenly made the proposal that they would bring food, if the Spaniards first tied themselves with ropes! But now, if any of these warriors were lurking near by, they dared not dispute the passage of the river with the men of Coronado.[7]

The advance party had taken a flock of sheep with them for provisions, but because of the "roughness of the rocks" many lambs and wethers lost their hoofs; finally it was decided to leave most of the flock behind at the Yaqui in charge of four horsemen, to be brought on to Cíbola later. Only a few of the herd were to survive that journey, even though they were driven no more than two leagues a day. The shortage of provisions for the flying column, which resulted in forcing them to live off the country like brigands, was to have a curious effect on the success of Coronado's mission.

Beyond the Yaqui the party swung to the left and reached a settlement of Indians who had straw huts and storehouses of corn and beans and melons.[8] The horsemen crossed one more toilsome ridge, and on May 26, after more than a month on the road, they came to the valley of Corazones, the place called Hearts in Cabeza de Vaca's narrative.

No dressed deer hearts or any other delicacies were offered to these hungry travelers. Although there was much tilled ground in the valley, and an irrigation ditch gave evidence of high agricultural skill, it was proving to be a poor season, and the Opata inhabitants, with their own many mouths to fill, had no food to spare for the Spaniards.

It had already been a belt-tightening trip for the men of Coronado. Some Indians and negroes of the party had died from hunger and weariness, and ten or twelve horses had died "because they were unable to stand the strain of carrying heavy burdens and eating little."[9]

Coronado's first need, therefore, was to find a food supply. Hearing that the Indians of the neighboring "valley of Señora" (or Sonora, which was the proper native name) had ample provisions, he sent the energetic Díaz on a peaceful trading mission into their territory. The "valley" was the next basin upstream on the Sonora River from that of Ures, in which Corazones lay, and was separated from it by a long and narrow gorge. Díaz obtained there a small quantity of corn by barter, bringing temporary relief to his famished comrades.

General Coronado rested several days at Corazones,

which he learned was a good five-day journey from the sea. Natives from the coast told him that there were seven or eight islands in the Gulf opposite this region, islands poorly supplied with food but heavily populated by savages—undoubtedly the filthy and ferocious Seris. The coast dwellers also gave news that they had seen a ship pass not far from the land. This, however, could not have been one of the fleet that Mendoza was sending forth; probably the natives were speaking of one of Ulloa's vessels sighted the previous summer.

The people of Corazones lived in mud-and-cobble houses and dressed in deerskins. The place seemed a friendly spot to Coronado, and he gave orders that the army on its way north should establish a Spanish settlement there. The site of this town, the Villa de San Gerónimo de los Corazones, was for various reasons later shifted twice, each time farther upstream, without any change in name.

The upper valley of the Río Sonora, which for centuries was to be the chief route for travelers from the west coast to the pueblo country and to California, is a chain of fertile basins, one above another, separated by gorges which the river has cut through the rock. Through this lovely part of the Mexican northwest the men of Coronado, somewhat refreshed and rested, now pushed forward. Leaving Corazones, they rode through the wild fifteen-mile canyon to "Señora," to which the Villa de San Gerónimo was soon to be moved. This valley, extending from Babiácora to beyond Banámichi, was well suited for settlement, although the fertile spots along the river bottoms were not extensive enough to support large numbers of Indians.

The explorers followed a trail that crossed and recrossed the stream a score of times. Overhead, the fretted and crenelated sandstone cliffs, undercut by the river, were fringed with emerald foliage; monstrous lizards and bright snakes moved at their feet; and strange birds filled the warm air with their songs. At the upper end of this pleasant valley the men passed the twelve-mile gorge of Sinoquipe, and so came to the broad basin which they called Ispa.[10] Then, at the northern end of the right fork of the Sonora, they found, "forty leagues farther toward Cíbola," the valley of Suya,[11] which was to become the third and final site of the town of San Gerónimo.

This Suya region attracted the lively interest of the observant foot soldier, Pedro de Castañeda. "The chiefs of the villages go up on some little mounds they have made for this purpose, and like public criers there make proclamations for the space of an hour, ordering those things that must be performed. They have some little huts for shrines, all over the outside of which they stick many arrows, making them look like hedgehogs. They do this when they are eager for war. All about this province toward the mountains there is a large population in separate little provinces containing ten or twelve villages. . . . The women paint their chins and eyes like the Moorish women of Barbary. The people are great sodomites. They drink wine made of the pitahaya, which is the fruit of a great thistle which opens like the pomegranate; this wine befuddles them. They make a great quantity of preserves from the tuna cactus; they preserve it in a large amount of its sap without other sweetening. They make bread of the mesquite, like cheese, which keeps good for a whole year. There are native melons in this country so large that a person can carry only one of them at a time. They taste like cooked dried figs; they are very good and sweet, keeping for a whole year thus dried. In this country there were also tame eagles, which the chiefs esteemed highly. . . . Between Suya and Chichilticalli there are many sheep and mountain goats with very large bodies and horns."[12]

Leaving Suya, the soldiers and priests marched for four days over the uninhabited grasslands cupping the headwaters of the Río Sonora. All about them were the heaped ranges of the border country. This high plateau is a natural boundary. So far, all the rivers that Coronado had crossed or ascended had flowed in a southwestward course to the Gulf coast. Now, on the mile-high tableland, for the first time they came upon a stream, which they called the Nexpa,[13] whose trickling waters would lead them northward, toward their long-dreamed goal. On its banks a few poor Indians[14] came out to greet the strangers with presents of roasted maguey and pitahaya cactus.

After the cool ravines of Sonora, the next stage of the journey must have seemed doubly hard to endure, for this southern part of Arizona contains some of the hottest and most Saharan deserts in the United States. Fortunately for the men of Coronado, the time of their passage was just after the snow-fed spring floods; at any other season, surface water would have been impossible to find. This was the domain of mirage, of the polychrome mesa shimmering in the crisp, dry air. It was the land of cactus and sage, mesquite and creosote bush; the home of the sand-colored snake, the scorpion, the bead-scaled Gila monster, the burrowing owl.

"We went down this stream [the Nexpa] for two days, and then left the stream, going toward the right to the foot of the mountain chain in two days' journeys, where we heard news of what is called Chichilticalli. Crossing the mountains, we came to a deep and reedy river, where we found water and forage for the horses."[15] The "deep and reedy river" was the great desert stream now called the Gila, on which was situated the famous landmark of Chichilticalli,[16] whose praises had been sung by Fray Marcos.

This great "red house" was a large earth-walled fortress, daubed with ochre, which had been built, according to Castañeda, by people who had separated from Cíbola, "a civilized and warlike race of strangers who had come from a distance."[17] But Coronado and his men suffered new pangs of disappointment when they discovered that the vaunted Chichilticalli was merely a roofless ruin of mud walls. It had been destroyed some time before by Gila River Indians—Apaches or a similar nomad tribe—who impressed Castañeda as "the most barbarous people that have yet been seen." They dwelt among the ruins in isolated huts, and lived by hunting.

Fray Marcos was questioned on another point. He

had stated in his report that from Chichilticalli one could view the sea. Coronado, anxious now for news of the fleet sent to support his land movements, took pains to investigate, only to make the bitter discovery that Indians of this region could not reach the coast, traveling at their best speed, in less than ten days. Sunburnt soldiers muttered and spat as the friar passed their campfires.

The men of Coronado rested for two days at Chichilticalli and would have stayed longer had they dared, but the food was rapidly giving out. The Gila Valley was not a pleasant camping spot, for the adventurers were continually exposed to the bronze heat of the desert sun and the ravages of strong sand-laden winds. They must push on. And ahead lay the increasingly rough and serrated mountains of the great Colorado Plateau, a wilderness so remote that it is still little known, and which in Coronado's day was almost completely empty of human beings.

Into this pine-covered mountain country Coronado led his men on St. John's Eve, June 23. Don García López de Cárdenas was sent a day's march in advance with fifteen horsemen, to scout for a passage.

The flying squadron forded the snow-fed Gila, swelled with brown floodwaters, ascended the steep Gila Range, and for the next fortnight pushed through sierra after sierra, stumbling dog-weary, losing men and horses, more horses than during all the previous march. "We found no grass during the first few days," wrote Coronado, "but a worse way through mountains and more dangerous passages than we had known previously. . . . The way is very bad for at least thirty leagues and more, among impassable mountains."[18]

Marcos, who was rapidly becoming an anathema, had said that on this part of his journey he had been bountifully supplied with game—deer, rabbits, and partridges—by his Indian guides; but the mounted party could not pause to hunt the reaches of the forest, and the only beasts that they saw were "gray lions and leopards"—pumas and wildcats. As the last of the supplies dwindled, manna in this wilderness was found in the form of pine nuts, which the soldiers soon learned to relish. Their Indian guides showed them how to make a sweet cake of acorns, and some watercress was found in springs. They also tried fishing for the Gila trout and mountain catfish.

Their route through the wilderness is fairly clear. It cut across the White Mountains, over the arroyos and gorges of the high Colorado Plateau, and through the upper drainage of the Colorado Chiquito, by way of the site of the present town of St. Johns, to the Zuñi River.

The first stream to be crossed after leaving the Gila was the Gila Bonito, which was christened the San Juan because the scouts reached it on St. John's Day. The next large stream, the Salada or Salt River, was rising when they came upon it some two or three days later, and, as they used rude rafts to cross it, the name of Río de las Balsas was given to it. Two days later they came to what they called the Río de las Barrancas, or River of

Ravines, an unidentifiable stream in the White Mountains, perhaps an upper branch of the Colorado Chiquito. Two days more and they reached the Chiquito proper; Jaramillo called it the Cold River, Coronado the River of Flax because of the plants found on its banks. Beyond the river they went by a "piny mountain," on the top of which was found a cool spring. There some of the Indian allies, several negroes, and "a Spaniard named Espinosa,"[19] all too famished to be prudent, died from eating poisonous herbs when their rations gave out. Two days beyond this point they came at last to the "river of Cíbola," which because of its muddy, chocolate waters, roiled by freshets, was given the name of Río Vermejo or Red River. The goal so hopefully envisioned during their arduous journey was now almost in sight of the famished soldiery.

Coronado and his men had now traversed the trails from Mexico City to the outskirts of Zuñi on the east-central border of Arizona, a distance of five hundred bone-racking leagues. But the general himself, it may be noted, was not the first explorer over any part of this route.

The trail was well known to Indian traders of one or another tribe for its full length, and at least one alien, black Esteban, had traversed it before Coronado came to the "river of Cíbola" in the early days of July, 1540. The southernmost roads along the Pacific coast had been discovered by the lieutenants of Cortés; Nuño de Guzmán had literally blazed the way as far as Culiacán; and Diego de Guzmán, Alcaraz, Samaniego, and others had pushed exploration as far north as the Mayo. Cabeza de Vaca, heading southward, had followed the old route down from the headwaters of the Sonora. Marcos, at the least generous estimate, had arrived at the sources of the Nexpa, or San Pedro, and perhaps had gone farther into the wilderness; Melchor Díaz on his winter sortie had won to Chichilticalli; and Esteban, as has been told, had gone the whole way to Cíbola, never to return.

On this road Coronado, whose instinct for scouting the route ahead was as strong as a good leader's should be, so far had not personally been in advance a single step of the way. Even when crossing the Colorado Plateau, he had kept Cárdenas always one day ahead to guard against surprise. Most of the later exploration out from Cíbola was to be made by his lieutenants, and not until a year had passed did Coronado himself act as a trail breaker on an unknown route.

Although not in the van, General Coronado had nonetheless successfully led an armed force of men across much dangerous country to the doorstep of the Seven Cities. Cíbola now lay before him. What could be done to ensure its seizure?

A bold stroke was necessary; and he had good cause to wonder just how powerful the forces at his command might be. As a military corps, the flying squadron was not impressive. The legion of Mexican Indians was badly weakened, and he knew they could not be depended upon to aid greatly. The Spanish party had been reduced by losses of men and animals; all were haggard and wayworn, many were in a starving state, and the repeated disillusionments where Marcos had prophesied great things had left more than one soldier in cynical mood. The fighting morale of the weary recruits might be shaky. And this puny force, less than a hundred white men in all, had to be relied upon to storm the famed walled stronghold of Cíbola!

The invaders had not even the advantage of surprise, for already the enemy knew of their coming and were fully prepared to resist. The scouts under Cárdenas had met four Indians on the bank of the Río Vermejo who made signs of peace and announced that they had been sent to welcome the white men. The very next day, they said, they would provide food for the whole troop. This sounded hopeful, and Cárdenas presented the men with a cross and told them to have no fear, because General Coronado came in the name of his great lord to help and defend the people of Cíbola. Word was sent at once to the commander; and coming up, he gave the strangers good words and presented them with some little cloaks.

But with good reason the Spaniards suspected that these overtures were false. Cárdenas was ordered to go forward with a guard and hold any narrow passes where the Indians might set an ambush. He found "a very bad place," which he occupied, and just in time. That night a force of natives came to the pass to secure it for themselves, and upon finding it defended, they flung themselves against the vigilant guards.

The Indians were soon beaten off, but retired in

good order, sounding the retreat on a small horn. The noise of battle aroused the main body of soldiers, and some of the young Spaniards were so frightened that in the turmoil of alarm they "saddled their mounts hind side before." The men of Coronado were soon to learn that these Cíbolans were no skulking cravens like some of the lowland tribes of Mexico, but were fighters who could be expected to make a sturdy stand for the defense of their homes. That night the hills were alive with signal fires, spreading the news to all the pueblos that the white masters of murdered Esteban had come from the south to avenge his slaying.

With these warnings of what he might expect, Coronado moved forward the next day with as bold a front as could be mustered, considering, as he said, "that we were in such great need of food that I thought we should all die of hunger if we continued to be without provisions for another day, especially the Indian allies, since altogether we did not have two bushels of corn. So I was obliged to hasten forward without delay."[20]

At dawn he marched. The day was Wednesday, July 7, 1540; and before it closed a battle was to be fought, the battle of Hawikuh, first and not least of the bloody series of fights between red and white men that have stained the history of the American Southwest from mid-sixteenth century almost into our own generation.

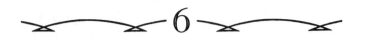
The Conquest of Cíbola
July, 1540

THERE IS NO DOUBT whatever that the Seven Cities of Cíbola, which Francisco Vásquez Coronado was about to enter, were the group of pueblos occupied then, as now, by the Zuñi tribe of Indians on the upper stretch of the river of that name, in the shadow of the dark ranges on the New Mexico side near the Arizona boundary.[1] The idea that there were seven of these villages was a preconception stemming from the old myth of Antilia; Jaramillo[2] truthfully recorded that there were only six.

Of these, the first that would be reached by a party ascending the Zuñi River, or Río Vermejo, the village where Coronado first came in contact with the Pueblo Indians, was named Hawikuh, the Ahacus of the Marcos report. The others, lying in the furrows of the Zuñi Range, were Kechipauan (or Kyanawa), Kwakina, Hálona (site of the present village of Zuñi), Kiakima, and Mátsaki. These were the only sizable Indian pueblos

---

[1] For notes to chap. 6, see pp. 340–343.

that could have been reached by the route laid down in the several contemporary accounts, and that fit the descriptions left by the conquerors. Several near-by places which were also described, such as Ojo Caliente and Zuñi Salt Lake, can also be located exactly.[3]

When the Coronado force came out upon the plain, they saw the walled village of Hawikuh lying before them. It was built on a rather low bluff above the sparse plain—a terraced jumble of cubical, flat-roofed cells rising three or four stories high and overlooking the irrigated fields on the southern side of the river. Its jutting polygonal walls made it look to Castañeda "as if it had been crumpled up together." Here at last was the silver city that Marcos, according to his story, had descried from afar, the place where Esteban had died, the goal of all the dreams of Mexico in that year.

Like other details in the friar's account, the town was a disappointment, the greatest disappointment of all. "I can assure your lordship," wrote Coronado to Mendoza shortly after, "that in reality he has not told the truth in a single thing that he has said, but everything is the reverse of what he has said, except the name of the city and the large stone houses."[4] Castañeda's dejection at seeing this prosaic realization of their dream of an argent City of God was even greater. "It is a little unattractive village. . . . There are mansions in New Spain that make a better appearance from a distance."[5] Many were the maledictions heaped upon the head of the friar! So bitter was the feeling against him in the army that he took the earliest opportunity to return to

Mexico. With the first party going south he was to re-treat in disgrace, leaving execration behind him.

Coronado, with the armed defenders of Cíbola ar-rayed before him in battle order on the plain, dared not turn back from the task of conquest, even had he wished. He had a tiger by the tail; he must go forward. Retreat would mean nothing but death from hunger or an arrow in the back.

But peaceful occupation of the place might still be possible could these belligerent red men be overawed by gilded mail, waving plumes, galloping chargers, or dignified words. The army-master, Cárdenas, and two priests were sent ahead with a few horsemen to notify the Indians that Coronado came on a lawful and holy mission.

Before the copper-skinned ranks of Cíbola, the *re-querimiento,* or formal "requirement," was read and interpreted. This was a ceremony incumbent upon the leader of every Spanish party when first coming in con-tact with the Indians of a newly discovered territory, and was a lengthy demand for submission to the claims of the Crown and the Holy Church.[6] In part based upon the Bull Inter Cetera of Pope Alexander VI bestowing upon Spain the right to the Americas lying west of the famous Line of Demarcation, it threatened that those who resisted the authority therein conferred would be treated as rebels. On the banks of the Vermilion River, the soldier Hernando Bermejo intoned the pompous Castilian words.

The solemn rigmarole failed to have the desired effect. If any of the Zuñis understood the rough translation given them, they showed no willingness to bow down to the demands of the strangers. The people of Cíbola were proud, and they could see that the force opposing them was small.

Unlike most savage tribes of the Americas, the men of Zuñi did not prostrate themselves in fear at sight of the horses; in the elk and buffalo they had seen beasts quite as terrible, and so were not dismayed. The men who rode these beasts were odd beings, to be sure, and seemingly covered with jointed plates like river crayfish; but anyone could tell that both the men and the beasts were shaky with hunger. It would be shameful to submit to their demands. Better to treat the newcomers as their forerunner Esteban had already been treated!

The demands of the army-master were greeted with derisive yells. An arrow swished through the gown of Fray Luis, and when Coronado galloped up his men he found the Indians ready in battle drawn. As a hail of arrows fell, the soldiers begged for permission to attack; but the general, mindful of his instructions, and hoping even at this hour to make a peaceful entry, restrained them.

Alas, peace was now beyond thought. The Indians, seeing that the white men held back, called them cowards and grew so bold that they came almost up to the horses to let fly their arrows. Now even the priests cried for action; and Coronado gave the word to charge, the old war cry of Holy Spain: "St. James and at them!"

At the first shock of the attack the Indians took flight, scattering over the plain and racing for the sheltering walls of their town. A few were killed, but Coronado held back his men from futile pursuit. The city must be captured, and speedily, before the famine-stricken soldiers were too weak to lift their weapons. There was only one place where food might be found—in the houses of the enemy. Forward, then, to the walls of the town!

The heights were lined with shouting braves, for all the old men, women, and children had been sent away to hide in a secret fastness. The entrance gate was to be gained only by a narrow and tortuous way; obviously, some strategy was called for. Coronado decided to distract the warriors by a frontal attack of crossbowmen and harquebusiers, while the cavaliers dismounted and attempted to scale the walls on another side by means of a ladder which the Indians had negligently left leaning there.

The bronze field guns were hauled into position, and a few haphazard shots were fired. But the sun-rotted strings of the crossbowmen soon snapped, and the musketeers could do little because they were so feeble from lack of food that they could hardly stand and fire. The hundreds of Indian allies were kept in the rear and took no part in the battle. Unsupported, the storming party was exposed to the full fury of the defenders of Cíbola.

General Coronado, with his gilded armor shining in the sun, was singled out as a gleaming target; as a result he suffered more serious injuries than any of his men. Several times he was struck in the face with arrows, and once in the foot, and twice he was felled to earth by torrents of heavy stones. His strong helmet saved him from death, but he was so bruised and prostrated that had not Cárdenas come to the rescue "like a good knight" and placed his body above the fallen leader, taking the brunt of the stones himself, the expedition might then and there have lost its commander.

"They all directed their attack against me because my armor was gilded and glittered," wrote Coronado afterward, "and on this account I was hurt more than the rest, and not because I had done more or was farther in advance than the others; for all these gentlemen and soldiers bore themselves well, as was expected of them."[7]

The wounded general was carried off the field along with the other casualties, which fortunately were few. Not a man had been slain, although several had been hit by arrows and stones, and three horses had been killed.

The general's staff consulted hurriedly. One more attack would do the trick! The defenders were weakening; perhaps their supply of rocks and arrows was running out. "St. James and at them!"

The final rally was sounded, and when the action was no more than an hour old the town was taken by storm. The Indians retired in good order, leaving their homes open to the conquerors. The Battle of Hawikuh was over.

The first act of the starving Spaniards was to scurry
to the storehouses. There, according to an anonymous
member of the party,[8] "they found that of which there
was greater need than of gold or silver, which was much
corn, and beans, and fowl[9] better than those of New
Spain, and salt, the best and whitest I have seen in all
my life." The victors of Hawikuh sat down to gorge
themselves on the raw spoils, to nurse their wounds
and forget the miseries of their eleven weeks of marching from Culiacán. On the plain below the village, the
evicted Zuñis sent out fleet messengers to all the provinces of Cíbola, to give warning that shining grim
strangers who fought with fire were abroad in the land,
and that the first stronghold of the ancient gods had
fallen.

Three days after the battle, a delegation of old men,
the spokesmen of the people who had fled from the
town, came to Coronado with proposals of peace. They
brought as presents some poor cotton garments and a
few turquoises. The convalescent general urged the Indians to return to their homes and become Christians. Pretending to agree, the people cautiously drifted
back. They came merely to gather their possessions,
with which, that same night, they fled to another town
near-by where they felt secure.

On July 19, when Coronado had recovered suffi-
ciently from his wounds, he made a visit to this town,
which was the largest of all the Cíbola settlements.
Castañeda called the place Macaque; it was the Zuñi

town of Mátsaki, or "Salt City," near the northwest base of Towayalane, or Corn Mountain, about three miles southeast of the present-day village of Zuñi.[10]

Several of the Zuñi towns, notably Hawikuh and Mátsaki, had the outer shape of a polygon, reminding the Spaniards of the buttressed, fortified towns they had seen in Europe. The rooms of the houses formed an irregular wall about the village; the walls were pierced on the outside only with a few loopholes, and the rooms could not be entered except from within the ring of walls, thus making defense easy, as the Spaniards were to learn to their cost. Some of the buildings of Mátsaki were seven stories high, rising well above the others; the walls of these buildings were cut with embrasures and loopholes to serve as bastions for defending the roof tops.

Coronado, who was not prepared to dislodge the Zuñis from this stronghold, merely asked to speak with their "king." This was a request which they were unable to comply with, for they had no supreme lord. Shortly after this visit an old priest did bring a few chiefs to parley with the general at the Spanish headquarters. In spite of Coronado's pacific arguments, the Indians refused to come out of hiding; nor would they embrace the Cross or even admit the sovereignty of Spain.

Some of them promised, however, that they would bring their children to be instructed by the friars. The Indians confessed, curiously enough, that it had been foretold among them fifty years before that a people such as the Spaniards would come to them from the south, and that the whole country would be conquered by the invaders. This prophecy may have accounted for the lack of determined resistance that Coronado found at Cíbola, a circumstance which enabled him to conquer the land with less than a hundred Spaniards.

The manner of Esteban's death was also verified by Coronado at this time. "The Indians say that they killed him here because the Indians of Chichilticalli said that he was a bad man," he wrote to Mendoza on August 3, "and not like the Christians, because the Christians never kill women, and he killed them, and because he assaulted their women, whom the Indians love better than themselves." But Marcos had reported that three hundred of Esteban's followers had been killed, and now the men of Cíbola said that not a single one of these had died. They had not even harmed a lad from Petatlán who had been Esteban's messenger and interpreter, but had kept him secretly and safely. "When I tried to secure him, they made excuses for not giving him to me, for two or three days, saying that he was dead, and at other times that the Indians of Acuco had taken him away. But when I finally told them that I should be very angry if they did not give him to me, they gave him to me. He is an interpreter; for although he cannot talk much, he understands very well."[11] Coronado was to have need of skilled interpreters, for he was henceforth to be dealing almost daily with the people of the pueblos.

The Zuñi settlements, where Coronado was to spend

some months directing the exploration of the surrounding territories, were the first towns of the sedentary tribes of the Southwest in which the members of the expedition lived, and of which they gave descriptions. Among all the achievements of the Coronado expedition, not the least is that he and his men first gave to the world an account of these Pueblo Indians, who still retain the name given them by the Spaniards.

The Pueblo Indians, like their ancestors, the cliff dwellers, sprang from the same basic stock as the other American races.[12] They did differ sharply from all other tribes of the continent north of Mexico in that they had forsaken the nomad life of hunters following herds of game over vast territories, and had chosen rather to settle in easily defended valleys and to depend on the soil for their living. The agricultural life that they led gave rise to differences still more marked; they built permanent houses, created a village society, were able to store up food and other forms of wealth, and had leisure to create works of art and to develop an intricate ritual of worship.

By 1540, when Coronado first met these descendants of the cliff dwellers,[13] the Pueblo Indians had developed a native American democratic culture of such deep-rooted strength that in spite of later vicissitudes it was never lost to them. The Coronado chronicles give an excellent picture of this culture. The Spanish records reveal a high respect for the Indian achievements, which is the more remarkable considering the fact that the invaders could have had only the vaguest notion of the true attainments of the Indians and their tribal aspirations.

It is one of the strongest traits of the Indian to be secretive regarding his feelings, or any of his activities which reflect religious or social ideals. Moreover, the Indian culture is almost Oriental in its mystical acceptance of religion and art as the predominating factors of life, in its traditional submergence of individual desire into communal welfare, and in its tranquil idealization of spiritual attainments and disdain of mere material advantage. Hence it was well-nigh impossible for a conquering European, coming from a crowded land of kings and priests and merchants warring for gains that could be made only at the expense of another's loss, to comprehend—or even to be aware of—the main currents in a way of life so markedly strange to him. What was one to do with a people without a "king," who had no rulers or aristocrats or conquerors or rich men or self-seeking individualists, whose meanest utensil was a work of art, who did not fear death and yet whose smallest act was always an act of worship?

Each of the pueblos was an independent republic. "They do not have chiefs as in New Spain, but are ruled by a council of the oldest men," wrote Castañeda. "They have priests who preach to them, whom they call *papas*. These are the elders. They go up on the highest roof of the village and preach to the village from there, like public criers, in the morning while the sun is rising, the whole village being silent and sitting in the galleries to listen. They tell them how they are to live, and I believe that they give certain commandments for them to keep, for there is no drunkenness among them nor sodomy nor sacrifices, neither do they eat human flesh nor steal, but they are usually at work."[14] There was little crime in the modern meaning of the word. Land, so often in other civilizations a cause of quarrels, was not held by individuals; all the lands were owned by the village, and allotted in accordance with family needs. In times of scarcity, the hardships were shared by everyone in the community alike, and none starved until all starved.

Although the village was divided into totemic clans (or clusters of families related through a common maternal ancestor), the community was the social unit. So far as is known, there has never been in the history of the Pueblo people any political group larger than a temporary alliance of tribes, which fell apart as soon as the common danger was past. The village was self-contained, and there was little trade with other provinces except in such things as the sacred turquoise. Another barrier to the mingling of tribes was the fact that within a small territory two villages might speak languages as different as French is from German, although, when necessary, the highly descriptive sign language that later amazed Coronado served as a lingua franca among the tribes.

Like all Indians, those of the pueblos worshiped the elements—in particular the creative sun, whose priests were to be seen praying at dawn. Sun and water and cloud manifestly dominated the destinies of these tillers of the arid lands. Even on the darker side, their religion was a fetishism based on fear of the elements; the medicine man and the greatly feared "witch" were looked upon as having power over natural events.

All their arts—and every pueblo dweller was an artist—were reflections of their spirit of gratitude and reverence for these life-giving forces. The great communal art was that of the dance—sun dances, rain dances, growing-corn dances—dramas accompanied by the music of pipes and drums, performed in ceremonial garments and symbolic masks, and prefaced by the making of priest-drawn "sand paintings" of vivid pigments and ground meal. The designs of their famous basketry and pottery were always symbolic, as were those of the laboriously woven, bright blankets of cotton. The lovely symmetry of the pottery was achieved by skilled handcraft, for the potter's wheel was unknown to them and even today is never used. Each stage of any of their work was done with deliberate perfection, for time meant almost nothing to these leisurely people who, unlike their southern brothers in Mexico, had never developed a calendar.

Even the hunting of beasts—deer, bear, mountain lion, buffalo, wild turkey, the humble rabbit—must be undertaken with proper ceremony. Fish, as sacred to the water gods, were never eaten.

Water was the great determiner of their lives, for in the bleached and dusty plateau land every drop is precious, and settlements are only possible along the trickling streams. The greatest dances, such as the Snake

Dance of the Hopis of Tusayán, were those imploring the life-giving rains. When these came, the intensive cultivation of corn, pumpkins, and beans could enable the growers to store up enough to feed themselves for another year or two.[15] Irrigation was practiced on a small scale, but any prolonged drought meant catastrophe. Every expedient to catch and store the precious fluid was used, and each village had a *tinaja,* or cistern, wherever there was a proper depression in the rock.[16]

Maize, their only cereal, was the staff of life among the Pueblos, and a good crop might last them for several years, for in the dry air the kernels did not rot. The corn at Zuñi in particular impressed the Spaniards greatly; many of the army had been farmers themselves and knew good plants when they saw them. "It does not grow very high," remarked Castañeda. "The ears start at the very foot, and each large fat stalk bears about eight hundred grains, something not seen before in our parts."[17] Coronado found it an appetizing staple of diet. "They make the best corn cakes I have ever seen anywhere," he wrote, "and this is what everybody ordinarily eats. They have the very best arrangement and equipment for grinding that was ever seen. One of these Indian women here will grind as much as four of the Mexicans."[18]

The Pueblo Indians were able fighters, although they did not expect to make a trade of fighting for gain, as did their wandering, raiding enemies the Apaches. There were also occasional battles between two or more of their villages, and the war chiefs were at such times the leaders in council. During aggressive raids—when the warriors often wore round-soled war sandals whose tracks would give no indication of the direction taken by the wearer—the young men obtained training in the arts of fighting, and at home had always to be continually on the alert against marauding bands. The Pueblos, like other Indians, took scalps; at Zuñi, the dried hanging scalps of victims were used as a gruesome sort of barometer, for the skin became soft and pliable at the approach of rain. However, by temperament the pueblo dwellers preferred to live in seclusion and peace, and they fought best on the defensive.

The home places of these town builders were always chosen for defensive reasons. Most of the villages were found in localities that were grim, almost barren, frequently sandy and hot, and at long distances from their hunting grounds. Many lovely forest glades of the Southwest show no trace of permanent Indian occupation; Coronado passed through the wooded country of the White Mountains, but found there only a few prowling savages. The reason for this was that in order to stay for any length of time in a region the southwestern Indian required not only availability of water, cultivable soil, and timber, but most of all security. The high forests of New Mexico and Arizona, aside from being hard to grub out for planting, as well as being exceedingly cold and snowbound in winter, provided excellent lurking places for nomad raiders. The village Indian was willing to carry his wood and water from a distance, and even to travel to fertile patches of land

and camp there through the growing season, so long as he could find protection when it was needed. For his permanent home, therefore, he built strong-walled houses that could withstand a siege.

It was not until the Spaniards came that the full strength of these fortress towns was fully tested, for most of the attacks of other Indians were of short duration. Protection was offered by some villages because they were built in out-of-the-way spots secluded from enemy observation. In some places, the walls of the houses blended into the rocky landscape and were not noticeable. Other towns were built on crags or mesas that were hard for an enemy to scale. Watchtowers were often erected on the borders of a tribal range so that watchers could give ample warning of the approach of a raiding party. Often a tribe unwilling to do battle would be able to abandon its houses and scatter to secret places of refuge for a few days, until danger was past.

The fortress towns of the Pueblos were always built in strategic spots, even though this might mean that most of their food and water, and even garden soil, had to be carried in jars and baskets up almost perpendicular trails worn deep in stone by generations of moccasined feet.[10] Much of their building material, especially the large framing timbers, had to be transported for great distances. Where building stone was plentiful, the Indians built in stone, selected for smooth shattered faces but not dressed with tools; otherwise they used puddled masses of sun-dried clay, joined with a native mortar and white-washed with chalky gypsum.

A village grew as adjoining rooms from time to time were added like the cells in a honeycomb.[20] Outer walls had neither doors nor windows; easily withdrawn ladders, which were removed to baffle attackers, led from terrace to terrace; the rooms of the various families were entered by openings in the ceilings, "like hatchways of ships."

The heart of the village was always the *kiva*—the Hopi Indian name for the chamber that the first Spaniards called *estufa* (literally "stove," but meaning also "hot-room" or "hot-bath"). These pine-pillared underground rooms were built only by the men and were always barred to women. Often rather spacious, the dark sanctums served as church, clubroom, school for boys, and lodge hall for male secret societies. Other small shrines were built in secret places out of doors.

The dress of these Indians was as distinctive as their dwellings. The typical garb of the male members of the Pueblo tribes was a short tunic, trousers, leggings, and moccasins, all of tanned deerskin, with a decorated skin cap. Robes of woven yucca fiber, rabbit skin, or mountain-lion skin were worn in cold weather, as well as feather cloaks or bright cotton blankets, woven by both men and women and worn on gala days. The men cut their hair in bangs in front, and plaited it on the side or held it back with a headband. The women wore a blanket-like woven garment thrown over the right shoulder and under the left, and belted with a wide sash; a woven shirt; and leggings and moccasins like those of the men. Their hair was usually parted in the middle and hung in braids; girls who had reached the marriageable age wore disk-shaped puffs on each side of the head. Both sexes decorated their persons with sacred turquoise and drilled-shell ornaments hung from ear and neck, or attached to belts and leggings. Earth pigments served for painting the body for the many dances and other tribal ceremonies.

To such a self-sufficient people, the invading Spaniards had little to offer in the way of "civilizing" implements or influences. True, they implanted in the country a diversity of domestic animals (the Indians had only the dog and the turkey), particularly the horse and the sheep.[21] But the exchange between red man and white has never been one-sided. If anything, the Pueblo Indian has given more than he has received. His lore and craftsmanship and painfully won wisdom of existence have passed into the American heritage. His way of building a home, for example, created a style that is still furnishing inspiration to architecture in the western states. The Indian culture, like his dwellings, has remained firmly rooted in the soil that Coronado's army trod. Today, any visitor to the American Southwest may see this enduring race living virtually as they lived when Coronado came, four centuries ago, and white men first whispered the magical names of Cíbola and Tusayán.

The Desert and the Canyon

Summer, 1540

WHEN HE STARTED NORTH, Coronado left orders with Don Tristán de Arellano to set out from Culiacán a fortnight later and lead the main body of soldiers on his trail. He promised that instructions would be sent back to the army as soon as the advance party had explored the Cíbola country enough to know where the men would be most needed for conquering and colonizing. The first orders that came directed the main force to build a strong garrison town in the valley of Hearts.

It so happened that the important discoveries were to be made by Coronado's hundred without the aid of the larger force, and thus the army was to be without occupation for most of the summer. So far as they knew, Coronado and the others had vanished into space beyond the Sonora Valley, and months were to pass before word of their exploits came to the expectant, restless soldiers of the main guard.

Some time in the first half of May, the army under Arellano took leave of their friends in Culiacán and turned their faces northward on the Cíbola road. All marched on foot, carrying their lances and other equipment, so that the horses might be available for conveying the provisions needed for so large a party. It had taken the flying squadron a month to reach the valley of Corazones, and the heavily laden army might well take twice as long.

No difficulties were met with other than the ordinary discomforts of travel in that barren country lying south of the Sonora. By the middle of the summer the soldiers had arrived at the Ures basin and were hard at work building the town of San Gerónimo—St. Jerome of the Hearts. Such labor must have been little to the liking of many of the volunteers, who had dreamed of sacking towns rather than of building them. This villa, the first Spanish settlement in the present state of Sonora, was destined to be moved several times and at last to come to an inglorious end.

While the town was building, Don Rodrigo Maldonado led a scouting party to the Gulf coast to look for the ships that had been sent out to support Coronado. No trace of the vessels was to be found, but Maldonado brought back with him a "giant" Indian from among the Seri inhabitants of the shoal waters. He was so tall that the best man in the army reached only to his chest; moreover, it was said that there were Indians even taller to be found on the coast.

The summer rains drenched the weary workers, and the shortage of food at this place was still as pressing as Coronado had found it to be in the spring. Therefore the town was abandoned when only half-finished, and the army moved upstream to the more friendly valley of "Señora," where the soil was somewhat more fertile. There they began anew the task of building a town, to which they again gave the name of San Gerónimo de los Corazones.

Time dragged on until the middle of September. Many of the soldiers had almost given up hope of hearing from their commander, when three white men descended upon the settlement from the north, to be greeted with lusty cheers. The three were Captain Melchor Díaz, Juan Gallego, the general's courier, and Fray Marcos de Niza.

Díaz carried orders to lead another exploring party from the new town to the coast in a final endeavor to make contact with the fleet. Gallego was to push on to Mexico with a letter for the viceroy which Coronado had written in Cíbola on August 3; the courier carried also maps and bundles of Indian handiwork. Fray Marcos was going with him; Mexico was a much safer place for the friar than Cíbola, where the walls resounded with the threats of disappointed cavaliers who felt that they had been duped by his tales.

The messenger and the friar were soon on the road again, but Díaz remained and took charge of the settlement with a firm hand. He had much to tell the eager garrison.

He related the story of the hungry march to Zuñi, the capture of the village of Hawikuh, and the establishment of headquarters in that town, to which Coronado had given the name Granada, in honor of Viceroy Mendoza's birthplace in southern Spain and also because he fancied it bore some resemblance to that famous stronghold of the Moors. So far, said Díaz, there had been no more battles with the Indians, but the natives had fled from their homes and would not come back or become Christians, believing that the Spaniards would soon have to return to the south whence they came. The lack of food was a serious matter, he said; supplies were badly needed, and they were completely out of sugar, oil, raisins, and wine, except a single pint which had been saved for use in communion.

No, there was still no sign of gold or silver, although a few turquoises had been taken. Juan Gallego was carrying south with him samples of the work done by the Cíbola Indians, who lived in strongly built stone houses and were as clever with their hands as any tribe in Mexico. As typical of their handiwork, the general was sending to Mendoza some painted skins, a dozen cotton mantles (one of them very beautifully embroidered), two crude Indian paintings of the animals and birds and plants of the country, the skin of some strange shaggy horned beast like a cow, turquoises and turquoise earrings, fifteen decorated Indian combs, two rolls such as the native women wore on their heads when they carried jars of water from the spring, a few woven baskets, and, lastly, some weapons—a shield, a wooden club, and a bow, together with several bone-pointed arrows.

Truly, the spoil of the Seven Cities was so far not very

impressive. But Don Francisco Vásquez had heard of another province of seven cities to the westward of where he was, and he had sent Pedro de Tovar with a party to explore it. Perhaps there was gold there. The country was large, and there might still be found enough wealth to make the whole army rich for life. They might shortly go to see for themselves.

Díaz had departed too soon to hear what Tovar had found in Tusayán, or "Tucano," as Coronado believed the other group of seven cities in the west was called. Nor could Díaz know of the equally important reconnaissances made during the late summer by García López de Cárdenas and Hernando de Alvarado. The achievements of these earliest western scouts and those of Díaz himself, as well as the voyage of Hernando de Alarcón up the Colorado River, were to make the summer of 1540 the greatest season of exploration in the history of the American Southwest. Before the winter set in, the captains of Coronado were to overrun the northern parts of Arizona and New Mexico, to venture into the buffalo plains eastward, and to blaze the overland trail from Sonora to California, laying the foundations for all later discoveries in the southwestern states.

The inner and more significant life of the people of Cíbola was almost a closed book to the alien Spaniards. But if the men of Zuñi were reticent about their own affairs, they were not at all backward in talking of their neighbors, and Coronado soon after his arrival elicited from them the information that to the west there was a tribe of pueblo dwellers living in seven towns much like those of Cíbola, and that this province was called Tucano, or Tusayán.[1] These were the sixteenth-century villages inhabited by the native people now known as the Hopi or Moqui tribe,[2] and were believed by Coronado to be the same settlements that Fray Marcos, when in the Sonora Valley on his first excursion, had heard of under the name of Totonteac.[3]

Melchor Díaz, on his scouting trip early in 1540, had received a good account of this region from the Indians living in the country south of Chichilticalli.[4] Totonteac was declared to comprise twelve villages lying seven short days' travel from Cíbola, and to be of the same sort of houses and people. It was reported that the inhabitants were famous cotton growers, although Díaz doubted that this could be true, seeing that the district was supposed to lie in very cold country. There is now no doubt that the Hopi people, whose lands sloped with a warm southward exposure, were expert weavers as well as experienced cotton growers, and exported both raw fiber and finished blankets to the other Pueblo tribes.

In order to explore this unknown region, Don Pedro de Tovar with seventeen horsemen and a few foot soldiers departed from Cíbola about the middle of July. He held a commission which permitted him to be gone on this errand for thirty days. He was accompanied by Fray Juan de Padilla, the missionary who had been "a fighting man in his youth."

The party struck northwesterly across the Zuñi plateau to the Río Puerco. The most direct route would have taken them through the now world-renowned Petrified Forest, a wonderland of fallen giant trees turned to agate of a myriad rich tints by submergence ages ago when the region was a vast inland sea of water instead of a sea of sand and wind-carved plateau. Such a miraculous work of nature would undoubtedly have been reported by the Spaniards had they glimpsed it, and one can only conclude that they did not see it. The forest of chalcedony, carnelian, and jasper represented to the Indians an imperial treasury—chips and shaped instruments from the rigid bright trunks are to be found in Indian ruins from Canada to Mexico—and there is every likelihood that the cunning guides of Tovar deliberately led the invaders as far as they could from the fallen silicified giants, in the region of which many remains of Pueblo life are still to be found.

After crossing the stream now known as the Puerco, the adventurers found themselves in the Painted Desert, an almost waterless high land of rainbow sand and rock, dotted with thorny greasewood and sage, stunted cedar and piñon. Here and there rose a fantastic butte which time had fretted by whirling, wind-blown sand into a glowing, pinnacled monument.

After three or four days of marching parallel to the canyon valley of the Colorado Chiquito, with the peaks of the San Francisco Mountains, the highest range in Arizona, looming to the southwest, the riders came out on a drab plain where faint trails led to the grainy talus at the foot of a sandstone mesa rising six hundred feet from the level ground at its base. This was Tucano, or Tusayán.

Hills of corn, planted five or six kernels to a hill so that each plant might help to shelter the others from the blasting sand particles driven by the wind, were the only signs of habitation. Then the eyes of the Spaniards picked out, on a lower bench of the mesa or else crowning a sand hill at its foot, a heap of dull stone that gradually took the form of terraced houses. These dwellings were much like those at Cíbola, except that the gray stone, quarried from the same hillside, caused the walls almost to melt into their background. The thick-walled cells were the homes of the Tusayán people, who seldom left them except to work in the cornfields or to carry a jar of water laboriously up the steep hillsides from the seeping springs below.

So well prote ted from hostile raids were the Hopis by reason of their remote and fortified location and by the dull coloration of their hill homes that they had not bothered to keep outposts on watch, even though they had learned that Cíbola had been captured by very fierce people who traveled on animals "that ate human beings." There was not a single watcher to cry a warning when, that night, Tovar led his men through the fields and clambered up the sliding slopes until they were so close under the walls of the first town that they could hear the inhabitants conversing inside.

Not until morning was the presence of the interlopers discovered. Then, at the alarm, orderly files of

Hopis, armed with bows, shields, and wooden clubs shaped like potato mashers, descended to defend their homes from these men "wearing iron garments."

Captain Tovar formed his men on the plain, and his interpreter began to read the formal requirement, to which the Hopis listened politely, for, as Castañeda observed, they were "a very reasonable people." But during the lengthy proceedings the Indians traced lines of sacred corn meal on the ground, as is still their custom when they are performing ceremonial rites and do not wish strangers to trespass.

Some of the Spaniards, like small boys who are afraid to take a dare, pretended that they were about to cross these lines, and one of the bolder Hopis, becoming indignant at this, struck the bridle check of a horse with his club. Friar Juan, grown impatient because of the time consumed in this parley, and stirred by memories of his martial youth, exclaimed: "In truth, I don't know what we came here for!"[5]

This was enough for the eager soldiers, who uttered the *santiago* and charged so suddenly that many of the Indians were run down by the horses before they could escape. Others were killed as they scrambled for the shelter of their walls; but before the slaughter had far advanced, the attack was stayed by a cry for quarter.

The chief men of the village immediately surrendered and made a plea for peace, giving to the captain and his score of troopers the allegiance of the whole province of Tusayán. They brought gifts of some cotton cloth, corn meal, dressed skins, pine nuts, and birds

of the country. The Spaniards established their headquarters near the first village, and that day all the
people of the province came together and submitted
themselves, inviting the conquerors to enter all their
villages freely. Soon a busy barter was being carried on.

The villages of the Hopis were built on the lower
ridges of three large mesas, or close to their bases.[6] The
way of life of these people differed in no essential from
that of the other Pueblo groups, although they were of
a rather different lingual stock.[7] They were a mixture
of tribes, and their villages had been settled at various
times; there is reason to think that some of these stone
towns had been founded by a wandering tribe coming
from the south. In many ways the Hopis are the most
interesting of the southwestern Indians. An intelligent
and well-behaved people who live modestly, they express their deep religious emotions in such famed ceremonials as the dance of the sacred rattlesnake, bringer
of rain. They are highly skilled in the toil of village
and farm. Above all they are artists who make a characteristic basketry and notably fine pottery, and their
woven blanket-robes, for centuries, were the most beautiful products of the loom that could be found in the
Southwest.

It is to be regretted that none of the Coronado chroniclers left a good contemporary description of Hopi.
The brief contacts which the tribe had with Tovar and
with Cárdenas (who was soon to pass through their
province on the way to the Colorado) made little impression upon the tribal life or tradition. When Span-

iards next came that way several generations later, the Hopis had so little memory of the Coronado expedition that they were considerably frightened by the horses.[8]

Pedro de Tovar had not been commissioned by Coronado to explore beyond Tusayán, but after his pacification of the villages he gathered all the information he could about the surrounding country before returning to Zuñi about the middle of August. One bit of news that he picked up was to the effect that there was a large river to the west of Tusayán, and that several days' journey down the river could be found some very big natives of great strength.

Coronado pondered this, and concluded, quite correctly, that this river must flow into the Gulf of California. By following its course downstream, his men might be able to get in touch with the fleet which had been sent out to explore the mouth of this river at the head of the Gulf.

Accordingly, he despatched from Cíbola, about August 25, a party of a dozen horsemen under Don García López de Cárdenas, with instructions to find and descend this important stream. Unknown to Coronado, on almost the same date the fleet of Hernando de Alarcón crossed the bar at the mouth of the Colorado River and started to ascend the great channel in boats.

Cárdenas rode first to Tusayán, where he was well received and provided with Indian guides who knew the country to the westward. These natives advised that plenty of provisions should be taken, as it was a journey of twenty days to the river, through uninhabited desert.

The small party crossed the parched Colorado Chiquito plateau of northern Arizona, and at the end of
their journey came out upon a view for which no explorer could be prepared. Below them was the Grand
Canyon of the Colorado, the most stupendous gash in
the crust of our planet, one of the wonders of the Western Hemisphere—three hundred miles long, a mile
deep, and from ten to fifteen miles wide from rim to
rim, a primevally eroded chasm in whose depths tower
hundreds of peaks taller than any mountain east of the
Rockies.

To speculate upon the emotions of these wandering
Spaniards of 1540 when confronted with this stupendous vista is tempting but futile. It is known that one
Pedro Méndez de Sotomayor[9] accompanied the Cárdenas party as official chronicler and that he presented a
written report of this mighty discovery, but no trace remains of any such account. The version which Castañeda put down from the lips of the men who were with
Cárdenas is therefore the first known record of the impression made by the Grand Canyon upon the minds
of white men.

"After they had gone twenty days," he reported, "they
came to the banks of the river, which seemed to be more
than three or four leagues across by airline. This country
was elevated and full of low twisted pines, very cold,
and lying open toward the north, so that, although this
was the warm season, no one could live there on account of the cold. They passed three days along this
canyon looking for a passage down to the river, which

looked from above as if the water was a fathom's width
across, although the Indians said it was half a league
wide. To descend was impossible, for after these three
days Captain Melgosa and one Juan Galeras and another companion, who were the most agile men, made
an attempt to go down at the least difficult place, and
descended until those who were above were unable to
keep sight of them because of the rock overhang. They
returned about four o'clock in the afternoon, not having succeeded in reaching the bottom on account of
the great difficulties which they found, because what
seemed to be easy from above was not so, but instead
very rough and steep. They said that they had been
down about a third of the way and that the river seemed
very large from the place which they reached, and that
from what they saw they thought the Indians had given
the width correctly. From the rim, some small pinnacles
on the sides of the cliffs seemed to be about as tall as a
man, but those who went down swore that when they
reached these rocks they were bigger than the great
tower of Seville."[10]

It is easy to imagine the amazement of Coronado
when such a report was made by Cárdenas on his return, and to picture the ineffectual efforts of his men
in later years at describing, in the face of ill-concealed
disbelief and tapping of foreheads, the awful grandeur
that they had viewed in the west.

The spot where Cárdenas discovered the Canyon of
the Colorado cannot be exactly located, so meager are
the records of his adventure on its rim four centuries

ago.[11] However, it hardly seems possible that the curious Spaniards would have been content with examining the rim of the Canyon at a single point, and it is likely that they spent not a little time gazing down from the many different headlands; probably they viewed, during the three days of their visit, most of the main stream lying within the present national park.

The party seems to have returned up the Havasu Canyon along the west boundary of the park, for it was mentioned that at this stage they "saw some water falling over a rock and learned from the guides that some bunches of crystals which were hanging there were salt. They went and gathered a quantity of this and brought it back to Cíbola, dividing it among those who were there."[12] The men who offered to get the salt had to be suspended over the edge by ropes to reach the clusters.

Below this place, the deep canyon ended and the desert began. The Spaniards did not venture farther along the river, because drinking water was lacking. Along the high rim it must have been a torture rivaling that of Tantalus to see the brown sheen of the river a mile below them, unreachable as if it had been on the moon. Although Coronado had issued a commission for eighty days, the period of exploration by Cárdenas was limited by the fact that each evening the men had to travel a league or two inland to find water.[13] The guides said that if the Spaniards ventured four days farther downstream they would be halted by thirst; in fact, when the Indians traversed this region they had to take women with them laden with gourds of water which were

buried at appropriate intervals along the way to provide a supply for the return journey.

It would be hopeless for the Spaniards, who traveled
only half as rapidly as the Indians, to attempt this waterless stretch; consequently, Cárdenas turned reluctantly
back, to report to General Coronado that exploration
westward must inevitably be halted by the titanic canyon barrier. After the departure of this daring band,
it was half a century before white men again saw the
Colorado, and more than two hundred years were to
pass before other men of an alien race gazed down upon
the Grand Canyon.

Both the Tovar and the Cárdenas parties journeyed
through the desert plateau of northern Arizona that
today is the chief range of the nomadic Navajo, now
the largest tribe in North America; but neither party
reported the existence of any inhabitants in this country except the people of Tusayán. If any Navajos lived
then in the territory that they were later to make their
own, they were merely a few prowling newcomers who
kept out of sight of the Spanish invaders.[14]

Nor did any of the early explorers of the Southwest
mention the discovery of the cliff dwellings that had
cradled the ancestors of the Pueblo tribes. Cíbola was
not far from the San Juan Valley, prehistoric home
place of the earliest builders among the Indians of the
Southwest. The Mesa Verde region had been inhabited
less than three centuries before the arrival of Coronado
in New Mexico; but about A.D. 1275 the combination
of a dreadful thirty-year drought and the persistent

ravaging of raiding nomads resulted in a great exodus southward.[15] So complete was the disappearance of these earlier civilizations of Mesa Verde, Chaco, Cañón del Muerto, and Cañón de Chelly—the last two are only about a hundred miles from Zuñi—that when Coronado came, some two hundred and fifty years later, not even a legend of the Great Houses reached him. Had they learned of these curious old dwelling places, the Spaniards, eager treasure seekers that they were, would surely have made some attempts to reach and explore them. But these abandoned, secret settlements were truly "lost cities," hidden in remote spots that even to-day are difficult to reach; hence the cliff dwellings clung in somnolent peace to their hillsides until they were discovered by western explorers of modern times.

Discoveries East and West

August 29, 1540 – January 18, 1541

GENERAL CORONADO had requested the pacified people of Cíbola to send word to the Indians of neighboring provinces telling them that Christians, who desired to become their friends, had entered the land. Accordingly, this message was relayed far and near to the tribes that traded with Cíbola. As a result, while Cárdenas was making his explorations to the westward, there arrived at the headquarters of Coronado a delegation from a land some seventy leagues to the east.

Outstanding among these emissaries was a chieftain whom the men of Coronado promptly nicknamed Captain Bigotes, or "Whiskers," because he was the proud possessor of a long mustache—an uncommon distinction among the smooth-lipped natives. Captain Whiskers was a tall and well-formed young Indian, with a friendly and agreeable manner, who said that he had come in response to the call and that if the army wished to travel through his country, which was called Cicuyé, they would be welcomed as friends.

He brought presents of shields and headpieces of tough hide, and the tanned hides of some strange animals with tangled wool like that of a merino sheep. The fleeces puzzled the Spaniards greatly, and they were unable to comprehend what sort of strange "cows" had borne them, even after they had carefully studied a picture of one of these curious beasts which a member of the delegation wore painted on his breast.

In order that some of his men might visit the region whence came Whiskers and his friends, and see the "cows" they told about, Coronado commissioned Captain Hernando de Alvarado to take twenty men and explore for a period of not longer than eighty days, after which he should return and report what he had found. At the side of the captain as the party left Hawikuh on Sunday, August 29, "the day of the beheading of St. John the Baptist," was Fray Juan de Padilla, who had by now returned from Tusayán, his martial ardor for the overthrow of the pagan still unquenched.[1]

The explorers struck eastward around the southern slope of Towayalane; after traveling a few leagues they found a chain of abandoned fortresses, and beyond these an ancient city, "very large, entirely destroyed, although a large part of the wall was still standing, which was six times as tall as a man, the wall well made of good worked stone, with gates and gutters like a city in Castile."[2] This had been the home of a recalcitrant branch of the Zuñis, and was called Makyata, the place that Fray Marcos had heard about in Sonora under the

---

[1] For notes to chap. 8, see pp. 346–349.

name of Marata. Marcos had been informed at the time that Marata was at war with the other people of Cíbola; this news was stale, however, for Marata had already succumbed to repeated attacks and now was a ruin.

A mile or two farther on was another ruined pueblo, which had been built with a foundation of "quarried" granite blocks. Here the trail divided, the fork to the left leading to the Queres village of Sía on the Jemez River and the right fork to another Queres town called Coco, or Acuco.

Alvarado chose the latter and set out toward that town, marching through a desert country dotted with dead-black craters and lava flows. He probably passed south of the famous El Morro or Inscription Rock, a towering butte with two ruined pueblos on the top; at any rate, he made no mention of it, and he would hardly have neglected it had he seen it even from a distance.[3]

Five days out from Cíbola and "thirty leagues" from there, Alvarado came in sight of the city of Acuco, or Acoma[4] as it is now known, the Acus of the Marcos report. It comprised some two hundred houses, and the people were said by Castañeda to be robbers, feared by all the inhabitants round about.

"The village was impregnable," he wrote, "because it was up on a rock out of reach, having steep sides and so high that it was a very good musket that could throw a ball so high. There was only one entrance by a stairway built by hand, which began at the top of a slope [an immense sand dune] which is around the foot of the rock. There was a broad stairway for about two hundred steps, then a stretch of about a hundred narrower steps, and at the top they had to go up about three times as high as a man by means of holes in the rock, in which they put their toes, holding on at the same time by their hands.[5] There was a dry wall of large stones at the top, which they could roll down without showing themselves, so that no army could possibly be strong enough to capture the village. On the top they had room to sow and store a large amount of corn, and cisterns to collect snow and water."[6]

The high city impressed another of the soldiers as "the strongest position that ever was seen in the world,"[7] and it is true that a few warriors at the top of the trail might easily have held the place against a much larger force than the score of Spaniards with Alvarado.

The villagers, on the approach of the party, swarmed down their giddy stairs and at first refused to listen to pacific arguments. Like the men of Tusayán, they laid lines of corn meal on the ground as a magical barrier. Had they decided to defend their citadel, it would have been hopeless for the Spaniards to attempt to storm the frowning height. But something happened to cause a change of heart before the opposing forces came to blows. Perhaps the good offices of Captain Whiskers, who was known to the people of Acoma, induced them to yield.

"They went through the form of making peace, which is to touch the horses and take their sweat and rub themselves with it, and to make crosses with their fingers. But to make the most secure peace they put their hands across each other, and they keep this peace inviolably."[8] This pacific reception accorded to Alvarado did not spring from fear or cowardliness, for the warriors of the rock were among the bravest fighters in all the pueblos.[9]

The white men were then invited to visit the village, and soon were painfully ascending the high trail, not without some trepidation, however, that they would be trapped in that rocky eyrie. They had cause to repent nothing but their toilsome climb, for the Indians treated them with true friendliness and made presents of turkey cocks, corn meal, bread, tanned deerskins, piñon nuts, cloaks of cotton, and turquoises. From the houses, three and four stories high, the Spaniards could see, not far off, the top of the twin rock of Katzimo, the Enchanted Mesa. According to Acoma legend this had been the first home of their people, a place which they had occupied until floods destroyed the single trail upward to its flat summit.

Leaving Acoma, Alvarado and his men turned northeast and after a march of twenty miles passed by a "lake or marsh" where the Indian village of Laguna[10] is now situated. Three days later, on September 7, after a tiresome desert journey they reached the banks of a large river. As it was the eve of the day of the nativity of the Blessed Virgin, the river was christened Río de Nuestra Señora, or River of Our Lady. It was the upper Río Grande, the lazy, giant stream of our southern border.[11]

From his camping place on the river bank, Alvarado sent a hurriedly made cross of peace to a populous group of pueblos called Tiguex, occupying the stretch between the present towns of Sandía and Bernalillo, and lying on both sides of the river.[12] There were fifteen of these villages within a circle of twenty leagues.[13]

The day after Alvarado sent this cross, people came to the camp from twelve Tigua pueblos, each village group being led by their chiefs in good order, and approaching the Spanish tents to the sound of a flute. The warriors, who later were to show their fighting mettle against the armored strangers, now came out peaceably, for, although they were feared throughout the region for their prowess and could have made sturdy resistance, they knew Captain Whiskers and welcomed the white men on his recommendation. An old man, acting as spokesman, extended greetings and offered gifts of food, skins, and cotton clothing.

The Río Grande Valley was reported to hold about seventy villages small and large, extending north and south along the stream for fifty leagues, and spreading east or west for as much as twenty leagues from the river. The two- and three-story houses were built like those at Cíbola, except that the walls were not of stone but were of puddled, sun-dried balls of mud, plastered on the surface. The people of Tigua Land grew quantities of corn and beans and melons, although they had no town markets for the exchange of goods. Those living in the settlements near the river grew a little cotton, from which they wove a plain cloth; when they wished more fancy cloaks they made them of feathers braided and tied with thread.

The fertile and populous lands of the upper Río Grande, sheltered by the heaped Sandía Mountains on the east and by the scattered mesas on the west, impressed Captain Alvarado so much that he immediately sent a courier back to Coronado at Cíbola to suggest that the army spend the coming winter at Tiguex. The news that the country to the east was better brought great relief to Coronado, for it was clear that the small resources of the Seven Cities would not support the main body of his army. As it turned out, the Coronado expedition was to spend two winters among the Río Grande pueblos, so that the soldiers had many opportunities to mingle with the Tigua races and to study their customs and ways of living—and also to learn at firsthand of their skill in warfare.

Leaving Tiguex, the Alvarado party pushed northeast around the Sandías, and passed two villages whose names they did not learn.[14] These towns were the dwellings of the now almost extinct Tano tribe. The Spaniards, ably led by guides who were hastening homeward, now headed for the Santa Fe Mountains, which they called the Sierra Nevada or Snowy Mountains—an apt name for the range whose peaks, the highest in New Mexico, are free of snow for only a few weeks in midsummer. In the heart of these hills they came to the home city of Captain Whiskers, the pueblo of Cicuyé, or Pecos.[15]

Baltazar de Obregón, who never visited Cicuyé, nonetheless left a remarkably graphic description of it, gathered perhaps from comrades-in-arms who had been with Alvarado. "It is built," he wrote, "on a high and narrow hillock surrounded on both sides by two stream beds and many groves of trees. The hill is cleared of timber, but half a league from the pueblo there are many clumps of cedars, pines, and oaks. The town has entrances to the east and west, and it has the largest and best buildings in any of those provinces, and the greatest number of inhabitants, who go clothed and raise much maize, cotton, beans, and squashes.[16] It is walled and ramparted all about, and holds large houses with tiers of galleries leading outside, and in these they keep their offensive and defensive weapons—bows, arrows, shields, spears, and clubs. On their round shields they have painted some red crosses like the emblems of a religious order."[17]

A more complete description of the wonders of Pecos was given by Castañeda: "Cicuyé is a village of nearly five hundred warriors, who are feared throughout that country. It is square, situated on a rock, with a large court or yard in the middle, containing the *estufas*. The houses are all alike, four stories high. One can go over the top of the whole village without there being a street to hinder. There are corridors going all around it at the first two stories, by which one can go around the whole village. These are like jutting balconies, and they are able to shelter themselves under them. The houses do not have doors below, but they use ladders, which can be withdrawn, and so go up to the corridors which are on the inside of the village. As the doors of the houses open on the corridor of that story, the corridor serves as a street. The houses that open on the plain are right back of those that open on the court, and in time of war they go through these inner ones. The village is enclosed by a low wall of stone. There is a spring of water inside, which they are able to divert. The people of this village boast that no one has been able to conquer them and that they conquer whatever villages they wish."[18]

At the approach of Alvarado, the warriors of Cicuyé swarmed out joyfully to greet their mustachioed chief, and led his white guests into the walled town to the sound of drum and flute. Generous presents were offered the Spaniards of cloth and sky-blue turquoises.[19]

At Cicuyé, where the party tarried for several days, Alvarado encountered the strange Indian who was to be the evil genius of the Coronado expedition—a smooth-tongued rascal whom the Spaniards called "The Turk" because he resembled their idea of the men of that nation. He was probably a stray Pawnee who wore the distinctive turban of this prairie tribe. At any rate, he was known to have come from out the limitless east, and his services as a guide were eagerly sought.

Flattered by this attention and hoping to twist it to his own advantage, this Indian was soon concocting fantastic schemes. The cunning fellow had quickly discovered the besetting lust of the Spaniards for gold. Out of this arose a fabrication that before long had developed into the myth of Quivira—according to The Turk, a fabulously rich region somewhere to the east. Under questioning, he admitted that Quivira was heaped with gold; in fact, was a city builded of naught but gold. It

THE "HUMPBACKED OX OF CÍBOLA"

To the Spaniards, the "most monstrous thing in the way of animals that has ever been seen." (From Hernández, *Nova Plantarum, Animalium et Mineralium Mexicanorum Historia,* 1651.)

was enough. His wily brain and glib tongue were to lead General Coronado on a far journey into the heart of the continent.

With this grotesque figure as a guide, Alvarado and his men impatiently pushed south around the mountains and into the plains of eastern New Mexico. It was thirty leagues, according to Castañeda, from Cicuyé to where the plains began. The men followed the ancient game trail some distance to the west of the Río de Cicuyé, or Pecos, but after a few days they came again to the stream. Fording it, they went along its bank toward the southeast, traveling into the plains for four days.

At the end of this time they found themselves among great herds of "cows," the teeming bison of the plains, the "humpbacked oxen" of Cabeza de Vaca's tale. A terrifying sight they were, "the most monstrous thing in the way of animals that has ever been seen or read about."[20] As they marched, the soldiers found more buffalo each day, until they were enshoaled by them, beasts as numerous as the fish in the sea. A few of the bulls were slaughtered, at great risk to the horses, until the men learned to attack at a safe distance with their pikes, finishing off with a harquebus if the thrust failed.

Hernando de Alvarado and his troop were the first white men to see the American bison.[21] But Alvarado did not linger very long to hunt these strange beasts. His appetite for treasure had been so whetted by the repeated exaggerations of The Turk that soon he turned back with his men, and hastened to the westward to carry the golden news to Coronado.

Posthaste he rode through Cicuyé and the Snowy Mountains, hurrying ever faster until he reached Tiguex on the sunny Río Grande. There he came upon the army-master, Cárdenas, who had just arrived, having been sent by the general to prepare quarters for the entire army in this rich region that Alvarado had found. Before long, General Coronado and all his officers were listening openmouthed to the tales of The Turk; soon they were making plans for the conquest of the new Eldorado of Quivira, the glories of which The Turk never tired of extolling.

Meanwhile, things were stirring in Sonora. Melchor Díaz was about to set out to explore the Gulf coast and to search for the ships of Alarcón, and the army, eager for action, had received orders to join their commander at Cíbola.

The army left their new town of San Gerónimo in the Sonora Valley in mid-September. They found everything quiet among the Opata towns, but they got into trouble nonetheless. In a province called Vacapán[22] the Indians had a large store of conserves made from the prickly pears of the saguaro cactus, which have always formed a large part of the native diet in the region. The friendly Indians were more than generous with this rich food, and the greedy army ate so much of it that many fell ill with headache and a fever which lasted for twenty-four hours. So badly disabled was the force because of this gorging that the natives, had they wished, might have fallen on them and done much harm.

But Don Tristán de Arellano led the main guard safely forward on the trail of Coronado, by way of the San Pedro to the Gila. Beyond Chichilticalli, in the plateau country, some men of the advance guard started up a flock of animals that resembled sheep.[23] On the banks of a river flowing through a ravine—probably the Gila Bonito—they found a monstrous horn which the men of Coronado had noticed and left for the main force to see. It was six feet long and as thick at the base as a man's thigh, and seemed like the horn of a goat.

Winter was now enfolding the high piny plateau land, and only a day's march from Cíbola the shivering army felt its wrath. An icy blast of wind came up in the afternoon, followed by heavy snow, and through this storm the men pushed ahead, until near nightfall they found some caves on a rocky ridge. In great danger were the Indian allies from Mexico, who were unused to cold and suffered so severely that when the day dawned they were unable to travel alone and had to be carried across the backs of horses.

In this sad plight the army limped shivering into the stronghold of Cíbola, where quarters had been prepared for their comfort. There they were greeted at last by their general, who was on the point of leaving for Tiguex. He told his faithful followers that as soon as they had rested they would follow him to a good land. Hernando de Alvarado had found a fine country to the east, and it was there that the Spanish army of occupation would make its winter headquarters.

Shortly after the army under Arellano started marching to the north, a party from the town under Captain Melchor Díaz began making ready to head toward the Colorado River in a last effort to get in touch with the ships of the fleet. Díaz was destined to arrive too late to meet the ships, which by this time were already filling their sails on the homeward journey from the river land that Captain Alarcón had discovered.

The seventy or eighty men who had been left under the command of Díaz at San Gerónimo were the dregs of the army, weak in body and spirit. Under his direction, however, everything was put in as good order as possible, and supplies were gathered to outfit his exploring party that was soon to leave for the Gulf. To be in charge of the town during his absence, Díaz appointed Captain Diego de Alcaraz. Alcaraz had been Nuño de Guzmán's most energetic slave-taker, and had once tried to kidnap the six hundred Pimas with Cabeza de Vaca. He was not a fortunate choice; he was, as Castañeda said of him, "a man unfitted to have people under his command," and his brutal treatment of the Indians at San Gerónimo was later to bear bitter fruit.

Toward the end of September, Melchor Díaz picked twenty-five of the best men and, led by Indian guides, traveled north and west from the Sonora Valley for one hundred and fifty leagues.[24] The party had to travel slowly, for a small flock of sheep was taken along to provide fresh meat.

When at length they reached a great river (which was the Colorado, some leagues above its mouth), they came upon a tribe of gigantic Indians, the Yumas, who have always been remarkable for their stature and strength. "When they carry anything," wrote Castañeda, "they can take a load of more than three or four hundredweight on their heads. Once when our men wished to fetch a log for the fire and six men were unable to carry it, one of these Indians is reported to have come and raised it in his arms, put it on his head by himself, and carried it very easily."[25]

The Yumas were described as living in large cabins built underground, like pigpens, with only the straw-thatched roofs showing. Entrance was gained through holes at each end, and in these long houses more than a hundred natives customarily would sleep. The women cooked bread on wood coals, making loaves as large as the great loaves of Castile.

These Indians went naked, and in the cold weather were accustomed to carry with them a torch to warm themselves as they went from place to place, shifting it from one hand to another. This curious custom was the origin of the name Río del Tizón (Firebrand River), as Díaz christened the Colorado.

Arriving at a place where the river was half a league across, Díaz had definite news of the previous exploration of the stream by the fleet under Alarcón. Ships had been seen by the Indians three days' journey toward the mouth of the river. "When he reached the place where the ships had been, which was more than fifteen leagues up the river from the mouth of the harbor, they found written on a tree: 'Alarcón reached this place; there are letters at the foot of this tree.' He dug up the letters and learned from them how long Alarcón had waited for news of the army and that he had gone back with the ships to New Spain, because he was unable to proceed farther, since this sea was a gulf which was formed by the Island of the Marquis that is called California, and it was explained that California was not an island, but a point of the mainland forming the other side of that gulf."[26]

After reading this helpful news, Díaz turned back upstream in search of a crossing. Five or six days of travel brought him to a place where he thought the river might be crossed by means of rafts. The natives at this place[27] were suspiciously willing to help; so much so that shortly a number of crude *balsas* of woven reeds calked with bitumen were constructed.

While these coracles were being built, a soldier strolling idly around the camp happened to see a large group of armed Indians cross the river and hide in the shelter of a hill on the other side. He reported this to Captain Díaz, who at once had a local Indian spirited into a quiet place and "pressed" for information.

Under torture—at the time a common method of obtaining evidence in European courts—the Indian revealed the treacherous plan: waiting until the Spaniards were in the midst of their crossing, with the force divided with men on either side and some in midstream, the natives were to fall upon them from both banks at once, and thus wipe out the entire party by arrows or drowning. And "if they had had as much discretion and courage as they had strength and power," remarked Castañeda, "the attempt would have succeeded."[23]

The unlucky Indian who had confessed was killed secretly and his body, weighted with stones, was sunk in the river so that the others would not learn from him that the plot had been discovered. But the next day the natives, their suspicions aroused by the actions of the white men, became convinced that they would not catch the Spaniards unaware and openly attacked the camp.

As showers of arrows fell among them, the horsemen charged with lances at point and the musketeers fired into the mob. In panic the Indians fled to the hills, and soon not a living enemy was seen in the camp. Then, having evaded this trap that would undoubtedly have wiped out the entire party had it not been discovered, the men under Díaz crossed the Colorado on the *balsas*, with their horses swimming alongside and the rafts being guided from the water by the friendly Indians from Sonora and their squaws.

After this crossing, the Spaniards headed downstream once more along the far bank. According to Obregón,[29] Díaz went beyond the river for fifty leagues, "where he found the country very sandy, windy, and full of large and high dunes, which move very frequently from one place to another, and the severe daily winds make them rise and fall to greater or lesser heights, so that the harsh circumstances and the fear of getting lost forced him to turn back"—a good description of the moving high dunes of the riverside, in whose arid, shifting expanses any traveler might go astray or die of thirst. After a while the party came to some "sandbanks of hot ashes which it was impossible to cross without being submerged as in the sea. The ground they were standing on trembled like a drumhead, so that it appeared as if there were lakes underneath them. It seemed wonderful, and like something infernal, for the ashes to bubble up here in several places."[30] They left this diabolic region as quickly as possible, and swung around it in search of water, extremely scarce on that sandy shore.

Captain Díaz desired to take back with him one of the California Indians, so that the viceroy might observe the great stature of this breed. But in trying to

get a good specimen, his men caught a tartar. Mota Padilla[31] has related that when they found a huge young
man and attempted quietly to kidnap him for their
laudable purpose he made such a determined struggle
that they had to let him go in order not to enrage his
compatriots, who were already far from friendly.

Not a great distance from this place they reached the
end of their journey of exploration in the peninsula
that Cortés had tried to colonize. Four days after they
crossed the Colorado, some time in Christmas week of
1540, an odd accident deprived the band of their beloved captain's leadership.

Díaz was out riding one evening on guard when he
noticed that a greyhound which the men had brought
along with them was harrying the flock of sheep. The
captain galloped forward and in anger threw his lance
at the dog. The lance stuck in the earth, and because
Díaz was unable to control his mount in full career the
butt of the weapon nailed him through the groin and
pierced his body, rupturing the bladder.

With their leader badly injured, the men decided to
turn back. Sadly they placed Díaz in a crude litter and
began the long journey home to San Gerónimo.

They made slow progress, hampered as they were
with their sorry burden, for the captain, in great pain
all the while, survived for twenty days. The recrossing
of the Colorado must have been no small feat, with the
vengeful Indians of the river country harrying the column daily. But the retreat was conducted so wisely that
not a man was lost with the exception of their leader.

Somewhere on the homeward line of march from Lower California to the Sonora Valley, on a little hill on which they erected a cross, the men buried on January 18, 1541, the remains of Melchor Díaz, mayor of Culiacán, explorer and soldier of Coronado. The expedition which he had led had failed to find the ships of Alarcón, but they had blazed a trail destined to become famous—from northern Mexico across the desert to the Colorado River crossing, the first overland route from New Spain to Alta California.

9

The Secret of the Gulf

May–November, 1540

THE CORONADO EXPEDITION by land was to be supported, according to the plan of Viceroy Mendoza, by
a fleet of vessels that would carry the heavy baggage and
collaborate with Coronado in every possible way.

The report of Marcos had led the viceroy to believe
that the road to Cíbola was close to the sea all the way.
His plan was undertaken with some knowledge of Francisco de Ulloa's unlucky voyage to the head of the Gulf
of California; Mendoza assumed that in order to reach
the supposed latitude of Cíbola it would be necessary
to ascend a river that was believed to empty into the
Gulf at the point where Ulloa had fearfully turned
back. Such a river had been heard of as early as 1529,
when Guzmán's men were exploring the Yaqui River
country.[1] But as this river had not been discovered and
its course was wholly unknown, Mendoza's confidence
in assuming that the land and sea parties could work in
conjunction is something to wonder at. If it did enter

---

[1] For notes to chap. 9, see pp. 349–353.

the viceroy's head that his plan was not feasible, he must have been willing to take the chance anyway and to leave no stone unturned to make the expedition of Coronado a success.

His scheme of coöperation was never to be realized. Many attempts were made by Hernando de Alarcón, commander of the fleet, to get in touch with the army at the river mouths along the west coast, and both Rodrigo Maldonado and Melchor Díaz led parties from the Sonora to scout for signs of the ships; but during the whole course of the explorations the land forces were never to catch sight of their supporting fleet. The expedition by sea is chiefly remarkable because on this voyage—which in point of time comes between that of Ulloa up the Gulf and that of Cabrillo up the California coast—white men first saw and sailed on the waters of the giant Colorado River of the West, and brought back reports of the customs and traditions of the Indian tribes that in the sixteenth century inhabited its banks.

"He who puts to sea," runs the Peninsular proverb, "believes in God."

The lot of the Spanish seaman in the New World was one of little glory but of much hard work amidst the hazards of sea, scurvy, broken bones, Indian arrows, thirst, empty bellies, cold, and shipwreck. Sad to say, the achievements of those tough seafarers who pushed their high-pooped, homemade vessels through the shoals and among the rocks of the stormy western coast of America have never been fully recognized.[2]

The difficulties of constructing ships on the west coast of Mexico, where almost all fittings, even nails, had to be brought over long distances, and where there were no skilled workmen and no tradition of shipbuilding, prevented the production of vessels that could compare at all favorably with those built in Europe. Also, the tropical waters in which the ships sailed caused encrustation of hulls, requiring frequent halts to careen and scrape; moreover, as the bottoms were not sheathed with metal, it often happened that a ship was endangered by the riddling of the dreaded sea worm, *Teredo navalis*. The coasts they sailed are subject at times to terrific storms which could easily strip an unwary vessel of its sails and rigging, or run it ashore on hungry rocks. In truth, the seamen who ventured out into the unknown Pacific may have felt—and with some reason—the same qualms experienced by the unwilling foremast hands who first sailed with Columbus into the Sea of Darkness.

In spite of a written code[3] which defined his status and itemized his duties, and even regulated his daily diet, when a common seaman signed on for a voyage by the simple act of shaking hands with his captain he was thenceforward completely under the dominion of that officer, upon the vagaries of whose temperament his future lot depended.

The frequent mutinies recorded on the expeditions sent out by Cortés and others reveal that the men were often willing to risk dire penalties in attempts to escape intolerable ship conditions and harsh treatment by officers. The sailor accepted the dangers of the sea with the resignation of a fatalist. He endured spoiled food and impure water, and rarely protested against the ever-present vermin. He was accustomed to living day and night in his sodden clothing.⁴ But a tyrannical captain such as Diego de Becerra could make the bold seaman forswear his solemn oath, and then mutiny flamed forth on the narrow decks.

The voyage of the three ships under Hernando de Alarcón in the summer of 1540, in conjunction with the Coronado expedition, was remarkable in that there is no record of oppression of sailors. So far as is known, the fleet returned to harbor without losing a man. Nor did the voyage end in futility and disaster, as did most of the sea ventures of Cortés and other early explorers of the Pacific coast.

To one who reads the record of his voyage, it is apparent that Alarcón, who had served Mendoza in the important office of chamberlain, was a capable leader, wise in expedients, a commander unwilling to send men where he would not go himself and firm but tactful in his dealings with his followers and with the Indians (with whom it would have been easy many times to engage in pitched battle). Alarcón was a sincere Christian without being the sort of zealot who, with a sword, would ram the Mass down the throats of the natives. So far as he was able, he carried out fully the spirit of his orders. Little or nothing is known of him either before or after his famous voyage, but his claim to renown is secure, for he was the discoverer and the first explorer of the Colorado River, the mightiest stream of the American Southwest.

"On Sunday the ninth of May in the year 1540 [thus Alarcón began his account],[5] I set sail with two ships, the one called 'San Pedro' being the flagship, and the other the 'Santa Catalina.'"[6]

They departed from Acapulco, a port on the Pacific due south of Mexico City, where one of the shipyards of Cortés had been. It is more than likely that the "San Pedro" and the "Santa Catalina" had been built by the orders of the Marqués del Valle for an expedition which Mendoza had not allowed to sail.

Alarcón's intention was to stop at the port of Jalisco, or Santiago de Buena Esperanza,[7] at the mouth of the Río Grande de Santiago to take on additional men who were awaiting him there. Before arriving at that port, a terrible storm overtook the ships, and the crew of the "Santa Catalina," which was captained by Marcos Ruíz de Rojas, "being more afraid than was need" cast overboard nine pieces of ordnance, two anchors and a cable, and many other necessities. The losses were made good, however, at Santiago, and after the new members of the expedition were taken aboard the ships headed for Aguaiavale, the port of San Miguel de Culiacán.

There Alarcón learned that Coronado's army had departed from Culiacán in May, leaving behind them the heavier equipment and surplus baggage; these things, with a supply of provisions contributed by the generous citizens, had all been loaded on a vessel called the "San Gabriel," which now joined the fleet. The three ships then proceeded along the Mexican coast, and in sailing near the shore, on the lookout for signs of the army, Alarcón and his men discovered several good havens which the fleet under Ulloa had missed.

At last, at the northern end of the Gulf, Alarcón reached the region of shoals where Ulloa had turned back in terror. So great was the peril of shipwreck among these treacherous mudbanks that the pilots and crews of Alarcón also clamored to return. But Hernando de Alarcón was so determined to find out the "secret of the gulf" that he swore he would see the very head, even should it mean the loss of all his ships.

Nicolás Zamorano, chief pilot, and Domingo del Castillo (who later made a map of the Gulf of California) were sent out in boats to sound the channel. The ships attempted to work in among the tortuous shallows in the wake of the pilots, but it was not long before all the ships were fast in the sand and unable to lend aid to one another because of the mighty sweep of the current.[8] Fortunately, with the return of the flood the vessels floated free, and crossing the bar wormed their way into the "very bottom of the bay," hedged with shifting, amphibious islands. They had entered the mouth of the great river.

Because it was out of the question to navigate the ships against the rushing ruddy torrent, the dogged commander decided to leave the vessels anchored and to push upstream with a small exploring party in the ships' boats. Accordingly, that same day, into two sailing boats, leaving a third for the use of those remaining with the ships, Alarcón loaded twenty men (including both the treasurer and the *contador* of the fleet), and some small cannon. Warning the crews to obey his orders strictly, especially in the event of an Indian attack, he started upstream. On this day, Thursday, August 26, white men first sailed on the turbid breast of the Colorado River.

On either side stretched away the shifting, chocolate-colored flats of the flood plain, fringed on the far horizon with the shimmering peaks of desert ranges. Before nightfall, the men had performed the laborious task of drawing the boats with hawsers from the bank for the very creditable distance of six leagues.

At dawn they were once more in harness, and on this day the Spaniards first came in contact with the Cocopa Indians, who then as now inhabited the lowest reaches of the Colorado where the water is fresh. A number of these natives rushed from their huts in evident fright, but when they showed signs of hostility, Alarcón withdrew to the middle of the stream and rode at anchor, cautioning his men to remain quiet. The Indians approached nearer and nearer, until at last more than two hundred and fifty were on the shore, waving bows and arrows, and banners such as those under which the Indians of New Spain were accustomed to do battle.

The Indian interpreter that the captain had brought with him could not make himself understood, but Alarcón, heading his boat toward the bank, resorted to the prehistoric language of gesture. Casting down his sword and buckler in the sight of all, he seized a handful of trade trinkets and bestowed them upon one daring buck who had entered the water and who was promptly embraced for the edification of the beholders.

Friendly relations were shortly established, and the Indians were persuaded to lay down their arms. Alarcón bravely went ashore with a few of the men from his boat, to mingle with the crowd; and cakes of maize and loaves made of mesquite seeds were brought for the refreshment of the mariners.

Some of the Indians now made signs that they would like to see one of the harquebuses shot off. When Alarcón gratified this wish, they were all frightened except two or three old men, who reproached their compatriots for such unmanly fear. One of these old fellows began to make a speech which seemed to arouse the martial ardor of the Indians; they reached once more for their discarded clubs and bows, while the speaker, having worked himself into a rage, thumped poor Alarcón resoundingly on the chest.

Discreetly the Spaniards retired to their boats, and taking advantage of a favorable wind passed upstream two leagues. There they evaded an ambush of a thousand warriors who vainly sought to lure them ashore. The boats were moored in midstream, and watchfully the men passed the night.

The next morning Alarcón, by gentle tactics, again persuaded the Indians to lay down their arms, and the day was passed in brisk bartering. Although the interpreter was still unable to understand the language of the natives, during that day and the day following Alarcón succeeded in gaining by observation a good understanding of the manners of the Cocopas. All these Indians were very large in body, but well proportioned, with good features. Many had their faces marked with hideous designs in charcoal, and some wore blackened masks and feathered helmets of deerskin. Others had ear pendants of shells and bones. The men wore girdles from which dangled a sort of tail made of feathers; the women were clad in nothing more than a girdle of painted feathers. The hair was cut short in front, hanging down to the waist behind. The men bore tobacco pouches attached to one arm and a small pipe of cane fixed to the other.

Alarcón was quick to notice that these Indians worshipped the Sun, and at once conveyed to them the idea that it was from the Land of the Sun that he had come—that he and his party were, in fact, Children of the Sun.[9] His reception immediately became overwhelmingly favorable. His boats were laden with gifts of food, and any native who approached him bearing a weapon was immediately disarmed by the others. The Indians also begged respectfully for the privilege of towing the boats, many of them contesting for places at the ropes, and thereafter the Spaniards were relieved of this wearisome labor.

Alarcón also happened upon another useful piece of Indian superstition when, as a token of his favor, he began to distribute to the natives little holy crosses.[10] The demand for these relics soon outstripped the supply of materials, and, as the captain reported later, "at length the matter grew to such issue that I had not paper and sticks enough to make the crosses."

As the boats proceeded up the river in the days following, Alarcón had his interpreter call out frequently in his native tongue to the people along the bank. This device was of good avail, for on Tuesday, the last of August, one of the local Indians answered, and began putting questions to Alarcón. When he asked who had sent them to this land, Alarcón cannily responded that they had been sent by the Sun.

After a lengthy catechism, in which Alarcón cleverly set the Indian's doubts at rest, he was met by a final question. Did the white man come to this country to be their lord and ruler? The captain answered that he had come rather to be their brother. Whereupon the native cried out in a loud voice to the astonished throng that this was truly the Son of the Sun, and that all should accept him as their lord.

The day passed in further worshipful parley, and when night came Alarcón managed to get his questioner into his boat, where he asked the Indian if he had ever seen or heard of other men like them. The native said that he had sometimes heard from old men that very far away there were other white men, with beards like theirs; but he had never heard of Cíbola or Totonteac. He added that had the Christians not come and enjoined them to keep the peace they would now be at war, which was their favorite occupation. He complained of a people who lived in the mountains beyond and frequently made great wars against them.

The next day the party went ashore, to be greeted by the chief, Naguachato, and to be loaded down with provisions. They watched an Indian medicine man make devotion to his deity in the sky, and then helped the Indians to erect a large cross of timbers, teaching them to reverence it with dutifully folded hands. Leaving the population rejoicing before this tall emblem of Christianity, the Spaniards started upstream escorted by dancing natives at the ropes.

From another old chief who had accepted his heaven-sent origin, Alarcón learned that the upper reaches of the river were thickly inhabited by many tribes with different languages,[11] and that in stone houses in the mountains lived a large and warlike nation who came to trade deerskins for maize. Before he left this stretch of the river, beyond which his escort dared not go for fear of enemies, a party of runners arrived from down-stream. They said excitedly that the cross which had been set up was in a place which was sometimes over-flowed by the river, and desired to know if they might have leave to remove it to a safer location. This permission was granted.

Sailing up the Colorado, Alarcón soon discovered another man who could speak his interpreter's tongue. This man, who had taken the forty-day journey to Cíbola merely to see its wonders, described to him the lofty stone houses of the inhabitants who, according to the informant, wore painted mantles and "oxhides" and azure stones, and lived under one governor. The lord of this country, he said, had a dog like the one which Alarcón carried with him, and also certain green dishes like those used by the Spaniards. These had been obtained from a "black man with a beard," who had come uninvited into the country and had been killed by the lord's order. In these words Alarcón first had news from the Indians of the death of the slave Esteban, who had arrogantly entered the Zuñi stronghold the previous year.

Beyond this place the voyagers came upon many other Yuma settlements, belonging to the lord of Quicama, where cotton grew. There, likewise, they distributed crosses and were greeted as Children of the Sun. A little beyond, at Coama, Alarcón met an old man who also had been to Cíbola, and who said that the people there possessed a metal like copper brought from a certain mountain where an old woman named Guatuzaca dwelt, and that they also worshiped the Sun.[12]

The old man was asked if the people of his country had ever seen or heard of men such as the Christians were, and he said they had not, but only of a black man who wore on his legs and arms certain things which rang. This was another description of Esteban, who had danced into the place of his death in the garb of an Indian medicine man.[13]

Shortly after this conversation, the old man leaped on shore and joined a crowd of people who were waving their arms excitedly and pointing at Alarcón. The official interpreter in the boat then discovered that, by a coincidence, news had just come from Cíbola that white men with beards had arrived there, bringing war.

The Indians on shore were now saying that it would be a wise thing to kill the boat parties so that the invaders of Cíbola, who also had swords and "things which shot fire," would not come to do harm among the river tribes.

The old man restrained his people, pointing out that Alarcón's behavior had been kind and good; but Alarcón was now in a ticklish position. This was the first news that he had received of the arrival of Coronado among the towns which the general had set out to find, and it was clear that his countrymen had already clashed with the natives. Having proclaimed himself a Son of the Sun, whose mission was peace, Alarcón did not wish to be linked in the minds of the river Indians with the fighting Coronado party, who had apparently also termed themselves Children of the Sun. Moreover, his instructions were to get in touch with the land forces as soon as possible; and he could not do this so long as the Indians were suspicious or openly hostile.

Asked point-blank if he would join with the Christians if they invaded the river country, Alarcón indulged in a bit of casuistry. "I answered them that they need not fear any whit, for if the men were the Sons of the Sun as they said, they must needs be my brethren, and would use towards all men the same love and courtesy which I used; whereupon they seemed to be somewhat satisfied."

At once Alarcón determined to send word to Coronado of his whereabouts. But even though he offered liberal rewards, not one of his men would agree to make the dangerous journey—which they understood would take forty days, the first ten through desert—except one negro slave whose motives were so questionable that Alarcón declined to send him.

While waiting for further news, the party pushed upstream once more. Although Alarcón was not able to confront the two Indians who had just returned from Cíbola, he now found a local Indian who had met them on their journey and who knew their story. According to this man, the Christians had fought with the people of Cíbola because of the killing of the negro Esteban. The white invaders had oxen "like those of Cíbola," and other little black beasts with wool and horns; and some of them had swift-running beasts which they rode upon. These two Indians had watched the procession of Coronado's army for a whole day, and had encountered two of the Christians who, upon learning that the Indians were from a far country, had given each a little cap to wear, and others to take to their countrymen.

This further certain news made Alarcón all the more impatient to join forces with Coronado. When his repeated urgings failed to elicit a single volunteer, he decided to make the journey himself, and accordingly asked the chief of Coama if he would supply men and provisions.

The chief, who was suspicious, raised objections. He pointed out that the warlike lord of neighboring Cumana[14] would not let them pass, and that the country would be defenseless if he and his warriors went with Alarcón. But, he suggested, if Alarcón would first help them to end the war with Cumana they would then be glad to go with him to the east. Alarcón declined to be a cat's-paw, and the discussion became so heated that soon both were in a great rage. Before long, however, Alarcón prudently decided to accept this setback, and notified the Indians that he was returning to his ships to leave some men of his who were sick. However, he made it plain that he would come there again.

He departed forthwith; and so swift was the current that in two and a half days he made the return journey over the distance which had taken the party, going upstream, fifteen days and a half to cover. As the boats speeded south, the Indians on the banks bewailed his going and begged him to turn back and to remain forever with them, to be their lord.

Upon his return to the ships, Alarcón found all his people in health and in good spirits, although the swift tide had chafed through four of their cables and they had lost two of the anchors, which were later recovered.

A haven was found on the coast; the flagship was careened so that the sides might be scraped, and there was a general refitting. Alarcón then brought his men together and informed them of his determination to sail up the river again, since perchance Coronado might have heard of their coming and sent a messenger in the meanwhile. There were the usual protests, but the captain was firm.

He decided to take all three boats on this cruise, and loaded them with trade goods, wheat and other seeds, and "hens and cocks of Castile." Before departing, he proclaimed that in the region around the mouth of the river, which had been called the province of Campaña de la Cruz, a chapel should be built to Our Lady of Buena Guía, and that the river should be called the Buena Guía also, in honor of Viceroy Mendoza, whose family arms bore this device.

On Tuesday, September 14, the boats pushed off, with the chief pilot Zamorano again taking soundings from the bow of the first boat. The following day they came to the Cocopa villages, where at first the Indians failed to recognize Alarcón, since his clothes were different, and also because the party now had a fifer and drummer aboard to make their progress more impressive. But the natives soon realized who their visitor was, and Alarcón gave them some seeds to plant. Three leagues beyond he came upon his official interpreter, who had got himself left behind—having been led away by some companions, so he said, to get some parrot feathers for the captain.

At Quicama the party was joyfully received by the lord of the country.[15] He gave allegiance to the Children of the Sun and promised to make war only in defense of his country. As a reward for his protestations, he was fed with sugar conserves and presented with some trinkets, seeds, and hens.

The next day they came to Coama, and were greeted with delight. There a Spaniard who had been left behind on the first trip told of good treatment received, and of how the natives worshiped the cross; on petition of the Indians, this man was allowed to remain there.

Farther up the river, Alarcón learned that two Indians had come from the wicked land of Cumana to urge a rising against the white men, but that they had been refused. The old man of the neighborhood was then persuaded to draw a chart of the river and its tribes.

The day after this, the boats entered unknown country, "between certain very high mountains, through which this river passes with a narrow channel." Here an enchanter from Cumana had set up on each side some magical reeds with the intention of barring their passage, but the heathen charm was of no avail. "Thus going forward I came to the house of the old man who was in my company, and here I caused a very high cross to be set up, upon which I engraved certain letters to signify that I was come thither; and this I did so that if by chance any of the people of the general, Vásquez Coronado, should come thither, they might have knowledge of my being there."[16]

At about the time that Alarcón was erecting this cross, the troopers of Coronado's army-master Cárdenas were surveying the titanic walls of the Grand Canyon many miles upstream; but a stretch of almost inaccessible desert intervened, and it was impossible for either party to have news of the other.

The explorers in the boats ascended the river no farther than the place where the cross was erected, and it becomes a nice problem to determine how far up the river this point was.[17] It is almost certain that the site of the cross was on the Colorado somewhere north of the Gila and south of the Williams River.

If, as almost surely happened, Alarcón passed above the Gila junction, he and his party were the first white men to look upon any region now comprised within the boundaries of the state of California. Had he been a little more explicit in his description of the place where he planted his high cross, all the history books might now mention him as the discoverer of that great state. But the view that he saw upon his left hand probably did not seem to him to call for superlatives. This fringe of Alta California is part of the Yuma zone, which has the highest average temperatures of any section of North America. Beyond the river bank lay castellated red cliffs eaten by erosion, with here and there along the stream beds sparse clumps of mesquite, cottonwood, and willow. Farther inland could be seen the dazzling breasts of white dunes rivaling those of the Sahara, stretching out to the cactus-dotted wastes of the Colorado Desert. The vista must have struck him as one leading to an inferno rather than to a paradise.

At this farthest point of his explorations, two emissaries of the Mojave lord of Cumana came to Alarcón to ask what his desires were toward those people. Alarcón told them that he wished their tribe would embrace peace as the other tribes had done, and said that he would return again and visit that country; as a token of his good will, he sent a cross to the chief. From these men he learned of many settlements beyond, and heard that the river went much farther into the land, so far in fact that they did not know where its headwaters lay, and that many rivers joined it above.

The adventurers now turned back downstream, with the swift current again in their favor. This return trip was enlivened by a little incident; a stowaway came aboard. An Indian woman leaped into the water, crying out that they should wait for her. Clambering aboard, she crept under a bench, from which place they could not get her to come out. "I understood that she did this because her husband had taken another wife, by whom he had children, saying that she did not mean to live with him any longer, seeing that he had taken another wife. Thus she and another Indian came with me of their own accord."

The boats reached the river mouth after a four-day run. Then, with all the members of the party at last aboard, Alarcón proceeded on the homeward passage, keeping the ships close to the coast and often sending men ashore in an attempt to get word of the whereabouts of Coronado. In formal style, the captain took possession of all the coastal regions, and brought home with him many *autos,* or acts of acquisition, for the lands he had discovered.

At the port of Santiago, which he reached early in November, Alarcón was surprised to discover at anchor the fleet of Pedro de Alvarado, governor of Guatemala, who was sending off an expedition of conquest to the spice islands of the East Indies. A galiot came out to Alarcón's berth on the other side of the haven and he was ordered to strike sail. This was an odd proceeding, and not understanding how things lay in New Spain since his absence Alarcón had about decided to refuse when luckily a boat containing some officials of the viceroy put out to him. To these men he entrusted his report of the expedition, so that it might be transmitted overland to the capital; and to avoid trouble with Alvarado, he sailed away in the night.

According to most writers, Mendoza was displeased with this report by Alarcón; however, since the fleet had made every effort to carry out the viceregal orders, it is hard to see what grounds he could have had for displeasure. Perhaps Mendoza had allowed his hopes of finding pearls and golden cities to outrun his common sense. The historian Torquemada is responsible for the story that Mendoza was angered because fuller reports of the river expedition were sent to the emperor than to himself, and because Alarcón tried to claim the honor that was due the viceroy. As a result, so Torquemada wrote, Alarcón retired in sorrow and disgrace to Cuernavaca, where he died. But all this seems apocryphal; there is no evidence that Alarcón lost favor with his master after his famous voyage.[18]

Aside from Torquemada's sad tale, almost nothing is known of the further activities of Hernando de Alarcón. Yet he had done much. Under his direction a Spanish fleet had explored and mapped the upper waters of the Gulf of California, had ascended the Colorado for a considerable distance, had first viewed the edge of Alta California, and had brought back valuable descriptions of the Indian tribes of southwestern Arizona and the lower Colorado. In conjunction with the land forces, the fleet gathered more information about the

Colorado River in the summer of 1540 than was to be discovered in the following three centuries. Alarcón had also clearly and irrefutably established what Ulloa had suspected—the fact that Baja California was not an island.[19] That this demonstration was forgotten in later generations certainly cannot be laid at the door of that careful sea captain Hernando de Alarcón.

The Winter of War

November, 1540–March, 1541

GENERAL CORONADO was deeply stirred by the reports
of Hernando de Alvarado from the Río Grande Valley.
Cold weather was rapidly setting in, and a snug refuge
must be found if the Spaniards were to live through the
winter months. Comparing Alvarado's promising tale
with the report that Cárdenas had brought of desolate
deserts and a great canyon barrier in the west, he decided that the army must move eastward at once. Tan-
talized by the iridescent legend of Quivira, Coronado
was to follow his questing star ever to the eastward, toward the sunrise land of myth.

Only a few days after the arrival of his main army at
Cíbola, Coronado had news of a province called Tutahaco, comprising eight villages lying to the eastward
and somewhat to the south. He might well visit this
place, he thought, on his way to the good warm towns
of Tiguex.

He therefore chose thirty men who were least fagged
by their march from the Sonora, and, accompanied by

his personal staff, set out in the early winter chill. Captain Arellano was instructed to wait twenty days and then, after posting a garrison to hold Cíbola for Spain, to bring the main army directly to Tiguex by the route that Alvarado had taken.

The way that Coronado followed, led by native guides, was roundabout.[1] It was a dry march, and a cold one. "On the journey it happened that from one day when they left their camping place until noon three days later, when they saw a snowy range[2] where they went looking for water, they drank nothing. Neither the horses nor the Indian servants could endure the cold except by great exertions."[3]

In spite of hardships, after an eight-day march Coronado came to the villages of Tutahaco.[4] The inhabitants proved to be an active and intelligent people, content to till the fertile soil of the river valley. While at Tutahaco, Coronado heard of some other towns to the south.[5]

The general found the people of Tutahaco at peace, and he left them at peace. He hastily ascended the river valley until he came to the towns of Tiguex. There he met Hernando de Alvarado, who was just back from his discovery of the buffalo plains.

Alvarado was proudly exhibiting the descriptive talents of his dark protégé, The Turk, whose stories were becoming more and more colorful with every telling. The general listened eagerly to the tales that this prairie Ananias recounted for his benefit, "as though," wrote Mota Padilla, "he had never seen a stage play."

---

[1] For notes to chap. 10, see pp. 353–354.

The Turk lived as a captured menial among the Ti-guas, and was probably a Pawnee, one of the very few tribes of Plains Indians who would endure the slave's lot. Before his capture, he told Coronado, he had dwelt in a home far to the east.

His was a wonderful country. There was a river in that place two leagues wide, in which the fish were as big as the horses of the Spanish cavalry. On the river the natives propelled large canoes, with figureheads of eagles made of gold; twenty oarsmen to a side rowed with their sweeps in oarlocks of gold; and the boats also carried sails. If a chief went by boat, he would sit in state on the poop, sheltered by awnings. Tatarrax, the gray-bearded king of the country, took his afternoon siesta under a great tree hung with little gold bells which lulled him by their music as they swung in the air. He was so mighty that he went out to war borne in a litter, and overcame his enemies merely by unleashing huge greyhounds that tore his foes to pieces. This king prayed before a cross and the image of a lady, the god-dess of heaven. The palace doorways were hung with blankets. The lowliest servants there ate from plates of wrought metal, and the jugs and bowls were of gold.[6]

A look of doubt clouded the face of Coronado, and The Turk paused in his gesturing, stammering narra-tive to meet the unspoken question. Certainly he knew what stuff gold was! He pointed to a ring on the gen-eral's finger. That was it. Then they brought him a bit of brass; he sniffed it knowingly, and shook his head. This was not the true *acochis*.[7] These baser metals were not worth a second thought by any son of Quivira. If the white strangers intended to visit Tatarrax and receive presents of yellow *acochis* from him, The Turk would advise them to take carts along, for the horses alone would not be able to carry all the gold that would freely be given them.

Even the perverted mind of the Machiavellian Pawnee could not have wholly invented this story that the Spaniards so much desired to hear. His tale had been compounded partly from hints given him by his greedy questioners. It is always easy for an Indian to nod a pleasant agreement to any suggestion that he does not understand. Some parts of the tale may have held a grain of truth;[8] but the rest could only have been a reflection of the Spaniards' own hopes. Their interpretation naturally was chiefly based on signs and gestures, and it was all too easy for the credulous gold-hunters to construe each answer as a gladsome affirmative. The captains who had listened to The Turk could not keep the story secret; it leaked through to the lower ranks of the soldiery, and of course lost nothing in the retelling.

As a final proof of his lies, The Turk offered another lie. He could, he said, show Coronado some gold of Quivira. When he had been captured by the warriors of Cicuyé, he had been wearing some gold bracelets, and these had been taken from him. Now that he had faithfully guided Captain Alvarado to the plains of the buffalo, he had a request to make on his own behalf. Would the Spaniards go to Cicuyé and get his stolen bracelets? Then they would see that he spoke truly.

Here, at last, was a clue to the precious metal that, if found, would make the expedition a marvel to all Europe! Coronado at once sent Alvarado hasting back to Cicuyé to demand the surrender of the stolen bracelets, trinkets which might well be the key to all the treasures of the American north.

Alvarado was once again received warmly in the town where he had so recently been entertained. But when he stated his mission, the people of Pecos raised their shoulders and replied truthfully that the whole story was but the fabric of a lie.

Alvarado, not ordinarily credulous, now chose to cling to his hopes. It did not suit the desires of the Spaniards that The Turk be proved a liar; ergo, he had told the truth. Those bracelets must be produced. Captain Whiskers and the "governor," or chief priest, of the village, an old man, must come to the Spaniard's tent to talk about this.

They came, and immediately they were put in heavy chains. It was the old Montezuma trick; the two were to be held as hostages.

The Cicuyans were loud in their denunciation. Alvarado, they swore, was a man with no honor, lost to any feeling of faith and amity. Huddling his two prisoners within the Spanish ranks, the captain hastened from the enraged townspeople amid an *adiós* of arrows, and so brought proud Whiskers and his chief priest back in shame to Tiguex. "This," wrote Castañeda, "began the want of confidence in the word of the Spaniards whenever there was talk of peace from this time on."[9]

The Turk, wily rascal that he was, must have chuckled at this first fruit of his troublemaking. He had put a slight and a vengeance on the tribe that had made him captive. It would not be hard, now, to make these gullible white men serve as cat's-paws in other things. Only a story of much gold would be needed! Serious as was the breach with Cicuyé over the mythical bracelets, it was the least of the harms that the clever Pawnee imposter was to work against the gold-blinded Coronado brigades.

This first misguided action of the Spaniards was to lead to other more serious errors in the treatment of the Pueblo people, until at last they were provoked to retaliation. Coronado's main force, marching from Cíbola to winter in the comfortable villages of the Tiguas, were soon to find themselves embroiled in a bitter war.

Well-fed and rested, the main body under Arellano, leaving a small garrison to hold Cíbola, set out once more on the snowy road. The first day they reached Mátsaki, where the people driven from Hawikuh were still on the defensive. The army did not try to force a way into the heavily fortified high pueblo, even though it had begun to storm, but contented themselves with camping in the shelter of the shedlike balconies extending out from the walls of the Zuñi stronghold.

When the snow stopped, Arellano led the way forward; but his men made slow progress, for it was well into December and snow fell nearly every night. Sometimes the trail was completely covered by drifts, but the guides knew the landmarks well and succeeded in leading the army by the straight route that Alvarado had followed.

When the Spaniards wished to make camp, the snow had to be cleared away or melted by heaped brushwood bonfires of juniper and pine. "It was a dry snow," wrote Castañeda, "so that although it fell on the baggage and covered it for half the height of a man, it did not drench it. It fell all night long, covering the baggage and the soldiers and their beds, piling up in the air, so that if anyone had suddenly come upon the army, nothing would have been seen but mounds of snow. The horses, although half buried, endured it as well as they could. Those who were underneath were kept warm by it rather than cold."[10]

They crossed the rugged Zuñi Mountains, where the pines were bent down under the weight of the snow, and came out on the windy plain and the beds of cutting lava. At last, through the snow flurries, loomed up the great rock of Acoma.

The people of the white rock welcomed Arellano as they had welcomed Alvarado, offering birds and other food. Some of the Spaniards ascended the trail to the village to see the magnificent view, climbing with great difficulty and passing their muskets from one to another, marveling all the while at the easy grace with which the natives sprang up their cliffs, the women water carriers hardly seeming even to touch the rocks with their hands.

After ten days on the march, the men of Arellano arrived at Tiguex. They were warmly greeted by their comrades, and were cheered by the camp gossip about wonderful Quivira, where cartloads of gold were to be found.

The post at Tiguex was badly in need of reinforcements. For reasons which the Indians had found sufficient, the whole province was in wild revolt; only the previous day, the Spaniards of the advance guard had captured and burned a Tigua town.

The people of Tiguex had been alarmed by the abduction of Captain Whiskers and the old governor of Cicuyé on what seemed clearly a false charge. If the Spaniards behaved thus to the Cicuyans, whose turn might it not be next? Moreover, they were smarting under greater grievances of their own.

For one thing, when Captain Cárdenas had received orders to provide quarters for the Spaniards he had solved the problem by ejecting the entire population of one of the villages,[11] sending the Indians out, empty-handed and with only the clothing they wore, to be dependent upon the charity of friends in other villages. This act enabled the Spaniards to spend the winter snug and well-fed, living on the stored provisions of the Indians, supplemented by the livestock driven from New Spain. But to observe the comfort of the invaders could only have heightened the misery of the natives who had been forced out of their homes in the middle of the winter. It was to be an unusually hard season, too, for the Río Grande was frozen solid from bank to bank.

Coronado, upon his arrival, likewise behaved in a summary fashion when he made requisition of Indian blankets and other clothing to protect his men from the winter's cold. He summoned one of the chiefs of Tiguex who had been on close terms with the Spaniards, and whom they had nicknamed "Juan Alemán" because he resembled a citizen of Mexico of that name,[12] and bluntly demanded that the people provide at least three hundred lengths of cloth for the needs of the army.

This requisition Juan Alemán was unable to meet, for the making of all such decisions was the duty of the chief priests of the villages, who would first have to consult and then apportion the quota that each town was to contribute.

The general, not wishing to wait, then ordered several of his lieutenants to visit each town separately and make the requisition; "as they came unexpectedly, they did not give the natives a chance to consult about it, but when they came to a village they demanded what they had to give, so that they could proceed ahead at once. Thus these people could do nothing except take off their own cloaks and donate them to make up the number demanded of them. And some of the soldiers who were in these parties, when the collectors gave them some blankets or cloaks which were not such as they wanted, if they saw any Indian with a better one on, they exchanged with him without more ado, not stopping to find out the rank of the man they were stripping, which caused not a little hard feeling."[13]

Another bit of callousness was shown when one of the

Spanish gentlemen, whose shameful name Castañeda was very careful to omit, dealt brutally with an Indian woman. Coronado had endeavored to avoid such affronts previously, for he knew that they would not be forgiven by the monogamous Pueblo men, whose ideas of morality were almost puritanical.

This nameless *caballero* found himself in a village about a league from the army headquarters, and, spying a pretty native woman above, he called her husband down to hold his horse and ascended to the roof. Shortly the Indian heard a commotion, but, as the terrace was a main entrance to the whole village, he suspected no wrong until after the Spaniard had departed. Then he went up and found that the cavalier had violated, or tried to violate, his wife.

He took this grievance to the chiefs of the village, who went to Coronado. The general at once had the entire army lined up so that the native might pick out the person who had harmed him. Either because the offender had changed his clothes or for some other reason, the Indian was unable to identify the guilty man; but he averred that he could identify the man's horse, because he had held the bridle. When the Indian was taken to the stables, he immediately picked out a certain soldier's mount. The owner of the horse denied the charge, and Coronado, in doubt, decided to do nothing to punish him. Angrily, the village delegation retired to their homes to brood over this failure to get satisfaction.

From brooding, they turned to action and a crude

reprisal. At dawn the next day, one of Coronado's Indians who had been guarding the picket line rushed in with the news that his companion had been killed and the Tiguas were driving off the army's horses. This was the first of many horse raids made by the Indians of the Southwest, and it was successful, for at least forty animals were run off and many of them were never recovered. Some of the general's favorite mules were also lost to him.

The day following this raid, Captain García López de Cárdenas led a party to talk with the rebels, but found the village shut by high palisades and the walls manned by natives, yelling defiance. Inside he could hear a great noise as the Indians harried the horses about, chasing them "as in a bullfight" and shooting arrows. The natives could not be drawn from their strong position, and it looked as if this town where the trouble with the woman had occurred might be the center of a general rebellion in the province.

Coronado therefore decided, when Cárdenas had reported this state of affairs, to make an example of the village. The operations against the town were to be directed by Cárdenas, assisted by Captains Zaldívar, Barrionuevo, Diego López, and Melgosa, all of whom had come with Coronado by way of Tutahaco.

These captains stormed the town in a surprise attack, and, in spite of the fact that many of their men were wounded by the Indians above, fought their way to the terraces of the first story of the pueblo. But the native villages were built too cleverly to succumb to the taking of a single line of defense. The Indians kept up a steady fire on the Spaniards exposed on the roofs. The storming party was held in check for a day and a night and part of the next day, although the men kept up a determined sniping with musket and crossbow.

Many of the Indians were concentrated in the underground *kiva* and could not be dislodged. Several plans were tried, and at last the Spaniards hit upon a successful one. While the cavalry screened the operation, the Indian allies of Spain mined the walls of the town beneath the *kiva* and built smudge fires. Burning green firebrands were dropped through the hatchway, and shortly the Tiguas were driven forth, choking with fumes—smoked out like a nest of wasps.

Even then the Indians might have carried on the fight. But they cried out for an armistice, and Captains Melgosa and Diego López, standing on the roof, replied by crossing their spears, making the Indian gesture of peace. The rebels then laid down their weapons, expecting that they would receive pardon.

The subdued warriors were now marched to the tent of Cárdenas, fearing at the most that they would have to make indemnity, but unprepared for the horrible fate that awaited them. Cárdenas had interpreted his orders to mean that not a man of the village should be left alive. He professed later to have believed that the Indians had submitted only because they were vanquished. Neither Melgosa nor Diego López disabused his mind, but stood by with folded arms, playing a Pilate's part; they did not feel called upon to tell Cárdenas that amnesty had been promised through their making the sign of the cross.

There was no trial, but sentence was swift. Cárdenas commanded that two hundred stakes should be prepared for burning the Indians alive, and faggots were heaped up. The smell of burning brought terror to the condemned. When the poor wretches saw their companions taken forth from the tents and lashed to stakes with flames rising about them, "beginning to roast," they realized their gruesome plight at last. Seizing the stakes and anything else that came to hand, they prepared for a last stand.

They had but the choice of two deaths. The tumult summoned all the Spaniards to the spot. The Indians were ringed about by the musketeers and the infantry with their swords, but still they fought, almost barehanded, against their butchers. It was one of the most terrible and cold-blooded massacres of southwestern Indians in all history, a horrible shambles that might well have turned the stomach of a Torquemada.

Only a few of the natives, slipping and stumbling in their own blood, broke through the stabbing ring of killers, to flee on the plain until they were brought down by the horsemen with their lances. "As the country was level, not a man of them remained alive, unless it was some who remained hidden in the village and escaped that night to spread throughout the country the news that the strangers did not respect the peace they had made, which afterward proved a great misfortune."[14]

Snow began to fall over the ruined town as if to blot out the sight, and the Spaniards wiped their weapons and marched back to headquarters through the whirling flakes. It had been a bad day for the Indians of Tiguex; it was a bad day likewise for Coronado and Spanish fame. The general could not in cold blood condone the rash act of his subordinate, Cárdenas; yet he could not well punish the man who was his chief aide and who had saved his life before the walls of Hawikuh. But when Cárdenas returned to Spain two years later, he was imprisoned, tried on a criminal charge, and heavily fined for his part in the abhorrent affair.

The massacre of the Tiguas was to be a stain upon the escutcheon of Francisco Vásquez Coronado to the end. That evil day was to lead to further tragic and senseless fighting between the white men and the red men among the old pueblos in the fertile Río Grande Valley.

The day following the massacre, the main body of the army reached their general's camp. But for the next two months, although the natives in all the other Tigua towns had risen against the killers of their friends, the snow lay so heavy on the country that further fighting was impossible.

Several times parties of Spaniards plunged through the drifts and tried to persuade these villages to keep the peace, but the Indians sulked behind their strong defenses. It was stupid for the white men to shout from below the walls that they came in amity, or to promise that all past acts would be pardoned. They might better save their breath to cool their corn porridge. Promises were broken arrows. The red men reminded the Spaniards that Captain Whiskers and the old governor of Cicuyé were still in chains, and that the villagers who had trusted the word of a Spaniard were lying unburied on the plain.

García López de Cárdenas, who had engineered the slaying, was among the peacemakers thus sent out. He should have been the last to be charged with this duty, for the appearance of this hated killer could only stir up further trouble. But with thirty men he marched to the main village to talk with Juan Alemán, erstwhile good friend of the Spaniards, whose attitude had now changed to one of bitter hostility.

There, after some argument, it was agreed that if Cárdenas would come before them alone, unarmed and at a distance from his troops, Juan Alemán and two of the other head men would parley with him. Cárdenas, who knew the risk, was willing to take it in the hope that he might, even at this late stage, pull the fat from the fire. Under the walls he met the three Indians, advancing toward them dismounted, swordless, and alone.

His overture of peace soon crashed into harsh discord. With Indian logic the natives had decided, if they could do so, to trap this man whom they considered their greatest enemy. Almost immediately, Juan Alemán grappled with Cárdenas, while his two companions drew out heavy clubs which they had concealed in their cloaks and felled him with stunning blows over the helmet. Their purpose was to capture him alive and torture his body, and they almost succeeded in dragging him into the village through a postern.

But several loyal troopers, suspecting that the Indians might be up to tricks, had not withdrawn as far as the others. These men galloped up just in time, and rescued their captain as he made a stand with his feet braced against the postern doorposts. The Spaniards were so close under the walls that the danger from arrows was great—a shaft passed through the nostrils of one of their horses—and some of the other soldiers who rushed up were wounded. But Cárdenas was saved.

After recovering from this brush with death Cárdenas, leaving the village of Juan Alemán under siege, took part of the army and went to another large town near-by, where the rest of the revolted Tiguas had gathered. There he repeated his plea for peace, and there likewise he was met with taunts and a cry of defiance. The whole province was up in arms; obviously, the day for promises or threats was long since past.

By the time he returned to the first town, a skirmish had already taken place. Pretending to withdraw under fire, the Spaniards had enticed some of the defenders out on to the plain. There they turned on the natives with the horses and captured several of the Indian leaders. But the others were not dismayed. The roofs were black with screaming braves, ready to die in defense of their citadel; and it became clear to Cárdenas that it would be a long, drawn-out affair to dislodge them. He could only return to the general and report that a direct assault in force would be needed.

Several days later, therefore, Coronado sent out his full army in siege array, armed with scaling ladders. Then began the long and bitter siege of Tiguex, which was to last for fifty winter days and to be fiercely fought on both sides, a struggle not unlike the beleaguering of some European walled town by a medieval army.

During the respite, the Indians had stocked their already well-filled granaries with more provisions, and had piled heaps of large rocks on the parapets.

With their first assault upon the walls the Spaniards, with bright Indian blankets over their rusting armor, made a determined effort to carry the place at all costs. But an avalanche of boulders soon battered them from above, and those on the ladders were stricken again and again by arrows. And it did little good to gain the first roof, for there the fire from towers and windows was even heavier.

They then tried to make a breach in the town walls, but soon discovered that these were palisades of tree trunks well anchored in the ground and woven together with branches, all daubed and plastered over with clay. These walls were tough and resilient, resisting the improvised battering rams used against them.

The Spaniards found their small field guns almost useless at this task, where artillery would have been of highest value. The amateur engineers of the army attempted one scheme after another. "One was to build some engines with timbers, which they called swings," wrote Mota Padilla, "like the old rams with which they battered fortresses in the times before gunpowder was known; but they did no good. Then, lacking artillery, they attempted to make some wooden tubes tightly bound with cords, on the order of rockets; but these did not serve either. Nor did they contrive to stow firewood against the walls and set them on fire. It seems to me that considering the cruelty with which they ended the lives of the hundred and thirty poor wretches before, they were unworthy of victory."[15]

Casualties were high. More than a hundred of the attackers received arrow wounds; and some of the men, because the surgeon with the army was a bungler, died of their wounds. Since the gashes festered and would not heal, it was believed that the Indians had poisoned the arrows by having the points bitten by caged rattlesnakes.

Several of the best men were slain at the opening of this senseless struggle. One was Francisco Pobares, a well-liked cavalier who was shot in the eye while attempting to plug up with mud a loophole from which an Indian sharpshooter was doing much harm. Another was the affable and distinguished Captain Francisco de Ovando, whose body was dragged into the village, to be found there many weeks later, his flesh perfectly mummified by the dry air of the plateau.[16] Francisco de Santillana, the volunteer blacksmith and veterinary of the army, got an arrow in his right shoulder which was to prevent him from practicing his trades thereafter. Juan Paniagua, a pious influence among the soldiers, got off with an arrow wound in the eyelid, and henceforth proclaimed that he owed his life to the fact that he was continually telling his rosary; his prayers, he said, had protected him.

The losses on the Indian side were crushing. Two hundred of the natives died to hold the roofs against the assaults of the besiegers. Their greatest affliction was the lack of water to supply the large population which had taken refuge in the town. Several times they were given a reprieve by a fall of snow, but this source supplied not nearly enough for their needs. In desperation, the Indians drilled a deep well under the village but did not strike water, and when the sides of the shaft collapsed, killing thirty of the workers, the attempt was abandoned.

The victory of Coronado, when it came at last, was sorry enough. In the end it was thirst alone that brought the defenders to disaster. After holding out for more than a month, the Indians called a truce, and said that since they believed the Spaniards would not harm the women and children they would like to send these forth from the village, so that they at least would not suffer from the lack of water.

This, as Coronado knew, meant that the warriors could hold out longer, but he agreed to the evacuation, hoping that by carrying out his part faithfully the confidence of the Indians might be restored and peace won at last. The white men as well as the natives had long since grown weary of this fight.

The occasion was marked by the chivalrous behavior of Don Lope de Urrea, a gentleman from Aragón. At the time agreed upon, about a hundred women and children—there were others who refused to be separated from their menfolk—left the beleaguered town. The little group of refugees was received graciously by Don Lope, who even took some of the smaller children in his arms. He pleaded earnestly with the warriors to lay down their weapons and receive pardon, but his entreaties were in vain. Never again would the men of Tiguex entrust themselves to the forsworn strangers, and when at last they were forced to come out it would be to die fighting.

As the cavalier continued to ride up and down before the village, voicing his appeal, the Indians warned him off repeatedly, threatening to shoot and calling out that he should replace his helmet, which he had put aside. He paid no heed until a native archer put an arrow between the forefeet of his horse, with a cry that the next would find its mark in the daring rider's brain.

He then gave up his efforts and rode reluctantly away, carrying with him the admiration of the watchers on both sides. When he reached his own lines, the Indians once more began to scream and shoot, signifying that now they would battle to the end. General Coronado decided to hold back his men for the rest of that day in the hope that an armistice might be negotiated; but it was of no avail. The struggle apparently was to be a fight to the death.

The besieged held out for a full fortnight longer, until the last of their water had been rationed out. One night a few spires of thick smoke began rising from the pueblo. The Indians had built bonfires and in them were burning their blankets, feather cloaks, and turquoise ornaments, so that their enemies should never enjoy these possessions.

Then, just before dawn, the entire tribe in desperation slipped silently from the sheltering walls, with the women in the center of the group, and tried to creep through the encircling ring of their enemy. In the dark they might well have got through, but guardsmen in the section of camp in charge of Don Rodrigo Maldonado were on the alert. A soldier screamed as he and his horse fell stabbed to death; another fell, but the alarm was sounded and the awakened troopers sprang to their stirrups.

Some of the Indians stood their ground, giving the others a chance to run like driven sheep as the rest of the army came up with flashing sword and pike. Before the stumbling natives there loomed, in the dim light of dawn, the frozen banks of the Río Grande. The river was filled with floating ice, cold as death itself; but on all sides the Tiguas were falling in their blood, destruction lay behind them, and there was no other path open. Only the hardiest spirits, however, plunged into the freezing waters; the rest died where they stood.

The next day some of the soldiers crossed the river and found the survivors of that terrible swim lying crippled and overcome by cold. A few were revived, to become later the servants of their captors. These were the only living beings to escape from the doomed village, except a few who had stayed behind the walls and were captured there soon after the flight.

The conquest of the province of Tiguex was complete, for the other village of refuge had already fallen, subdued by a troop under Captains Guevara and Zaldívar. Some of the Tigua braves of this town had been making regular dawn forays against the camp guards, and a squadron of Spaniards was sent out one morning to watch for their coming and ambush them. This party, on the alert, were startled to see a line of natives stream from the village in full retreat. At once the soldiers fell on the flanks and started killing. Shortly, and without much show of resistance, the entire band was slaughtered. In the defenseless village they had left, the Spaniards found a hundred women and children. These they made prisoners, and then plundered and burned the place.

Tiguex was now wrapped in the peace of the vanquished. Never again would a Tigua dwell within sight of the army of Francisco Vásquez Coronado. The tribe had fought, like the Trojans of old, over the honor of a woman; and like proud Troy their stronghold had fallen and been leveled to the plain.

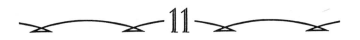

The Devil in the Jug
April, 1541

THE WINTER WAR, which ended in the closing days of
March, 1541, was a blow from which it took the Tigua
nation long to recover. They had created the largest
and the most gracious of all the Pueblo communities,
and their rich river valley naturally had attracted the
greedy strangers from the south, who had precipitated
a conflict ending in conquest.[1] For generations, anger
against the Spaniards was to rankle in the hearts of the
natives of Tiguex.

The home place of the Tigua tribe, in the middle of
Pueblo Land, was the most fertile spot in all the Southwest. It was the only region between the middle prairies
and the Pacific coast where maize grew abundantly,
making it the chief granary of a region two thousand
miles wide. Their villages lay where the north-and-
south highway of the Río Grande intercepted the great
trails leading from the Mississippi to the west. For some
centuries this land was to be a crossroad of adventure—

---

[1] For notes to chap. 11, see pp. 354–355.

a journey's end for migrations, a trading center, a battleground, and a place of frontier settlement where three civilizations mingled. Even in Coronado's day, this province on the upper Río Grande was the most populous part of the Southwest. The Tiguas were great builders and artists, and many descriptions of their achievements are to be found in the Coronado chronicles.

Unlike most of the other tribes, the Tiguas built with sun-dried clay balls rather than stone or rubble. "They all work together to build the villages," wrote Castañeda, "the women being engaged in making the mortar and the walls, while the men bring the timbers and put them in place. They have no lime, but they make a mixture of ashes, coals, and dirt which is almost as good as mortar, for even when the house is to have four stories, they do not make the walls more than half a yard thick. They gather a great pile of twigs of sagebrush and sedge grass and set it afire, and when it is half coals and ashes, they throw a quantity of dirt and water on it and mix it all together. They make round balls of this, which they use instead of stones after they are dry, fixing them with the same mortar, which is worked into a clay-like mass."[2] A similar method of building may be observed today in the Tigua pueblos.

The heart of the village, as at Cíbola, was the ceremonial chamber, which the Spaniards called the *estufa*. "The young men live in the *estufas*, which are in the courtyards of the villages. These are underground, square or round, with pine pillars. Some were seen[3] with twelve pillars and with four in the center as large as two men could stretch around. Usually they had three or four pillars. The floor was made of large, smooth flagstones, like the baths which they have in Europe. Inside they have a hearth made like the binnacle of a ship, in which they burn a handful of sagebrush at a time to keep up the heat, and they can stay in there just as in a bath. The top was on a level with the ground.' Some that were seen were large enough for a game of bowls.

"The houses belong to the women, the *estufas* to the men. If a man repudiates his wife, he has to go to the *estufa*. It is forbidden for women to sleep in the *estufas,* or to enter these for any purpose except to give their husbands or sons something to eat. . . . Before they are married the young men serve the whole village in general, and fetch the wood that is needed for use, putting it in a pile in the courtyards of the villages, from which the women take it to carry to their houses. . . . The men spin and weave. The women bring up the children and prepare the food.

"The country is so fertile that they do not have to grub it out the year round, but only have to sow the seed, which is presently covered by the fall of snow, and the ears come up under the snow. In one year they gather enough to last for seven. A very large number of cranes and wild geese and crows and thrushes live on what is sown, and for all this, when the people come to sow for the next year, the fields are covered with corn which they have not been able to finish harvesting.

"They keep very clean the separate houses where they prepare the food for eating and where they grind the meal. There is a separate room or closet where they have a trough with three stones fixed in stiff clay. Three women go in here, each one having a stone, with which one of them breaks the corn, the next grinds it, and the third grinds it still finer. They take off their shoes, do up their hair, shake their clothes, and cover their heads before they enter the door. A man sits at the door playing on a fife while they grind, moving the stones to the music and singing together. They grind a large quantity at one time, because they make all their bread of meal diluted with warm water, in the shape of wafers."[5]

The picturesque dress of the Pueblo women was well described by Mota Padilla. "They wear white blankets, which cover them from the shoulders to the feet, and although they are all covered up, they find places to put out their arms. Moreover, they are accustomed to wear over these blankets others which they throw over their left shoulder, with an end slung diagonally under the right arm like a cape. They make much of the hair and always have it well combed, gazing at themselves in a cup of water as in a mirror. They part the hair in two braids, tied with strips of colored cotton, and on each side of the head they form two disks or circles, which rise up at the back, leaving the ends of the hair lifted like a crest, and on little sticks of some three fingers' breadth they fasten in some green stones that they call *chalchihuites* [turquoises].

"It is the custom that when a young man wishes to woo a maiden, he awaits her where she goes to carry water, and takes her pitcher, by which act he makes known to her kindred his wish to marry her."[6] Another courting ceremony was noted by Castañeda: "When any man wishes to marry, it has to be arranged by those who govern. The man has to spin and weave a blanket and place it before the woman, who covers herself with it and thereby becomes his wife."[7]

The Pueblo Indians customarily had only one wife. In Tiguex and Cicuyé in particular, the marriageable young maidens went entirely naked, for a curious reason that Castañeda explained: "I found out several things about them from one of our Indians, who had been a captive among them for a whole year. I asked him especially for the reason why the young women in that province went completely naked, however cold it might be, and he told me that the virgins had to go around this way until they took a husband. . . . They say that if they do anything wrong then it will be quickly seen, and so they do not do it; nor do they need to be ashamed, because they go around just as they were born."[8]

There were no idols, the Spaniards reported,[9] nor any temples except the *estufas*. On the contrary, it seemed to the conquerors that the natives worshiped the Sun and Moon, led in this worship by priests[10] praying and preaching at dawn; at one time in Tiguex an eclipse brought great wailing and sorrow to the Indians. But it also appeared that the cross was held in high veneration, for Captain Alvarado wrote that crosses raised by the Spaniards were worshiped by the natives with great ceremony: "They made offerings to them of corn meal and feathers, and some left the blankets they had on. They showed so much zeal that some climbed up on the others to grasp the arms of the cross, to place feathers and flowers there; and others bringing ladders, while some held them, went up to tie strings, so as to fasten the flowers and the feathers."[11]

The Pueblo dead were buried in the earth.[12] Castañeda related that "in a graveyard outside the village at Tutahaco there appeared to have been a recent burial. Near the head was a cross made of two little sticks tied with cotton thread, and dry withered flowers." These prayer sticks are often found in excavations of Pueblo graves, along with stone pipes, beads, arrow points, and sacred pigments. The food and water pots buried beside the bodies were always "killed" by puncturing or violently cracking them.

Turquoises, especially of the pure sky-blue tinge, were held as sacred and were the chief articles of Pueblo ornamentation when polished, drilled with a bow spindle, and worn in necklaces. Larger pieces were embedded in lintels beside the hatchway entrances to rooms and *estufas*. These were the "emeralds" that had fired the imaginations of the Spaniards when they heard of them through Cabeza de Vaca and Fray Marcos. Most of the ancient supply came from Mount Chalchihuitl near Los Cerillos, between Tiguex and Cicuyé.[13] Spanish parties passed near the place several times, but naturally the Indians were careful not to guide them to the chief source of their mineral wealth and most ready article of barter.

Had Coronado discovered these old mines, he might have been less ready to embark, purely on the basis of rumor, upon a long and dangerous journey toward a far land in the quest of metallic wealth. But the lure of Quivira was strong, and with the siege of Tiguex ended, there was little to keep Coronado from the eastern road.

Even while the siege was still in progress, Coronado had given a thought to the people of Cicuyé, whose hostages he had kept under close guard all the while. He intended, as soon as the Tiguas were subdued, to start for Quivira, and he had no wish to fight another war to clear the road to that fabulous region. Moreover, it was possible that the Tiguas might enlist the aid of the Cicuyans to attack the besiegers from the rear.

To mollify the easternmost of the Pueblos, therefore, General Coronado braved the winter weather and made a journey to Cicuyé. The Río Grande was frozen over, and the horses crossed on the thick ice. As an earnest of his good will, Coronado took the old governor along, and restored him to his rejoicing people with the promise that Captain Whiskers would also be returned to them when the army came through later in the spring. After examining the pyramidal houses of the village, which he now saw for the first time, Coronado returned to Tiguex, leaving the warriors of Cicuyé friendly and on their best behavior in the hope of having their beloved chief restored to them.

The subdual of Tiguex enabled Coronado to make friends with the Queres, a tribe dwelling some leagues to the north. They were of the same stock as the people of Acoma. A captain was sent to Sía, a Queres town on the Jemez River sixteen miles northwest of Tiguex. This "fine village with many people" had sent word that they were willing to submit to Coronado. Hoping that the need for severe lessons to the natives was over, Coronado made friends with the people of Sía and bestowed upon them the honor of guarding the army's ordnance—four moldering bronze field pieces whose complete worthlessness had been demonstrated before the stubborn walls of Tiguex.

Six of the gentlemen of Coronado's army visited "seven" other villages in the province of Quirix.[14] These natives were excellent farmers and potters, deeply religious and accustomed to minding their own affairs. At the first village the Spaniards came upon, the inhabitants, numbering about a hundred, fled in terror; but by gently heading the Indians off and herding them back, the mounted men were able to halt the panic, and shortly all the Queres were in a friendly mood.

Along the road from Tiguex to the Snowy Mountains there were seven other villages—again seven—all of which acknowledged the control of Cicuyé, although the people were Tanos, who spoke a different tongue. Overtures of peace were made to these towns, but without much success; all the inhabitants shut themselves within their walls and refused to parley. One of these towns was called Ximena by the Spaniards.[15] Another, called Coquite by Mota Padilla, was partly in ruins, having recently been attacked. The soldiers named this place the Town of the Silos, because there they found large underground cellars stocked with corn.

Farther on the men came upon another settlement, which had been completely destroyed. Lying in its empty courtyards the Spaniards found a number of immense stone balls, big as twelve-quart jugs, which they thought must have been thrown there by gigantic catapults—although no such engines of war had been heard of in the new countries.

Castañeda inquired about the people who had made this attack, and learned that some sixteen years before a tribe called Teyas had come down from the north in great numbers and had worked this destruction. They had also besieged Cicuyé, but had not been able to make a breach in its high ramparts. Later, it appeared, the Teyas had made peace and now came regularly to trade with the Cicuyans and to spend the winter among the settlements; but the people of Cicuyé did not trust them and permitted them merely to camp under the overhanging outer balconies, while above them sentinels paced continually, sounding trumpets and calling to one another "just as the guards do in the fortresses of Spain."

The sight of the stone balls which they found in the ruined village may have set more than one soldier's heart to thumping; the appearance of a large Indian army capable of operating huge catapults might well put a stop to all further explorations in the new countries. But the Teya tribesmen that the army was later to meet, although fierce fighters, were wandering buffalo eaters who knew nothing about building towns, let alone constructing huge war engines; and the mystery of the village that had been bombarded by round shot has never been solved.

Although Pueblo Land was at last quiescent, Coronado now heard that trouble had arisen at the army's base on their line of communication to the south, toward Mexico.

At about the time the siege of Tiguex ended, messengers arrived from "Señora" bringing news from Captain Diego de Alcaraz, who was now in sole command there. He wrote of the expedition of Melchor Díaz and its fateful conclusion, and added that the riffraff left to garrison San Gerónimo were becoming more restive and mutinous every day. Two of the worst offenders among the soldiers had been sentenced to the gallows, but through the carelessness of their guards they had escaped.

This state of affairs was rightly considered by Coronado to be serious. At once he sent Don Pedro de Tovar to straighten out matters in Sonora and to weed out the malcontents in the garrison. With Tovar were sent messengers with a letter for the emperor, written on April 20, describing the latest events in the pueblo country, and dwelling in glowing terms upon the stories of The Turk about the province of Quivira.[10]

Affairs at the Sonora town required a strong hand.

With his usual ineptitude at dealing with the natives, Alcaraz had managed to provoke the friendly Opatas to enmity. Their opposition would be deadly, for they possessed an arrow poison which made the slightest scratch fatal. One soldier had been struck by an arrow and had died, although the arrow had made only a slight wound in one hand. Several of the Spaniards who went to investigate the attack upon this man were met with jeers and threats.

A tribe living in the hills were especially troublesome, and Tovar, upon his arrival, ordered Alcaraz to take a force and bring in as hostages the chieftains of the place, which the Spaniards had christened the Valley of Knaves.

This should have put an end to the trouble. But on the way back from this errand Alcaraz, whose wanton ignorance of Indian psychology was to bring about more deaths than his own, with criminal shortsightedness bargained to let the hostages go in exchange for some thread and cloth and other things that the Spaniards needed.

No sooner were the chiefs released than they rallied their tribesmen, fell upon their former captors, killed no less than seventeen of them, and harried the retreating party so successfully that only the staunch stand of the Indian allies from New Spain saved the troop from complete destruction. Alcaraz hurried his men back into the shelter of the town, leaving the bodies of his dead along the mountain trail. The poisoned arrows had done their work. "They would die in agony from only a small wound, the bodies breaking out with an insupportable pestilential stink."[17]

So menacing was the threat of the aroused Indians that Tovar, whose comments on the folly of Alcaraz may be imagined, decided that the district was too dangerous to remain in longer. Accordingly, he ordered the town shifted upstream for a second time, where it was rebuilt in the valley of Suya, forty leagues farther toward Cíbola. The Spaniards still called the villa San Gerónimo, but the new location[18] was to prove no safer for the feeble and mutinous garrison, whose morale was now thoroughly shattered. Coronado was to hear nothing of these men but scandals and disasters from that time forward.

The general had made all his preparations for leaving Tiguex and marching, foot and horse, to Quivira at the end of the rainbow, for the ice was off the river and the ford open to the east.

Just before his departure, some of his men came from the post at Cíbola, asking for orders. To them Coronado entrusted letters for the guidance of Captain Tovar when he should come out of Sonora bringing reinforcements; the general gave the direction of march that the army would take, and promised Tovar that other messages would be left buried under crosses erected along the trail. Coronado was impatient to be off on that road, and consulted frequently with The Turk, who was to be chief guide.

The Turk was now making a few additions to his famous story. Cartloads of gold could be had at Quivira—that was true as he had said. But beyond Quivira there were other places, named Arache and The Guas, whose riches would put those of Quivira to shame.

Rumors about The Turk and his yarns kept the camp gossips busy. A soldier named Cervantes, who had been the Pawnee's jailer during the siege, had a story to tell that instilled some doubts in the minds of the Spaniards regarding the source of The Turk's inspiration.

Cervantes asserted that once his captive had asked him how many of the Christians had been killed by the people of Tiguex in the siege. None, Cervantes had replied staunchly.

"You lie," The Turk had calmly responded; "five are dead, including a captain."

The jailer had to admit that this was true. Since The Turk had been kept under lock and key all the while, Cervantes pressed him to know how he had received the information. The rascally Pawnee said that he needed no one to tell him, for he had a way of finding out things for himself.

His curiosity thus aroused, Cervantes watched The Turk stealthily through the door. Later, he solemnly swore that he had heard the Pawnee conversing with some familiar demon in a jug of water.

There were many of the soldiers ready to say that The Turk had been talking to Satan himself in that jug, and that it was the Devil who had prompted all his story of the wonders of Quivira. And perhaps they had the right of it.

12

Astray in the Buffalo Plains
April 23–May 26, 1541

SPRING HAD COME to the pueblo country, and at last the army was on the march to the fabulous land of Quivira.

Not a single man wished to be left behind, although a few of the captains suggested that it might be wise to send a small scouting party to verify the Indian stories before setting the whole force into the field and abandoning the well-provisioned villages between the Río Grande and the Pecos. But the men were stirred by gold-hunger and the zealous preachments of the friars. Everyone wished to be off at once for the east.

Coronado himself had the most compelling reasons for putting the stories of The Turk to the test. So much hoped for, so little yet to show for his labors except battered headpieces and arrow scars! So great an outlay for the expedition, and thus far not a crumb of gold in recompense! The general, well knowing what his reception would be were he to return to Mexico empty-handed, was willing on the slimmest chance to risk all his powers in a final cast of fortune. The hunt for Quivira was to lead him on a far journey into the heart of the American continent.

On the twenty-third of April[1] (at about the same time that the army of Hernando de Soto was first viewing the mighty Mississippi) Coronado left Tiguex, to march to Cicuyé. At the Pecos town, Captain Whiskers, who by now was going about freely among the soldiers with only a single guard, was restored to his overjoyed compatriots. In gratitude, provisions were offered to the army and undoubtedly were accepted, although The Turk protested that it was useless to burden the horses with supplies; they might become too weary to bring back full loads of gold and silver from Quivira!

Friendly Captain Whiskers made a present to Coronado of two other "Indians of Quivira" who were serving as slaves at Cicuyé. One of these was a young fellow named Xabe, who said that there was gold and silver at his home place, although not as much as The Turk maintained there was. The third member of this corps of Quivira guides, however, differed sharply in his statements from the two Pawnees. This native, called Sopete or Ysopete, was of the Wichita tribe, a "painted Indian" who bore the distinctive tattoos encircling the eyes and lids which gave the Wichitas their tribal name of Kidi Kidesh, meaning "Raccoon Eyes." Sopete said outright that The Turk was a liar. But the Spaniards wished to believe in the gold of Quivira, and at this time Sopete was given little credence.

With these three strange guides at the general's el-

---

[1] For notes to chap. 12, see pp. 356–357.

bow, the great army column, followed by hundreds of friendly Indians and large herds of cattle and sheep, set out from Cicuyé to skirt the mountains and reach the plains where Alvarado had previously explored. They descended the west bank of the Pecos, or Río de Cicuyé.[2] The river was heavily swollen by spring floods, so that the army was forced to remain in camp for four days while a strong bridge was being built across it.[3]

It is impossible to locate with precision, four centuries later, the trail of Coronado's army from the Río de Cicuyé to the province of Quivira. Landmarks on the vast Staked Plains that they traversed are few; in fact the general was not far wrong when he wrote to his king afterward that there was "not a stone, not a bit of rising ground, not a tree, not a shrub, nor anything to go by."[4] Furthermore, the reckonings of direction in those days were clumsy. Consequently the wake of the army in 1541 on the ocean of prairie has forever vanished, even though its point of departure and ultimate landfall are known with some degree of certainty.

On those empty plains even the roving natives sometimes became lost; certainly it would not be surprising if Coronado's soldiers went wide astray in their march toward an unknown haven. There was not a hillock that would measure three times the height of a man. Landmarks were confined to a few small round lakes and buffalo wallows, a few clumps of dusty cottonwoods at the bottom of an occasional deep gash in the dead earth, a few rutted bison trails radiating from the infrequent water holes. In that vacant immensity, even

the army of Francisco Vásquez Coronado could be completely engulfed.

"Who could believe," pondered Castañeda, "that a
thousand horses and five hundred of our cows and more
than five thousand rams and ewes and more than fifteen
hundred friendly Indians and servants, in travelling
over those plains, would leave no more trace where
they had passed than if nothing had been there—nothing—so that it was necessary to make piles of bones and
cow dung now and then, so that the rear guard could
follow the army."[5]

Into those plains, "like the inside of a bowl, so that
wherever a man stands, the sky hems him in at a bow-
shot's distance away," ventured the army in its full
strength; and there, in the wide region west of the Mississippi and south of the Missouri, the summer of 1541
was to be passed in exploration. The accounts left by
these Spanish adventurers describing the prairies they
crossed, and the beasts and peoples they met there, are
as authentic and graphic as any that have since been
written.

The first boundary that Coronado crossed was merely
a shifting, nebulous line of demarcation—the edge of
the range of the buffalo. Eight days after marching over
the bridged Pecos River the army found itself surrounded by the monstrous grazing herds. These creatures were later to become of great importance to the
Spaniards, who could not have survived without the
meat obtained by hunting them.

"They have a narrow, short face," wrote Castañeda in

"ANIMAL FEO Y FIERO"

The American buffalo, as drawn by an artist who had never seen one.
(From Gómara, *Historia General de las Indias*, 1554.)

what is considered to be the best early description of
the bison, "the brow two spans across from eye to eye,
the eyes sticking out at the side so that, when they are
running, they can see who is following them. They have
very long beards, like goats, and when they are running
they throw their heads back with the beard dragging
on the ground. From the middle of the body rearwards
they have tapering waists. The hair is very woolly, like
a sheep's, very fine, and in front of the girdle the hair
is very long and rough like a lion's. They have a great
hump, larger than that of a camel. The horns are short

and thick, so that they are not visible much above the hair. In May they change the hair in the middle of the body for a soft pelt, which makes perfect lions of them. They rub against the small trees in the little ravines to shed their hair, and they continue this until only the fuzz is left, as a snake changes its skin. They have a short tail, with a bunch of hair at the end. When they run, they carry it erect like a scorpion. It is worth noting that the little calves are red and just like ours,[6] but they change their color and appearance with time and age."[7]

There were several things about the buffalo herds that puzzled the Spaniards greatly. For instance, the grown bulls that were killed by the army all seemed to have their left ears slit, although the calves bore no such mark. Another thing noticed was that large numbers of bulls traveled in bands apart from the cow buffaloes; in fact, there might be forty leagues between the place where the army began to see the bulls and the place where they began to see the cows. The explanation for this phenomenon of course is that the expedition came to the plains at calving time, when the cows always withdrew by themselves and the bulls herded to form a defensive outer ring until the small calves were strong enough to travel.

It is difficult today to conceive the multitude of buffalo that coursed this region in the earlier centuries. Sometimes the army, finding a sea of tossing shaggy heads blocking their way, would start to push through the mass of animals and in the end would have to make a long circuit around the beasts. From the time when

Coronado and his men first met the herds until they reached Quivira, they were never out of sight of buffalo for a single day.

At one place, in northwestern Texas, the army came upon an isolated salt lake, on the edge of which they found a pile of buffalo bones "a crossbow shot long, or a very little less, almost twice a man's height in places, and some eighteen feet or more wide." This was in a region where there were no inhabitants who could have heaped up the pile, and "the only explanation of this which could be suggested was that the waves which the north winds must make in the lake had piled up the bones of the cattle which had died in the lake, when the old and weak ones who went into the water were unable to get out. The remarkable thing is the number of cattle that would be required to make such a pile of bones."[8]

"The bulls are large and brave, although they do not attack very much; but they have wicked horns, and in a fight use them well, attacking fiercely," wrote one of the soldiers of Coronado. "They killed several of our horses and wounded many."[9] The ranging beasts made a tremendous impression upon all the Spaniards. At first they called the animals "cows of Cíbola"; later the term was shortened to *cíbolo,* which is still the Spanish word for the bison.

Soon after Coronado's army came among the "cows," some of the soldiers out scouting through the ground fogs of early morning discovered marks like those that would be made by dragging lance heads on the ground.

Following this strange track, they came upon a village of Querechos.[10] These wandering Indians, together with another branch of Plains Indians called Teyas, were the sole human claimants to the broad Llano Estacado, or Staked Plains of western Texas. In truth, the very name of the great state of Texas owes its origin to the Teyas.[11] The Coronado chroniclers gave to the world the fascinating first descriptions of these gypsies of the prairie.

The Querechos and Teyas could not have existed except by preying upon the immense buffalo herds. These Indians had no fixed dwellings, but followed the bison from range to range, dragging all their possessions with them. In their mode of transportation these natives had made an advance over those of the settled regions, for they were the only Indians except those of Peru to use beasts of burden. Teams of dogs were harnessed to a pair of long poles on which were lashed the tents and food of the nomads. The ends of one of these contraptions—the well-known *travois*—had made the marks on the ground which had first led the Spaniards to the Querecho camp.

"They travel just like the Arabs," observed Castañeda, "with their tents and troops of dogs harnessed up with saddle-pads and pack saddles with girths. When the load gets disarranged, the dogs howl, calling someone to straighten it out."[12] According to Obregón,[13] the dogs were kept muzzled by their masters so that they could not gobble the meat in their loads.

The skin tepee of the Plains Indians was a type of

dwelling very different from the stone terraces of the Pueblos. "They do not live in houses," wrote Jaramillo, "but have some sets of poles which they carry with them to erect huts at the places where they stop, which serve them for houses. They tie these poles together at the top and stick the bottoms into the ground, covering them with some cowskins which they carry around; and these, as I have said, serve them for houses."[14]

The tents were made of buffalo hide with the hair removed; and almost every other need of living was supplied by the great beasts that the Querechos and Teyas hunted afoot with bow and arrow.[15]

The utter dependence of these Indians upon the buffalo was succinctly described by one of Coronado's friars. "With the skins they make their houses, with the skins they clothe and shoe themselves, of the skins they make rope, and also of the wool; from the sinews they make thread, with which they sew their clothes and also their houses; from the bones they make awls; the dung serves them for wood, because there is nothing else in that country; the stomachs serve them for pitchers and vessels from which they drink; they live on the flesh."[16]

As they planted no corn, the wanderers existed on an almost unrelieved diet of meat, which sometimes was partly roasted over a fire of dried dung, or "buffalo chips," at other times hacked raw from the body of the kill. The blood was drunk warm, or else poured into a cleaned length of gut and carried about the neck like an immense sausage until the bearer thirsted. As soon as a beast was killed, the Indians customarily opened the stomach, squeezed out the half-digested grass, and drank the remaining juice—a primitive method of obtaining the vital vegetable juices that these meat eaters craved.

The Plains Indians were dexterous at skinning their quarry, cutting it open up the back and pulling the hide off over the limbs, deftly using in the process a small saw-edged flint tied to a short stick. Jerked meat was made by slicing the flesh as thin as a leaf and drying it in the sun; then the strips were ground into a powder which, when seasoned with fat, formed a sort of pemmican that could be boiled up quickly into a thick, nourishing soup.

The hide of the buffalo, tanned with the hair on by treating with a mixture of brains and earth, made a robe which was the chief article of merchandise for the Plains Indians. It was reported that they would load their packs and travel not only to Cicuyé and Tiguex, but also to Quivira and the countries toward Florida, to barter.

The pelts of other animals were also obtained in abundance by these forerunners of the western trapper. Great packs of fierce "white wolves" preyed on the buffalo, pulling down any unwary calf separated from its mother; the Indians in turn preyed upon the wolves. Antelope were also to be found on the prairies, "pied with white," their hides so loose on their bodies that while the carcass was still warm the hide could be pulled off as easily as a Mexican rancher might skin a pig. Jack rabbits were very plentiful, and so stupid that a mounted man could easily knock one over with a lance; apparently the rabbits could not distinguish between a horse and a wandering deer or buffalo, but a man on foot was sensed as an enemy, and then the small game bounded speedily away.

Animal skins formed the sole garments of the Texas tribes. "The women go dressed in some overskirts of deerskin from the waist down," wrote Mota Padilla, "and cover themselves with cloaks or *vizcaínos* of the same skin. They have leggings of tanned hide and sandals of rawhide. The men go naked, and when the cold begins to bother them, they cover themselves with tanned hides. Neither the men nor the women have long hair, but close-cropped, and in the middle of the head over the brow have it shaved with a knife."[17]

The men of the army were very favorably impressed with these buffalo chasers, in spite of their uncouth appearance. Coronado himself said that they had the best bodies of any people he had seen in the Indies, and Castañeda extolled them as the finest appearing, most warlike, and most feared of all the Indians they had met. "They do not eat human flesh; they are a gentle people and not cruel; they are faithful friends."[18]

Thus were described the Apache Indians at the time when white men first came in contact with them. In the years intervening between the journey of Coronado and the early settlement of Texas by Anglo-Saxons, either the Apache temperament or that of the white man had changed, for, under the names of Jicarilla and Mescalero, the descendants of the free-living Querechos were shot at sight by American ranchers as one would shoot a murderous prowling beast.

The Coronado army first saw the Querechos in the Llano Estacado of the Texas panhandle ten days after crossing the bridged Río de Cicuyé. They came upon a small band of about fifty nomads, who apparently had been forewarned by their scouts, for they showed no signs of fear at the coming of the white men. The Indians stared at the army with evident lack of curiosity, and later strolled over to parley with the strangers.

The Querechos were so adept in the Indian sign language that the use of interpreters was almost unnecessary, as a few expressive gestures could make their simple ideas quickly comprehensible. So flexible was this sign manual, originated because of the great tribal differences in language, that adepts could silently converse by the hour, and even tell complicated stories by this dumb show.

Some of these natives were called to speak with Coronado, who hoped to get from them a confirmation of The Turk's reports. The Querechos told the general, in their picturesque sign talk, that there was a very large river over toward where the sun came from, and that one could go along this river through an inhabited country for ninety days without a break from settlement to settlement. The first of the settlements was called Haxa,[10] and the river was more than a league wide and had many canoes on it.

These words must have been confirmation enough to settle the general's doubts for the moment. But the contingent of scoffers in the army was growing larger as a result of the repeated protests of Sopete, the Wichita, against the barefaced tales of The Turk; and more than one soldier remarked that the corroboration had resulted from the fact that The Turk, who traveled with the advance guard, had been allowed to talk first to the Querechos in their own tongue.

The next day the Querechos silently struck their tents, hitched up their dogs, and departed to the westward; and Coronado's men set out in an opposite direction, "that is, between north and east, but more toward the north." Two days later they met incredible numbers of buffalo and more roving Querechos. These Indians confirmed the report of settlements to the east.

It was at this point that one of the Spaniards went off hunting and became lost on the boundless plain. He was the first, but not the last, of Coronado's party to vanish into the desert of grass. Once separated from the cavalcade, a strayed soldier met a fate grim and sure; he would circle wildly until thirst and fatigue caused him to drop exhausted, soon to fall prey to the sharp-eyed vultures soaring tirelessly above.

Now The Turk was saying that Haxa was only two days ahead. Because Captain Cárdenas, the army-master, had just broken an arm when his horse fell with him, Coronado decided to send Diego López ahead with ten men to travel lightly equipped and at full speed toward the sunrise to find the elusive place. He was then to return and bring up the army, which was advancing at a slower pace.

Marching thus, some men in the van of the army at one place found themselves surrounded by an immense herd of bull buffalo, and decided to kill a number for provisions. They fell upon the animals and slew many, but the shouts and confusion created a terrifying stampede. The entire herd dashed madly ahead. The animals in advance plunged headlong into a low ravine in their path, and before they could right themselves and clamber out on the other side others crashed over the edge. In an instant the gulch was filled with wildly churning buffaloes. The remainder of the herd swept over on the backs of the struggling beasts. The Spanish hunters failed to see their peril in time, and before they could check their wild pursuit they and their mounts tumbled into the midst of the writhing, kicking mass. The men and all but three of their horses managed to extricate themselves. The three horses, all saddled and bridled, disappeared into the bloody jumble and perished.

Expecting the return of Captain López at any time now, the general sent six men upstream along the banks of this little arroyo and a like number downstream, to look for tracks of the horses; but traces were hard to find, for the grass was so short and wiry that it straightened up again as soon as it had been trodden. The López party was finally located some distance upstream by some of the Indians with the army who had gone out to look for fruit.

López reported that he had found no sign of any settlement. In the more than twenty leagues that he had covered, he and his men had seen nothing but buffalo, prairie, and sky.

Coronado tried another cast ahead, this time using the troop of Captain Rodrigo Maldonado, with somewhat better success. After four days' travel Maldonado reached a settlement at the bottom of a large ravine similar to the yawning gashes at Colima on the Pacific coast of Mexico. The location of the great ravines, in which the army was to pass several weeks, was most likely on one of the upper branches of the Brazos River of Texas.

Maldonado sent back some of his men to guide the army to the ravines, for, although he had been making trail markers of piled stones and buffalo chips, he feared that the army might still miss the way.

The men who returned to act as guides had a curious story to tell the army. It seemed, they said, that Cabeza de Vaca and his comrades must have passed this way on their famous overland journey to Mexico, for the Indians who lived in the ravines had come out to greet the white men and had piled up all their goods, tanned hides and other things, and a tent as big as a house, as gifts to the white strangers.[20]

Unfortunately, the Indians did not have the gentle Cabeza de Vaca to deal with this time. When Coronado came up to the native encampment, he decided to divide the skins among the men of the army for sleeping robes.

A guard was placed over the heap; but when the remainder of the army arrived and saw certain favored soldiers selecting the best of the hides for their personal use, the men were angered because the division was not being fairly made. They made a rush under the arms of the guards and grabbed pell-mell, and, "in less than a quarter of an hour, nothing was left but the empty ground."[21] Aroused by a great crying from the women and children, some of the native men also joined in the scramble, in an effort to retrieve their possessions, for these "Indian givers" had innocently believed that Coronado would merely bless their treasures and return them to the owners.

The army spent several days resting in the ravine. It was lucky for them that they did so, for one afternoon a tornado came up, a terrifying tempest of wind with hailstones as large as nuts, as large as duck eggs, falling like raindrops and covering the ground two or three spans deep in some places. Had the Spaniards been encamped on the open prairie, it would have gone very much worse with them.

As it was, it was bad enough. The horses, unable to protect themselves, were in great danger, and many were sorely bruised by the great hailstones. Almost all of them broke their picket ropes and dashed madly up the steep sides of the ravine, whence they were got down with great difficulty. Had this not held them back, all the horses might have been lost, which would have put the army in a bad predicament. A few of the mounts were shielded by negro servants who held bucklers and helmets over them, but all the rest were terrified, and hardly a one escaped injury from the hailstones. The soldiers' tents were damaged, armor was dented, and all the crockery of the army was broken—by no means a trifling loss, for the natives of the plains had no vessels but those they made of skin or gut.

After the Texas twister had passed and the camp had been set to rights, Coronado sent out another scouting party which, four days later, discovered a larger settlement called Cona. This was a cluster of tepees held by the Teya tribe, who much resembled the Querechos but who were frequently unfriendly toward them.[22] The Teyas painted or tattooed their faces, and the women decorated their eyes and chins "like the Moorish women." "These people," wrote Castañeda, "are very intelligent; the women are well-conducted and modest. They cover their whole body. They wear shoes and buskins made of tanned skin. The women wear cloaks over their small underskirts, with sleeves gathered up at the shoulders, all of skin, and some wore something like little *sambenitos*[23] with a fringe, which reached halfway down the thigh over the petticoat."[24]

The Teya settlements extended along a canyoned stream for three days' journey, and the army was led to a place where the river banks were almost a league wide with a little trickle of water running between. There they found groves of mulberry trees, nut trees (pecans), and a kind of rosebush. The Indians raised *frijole* beans, prunes, and grapes from which verjuice was made, and kept "fowls like those of New Spain."

While the army rested, scouts were again sent out, but found no promising signs. The expedition by this time was in a serious plight, and if they attempted to continue in the same direction there was a great chance that they would soon find themselves altogether lost.

It was nearing the end of May. The army had been on the road for thirty-seven days, and had made the very respectable speed of six or seven leagues a day, according to the calculations of one member of the party who had been told off to count his paces during each day's march. They had therefore come some two hundred and fifty leagues, and Quivira, if the place actually existed, must still be some distance off.

Hunger was among the men. Their provisions of corn had given out, and no one knew where more might be procured. Some of the men were becoming ill from an unrelieved diet of meat, and the horses had grown bony for lack of corn. Thirst was always with them. On the march, as Coronado wrote, "I was in great need of water, and often had to drink it so poor that it was more mud than water."[25]

In this desperate situation Coronado called a council, on Ascension Day, May 26, to discuss with his staff and friends what should be done.

Suspicion of The Turk and his stories had been steadily growing. Some of the Teyas who had not been given a chance to talk with the rascal gave a discouraging account of what lay ahead. Quivira, they said, was a place where corn was grown by people living in thatched houses. But it lay to the north and not to the east, and there was no good road thither, for the army was far south of the usual route.

Sopete, who had been asserting this all along, now had an excellent chance to say "I told you so!" He prostrated himself before Coronado and indicated by signs that, even though they should cut off his head, he still maintained that their road should be toward the north.

The concensus of the council was that Coronado should take a small party of light-horsemen and make a dash northward to find Quivira, while the remainder of the army should retrace its steps to the Río Grande pueblos.

When this decision was made known to the lower ranks, many a protest arose. Deep in the melancholy induced by the gloomy, sun-baked monotony of the plains, the men pictured themselves in a leaderless retreat, and begged the general not to desert them. They were willing to die in a lost march, if need be, but they must not be separated from Coronado! Others, less sentimental, feared that the advance party might gobble up all the gold and leave none for later adventurers.

All their remonstrances were useless. Coronado had made his decision, and would follow it to the end. His only concession was to promise that if his advance party found favorable signs he would send back messengers after eight days with orders to bring up the main army; with this the objectors had to be content.

The Conquest of Quivira

Summer, 1541

THIRTY HORSEMEN and half a dozen foot soldiers, the best equipped of all the army, were chosen by Coronado for his northward dash. Diego López, "the alderman," was made provost of the little force; but now for the first time Francisco Vásquez Coronado in person was leading the van of an exploring force into unknown country.

His staff of guides included a group of local Teyas, The Turk (now in disgrace and draped in chains), and Sopete, the Wichita, who had been made the official trailfinder and who had been promised his freedom if he would lead them truly to Quivira. Xabe was to remain with Arellano to guide the army back to Tiguex.

The main guard was deeply dejected as they watched these riders depart. Shortly afterward they sent two horsemen posthaste to ask if Coronado might not have changed his mind about having the whole force accompany him.

In a few days Diego López reappeared at the ravine

camp. The soldiers' hopes soared, only to be quickly dashed when López announced that he had come back merely to get more guides (which the chiefs at the settlement cheerfully supplied) because the Teyas with Coronado had all run away. López reported that Coronado continued obdurate in his decision, but the army remained encamped for another fortnight, still hoping that the general might have a change of heart.

The soldiers passed the time by killing more than five hundred bull buffalo and making jerked meat for the return trip. Hides were also needed, for clothing, shoes, and harness repairs. Even as the natives found their sustenance in the wild beasts of the plains, so now must the strayed Spaniards.

During the hunts a number of the army became lost on the prairie and did not get back for days, "wandering about the country as if they were crazy, in one direction or another, not knowing how to get back to where they started from, although this ravine extended in either direction so that they could find it."[1] Each night the roll was called to learn who might be missing, and the men in camp built fires and shot off their guns and sounded drums and trumpets in the hope that the wanderers would be guided back safely. The men soon learned that when they became lost the wise thing to do was to go back to where the game had been killed and cast about from there in all directions for signs, or else wait until the setting sun gave a clue to the direction of the river.

[1] For notes to chap. 13, see pp. 358–361.

After their food supply had been obtained, the army, led by Don Tristán de Arellano and guided by friendly Teyas, regretfully began the return march, with many a glance toward the north where the gilded casque of their general had vanished over the grass-rimmed horizon.

Coronado and his light-horsemen, accompanied by the indefatigable Fray Juan de Padilla, were in the meantime riding steadily north, guided by the compass needle—a bit of magnetized iron hung from a silken thread. Following along the hundredth meridian, they traveled for thirty days through the open country of northern Texas, across Oklahoma, and into south-central Kansas. They sometimes suffered from lack of water but were always able, from the buffaloes that were to be found on every side, to provide themselves with fresh meat, which they cooked over a fire of dried dung. In the hunts, however, they lost several horses, impaled by the horns of the buffalo.

On June 29, the feast day of Saints Peter and Paul, they came to a river which they called the Río de Pedro y Pablo.[2] This stream they followed for thirty leagues to the northeast.

After three days' travel down the river, the troop encountered a small band of Quivira Indian hunters with their wives, engaged in killing buffalo. The startled natives, who apparently had had no news of the coming of the strangers, as had the Querechos, were recalled from terrified flight by the shouts of the happy Sopete, and shortly were fraternizing with the Spanish riders and the other Indian guides.

At this point The Turk, who had been kept under close guard in the rear so that the sight of him would not infuriate Sopete, was dragged forth and questioned. Because it was now apparent to all that he had lied throughout, the dejected Pawnee made full confession of his treacherous plans. The scheme he revealed was horrifying enough to Coronado, who could easily imagine how it might have brought complete disaster to the army he commanded.

The Turk admitted that he had told the Spaniards anything which he thought might excite their desire, in order to draw them out into the boundless plains, there to die of hunger and thirst. He had advised against loading the horses heavily with provisions, hoping that the Spaniards would be unable to exist without corn; he evidently had overlooked the possibility that they would be able to kill the buffalo for food. In all his contriving he had been encouraged by the Pueblo people, who likewise wished that the white conquerors might be led astray to perish with their horses, or else, if they did get back to the terraced villages, to return so weakened that they would fall an easy prey to the seekers of vengeance from Tiguex and Cicuyé.

The Turk had thought to slip away and travel back to his home country, but he had been too closely guarded, and now he did not seem to care what happened to him. As for gold, he did not know where any was to be had. His failure to carry his murderous plan to a conclusion had made him sullen and malignant, and he was more closely watched than ever.

The Spaniards, in spite of their bitter disillusionment, were somewhat more cheerful as they pushed ahead into the comfortable country of rolling hillocks and small fertile valleys toward the Quivira villages. Although The Turk had confessed himself a liar, Coronado could not forget his mention of a grey-bearded king of Quivira and his story of boats with sails. Somehow, he had gotten the notion that the ruler of the provinces of Quivira and Harahey was a white man, a Christian survivor of the wrecked Narváez party. To this personage the general addressed a letter in round Castilian, sent forward by the obliging Sopete, telling of the coming of their expedition, begging full information about the country ahead, and asking eagerly what should be done to free the white castaway from his bondage among the heathen.

Coronado had now reached the point on the Arkansas River where, at the town of Great Bend, the river alters its course. There he left the stream but continued his northeasterly path down the valley of the Smoky Hill River. The Spaniards found themselves among six or seven settlements strung along between the Arkansas and Kansas rivers, where then and for centuries after lived the Wichita Indians. They had reached Quivira.[3]

The confession of The Turk had partly prepared them for disappointment, but it was a rude shock to discover that the grand houses of their dreams were small thatch-roofed cabins like beehives of grass and earth. No golden-prowed argosies cut the limpid waters of the river; no proud emperor drowsed to the tinkle of golden bells; and the jars on the shoulders of the burdened squaws were only of dull clay. Perhaps the rich kingdom of Tatarrax lay beyond?

They hurried ahead down the Kansas River. "We reached," wrote Jaramillo, who was one of the Quivira party, "what they said was the end of Quivira, to which they took us, saying that the things there were of great importance."[4] They were of importance to the Indians, for these river lodges, contemptible as they might be to the men who had hardly been stirred by the sight of the high walls of Cíbola and Cicuyé, were the center of culture for all the Plains Indians, the homes of great medicine men and painted lordly chiefs. In Quivira food was to be found in abundance; the province had flint deposits from which keen arrowheads were made; and it served as a base from which to sally forth and hunt the buffalo.[5]

The "end of Quivira" was most likely on the Kansas somewhere near Junction City. "Here there was a river," continued Jaramillo, "with more water and more inhabitants than the others. Being asked if there was anything beyond, they said that there was nothing more of Quivira, but that there was Harahey, and that it was the same sort of a place, with settlements like these, and of about the same size."[6]

In the capital of the Wichitas, which one chronicler[7] called Tareque, Coronado summoned the chief of the Quivira people, who came forthwith to greet him. This ruler was not, as the general had pictured him, a strayed Spaniard reigning in sultanic grandeur, but a large-bodied Plains Indian whose retinue numbered no more than two hundred naked followers armed only with bows of *bois d'arc* and well-made arrows. They had "some sort of things on their heads," possibly the ridge of plastered hair rising from their shaven pates that was the mark of some of the Wichitas and their close relatives the Pawnees. Many of the group were, in fact, Pawnees of Arache or Harahey, and a few of these were later used to guide a party of Spaniards to their province to the north.

The Wichitas of the Great Bend country were the aboriginal inhabitants of the fertile valleys of the Arkansas and Kansas rivers. No other tribe of the southern plains lived in permanent houses or practiced agriculture before the coming of the white man. They wore ornaments of bone, seeds, pipestone, and shell, and painted their faces. From the custom of tattooing themselves on eyelids, chin, and breast by the use of cactus spines and charcoal, they were later called by the French explorers the *Pani Piqué,* or Tattooed Pawnees. They were closely related to the Pawnees, who lived in Harahey.[8] Both Wichita and Pawnee were of Caddoan stock, and were allied in constant warfare against the wild Apache and Comanche wanderers. Their relations with the "Guas," the Kaw or Kansa tribe of the lower Kansas River, were equally hostile.

The disappointment of Coronado over this goal of his journey is clearly evident in his letter to the king written shortly after the general returned to Tiguex. The people of Quivira, he said, were just as barbarous as those he had met elsewhere in the new lands. They were polygamous and used their wives as slaves of burden. They ate raw buffalo flesh like the Teyas and Querechos, dressed in skins, lived in houses thatched with grass, and worshiped the Sun. There were in all this country not more than twenty-five little villages, and in each the inhabitants apparently spoke a different dialect. The houses were round, and had one story like a loft under the roof, where the people slept and kept their few belongings. The straw walls reached to the ground, and attached to most houses was a sort of chapel or sentry box; these were merely grass-roofed arbors or drying frames.

The natives were tall; Coronado had several of them measured and found them to be ten spans in height— about six feet eight inches! The features of the women seemed more Moorish than Indian.

The country itself, which Coronado said was nine hundred and fifty leagues from Mexico and lay in the fortieth degree of latitude,[9] was fertile, "the best I have ever seen for growing all the products of Spain, for besides the land itself being very fat and black and being very well watered by the rivulets and springs and rivers, I found everything they have in Spain, and nuts and very good sweet grapes and mulberries."[10] Other plants seen were pennyroyal, oats, melons, and wild marjoram; much flax was found, but the Indians did not know how to use it. Jaramillo also was much impressed by the agricultural possibilities of the country; the business of exporting buffalo meat alone, he believed, would bring a fortune to a good cattleman.

But Coronado had come seeking gold, and there was no gold. The chief of the country wore a copper plate around his neck, which he prized highly[11] but which he was persuaded to turn over to Coronado for delivery to His Majesty Charles V as the sole metallic plunder of Quivira. A momentary surge of hope came when one of the Wichitas exhibited a small bit of what seemed to be gold; but this dream vanished with the rest when no place from which it might have come could be found, and Coronado finally decided that the piece had been obtained by its owner from one of the Indians in the Spanish party!

Twenty-five days were passed in exploration in several directions. Some of the scouts sent toward Harahey may have traveled as far north as the Nebraska boundary—the high-water mark of the Coronado explorations—but little of importance was found.[12]

Aside from the fertility of the soil, General Coronado considered the Kansas provinces of little value, although he carefully claimed the whole territory for the Crown, and caused to be erected a large cross on which were chiseled the words: "Francisco Vásquez de Coronado, general of an expedition, reached here."

The devout Fray Juan de Padilla swept the place at the foot of the cross and taught the natives how to fold their hands and pray to the God of the Christians. There was a fatal power in that wooden emblem, for a year later it was to draw Fray Juan back to Quivira, and eventually cause him to give up his life as a testimony to his faith in that God.

After almost a month had been passed in fruitless search for metal, Coronado once more called a council. Although it was then only the early part of August,[13] the horror of being caught unprepared in this land by the snows of winter, far from their companions in the army, filled every mind. It seemed to the captains that Coronado should order the return to Tiguex, where they hoped the army would be found in safety and well provided with food. At the opening of spring, they argued, the whole force could come back to consolidate their discovery of Quivira and colonize the province.

This seemed wisdom to them, and Coronado nodded agreement without appearing to be too eager to retreat. The general was having a touch of homesickness. Nine hundred and fifty leagues was too far a separation from Doña Beatriz and the comforts of the little estate at Tlapa.

Another danger was uncovered before the Spaniards left. The Turk, feeling that he might as well be hanged for a sheep as a lamb, had been busy conspiring behind their backs with the people of the country, stirring them to rise against the thirty white men and kill them.

The discovery of this plot was the last straw. That night The Turk was garroted in his sleep. It was a poor satisfaction for the repeated betrayals he had contrived, even though his fanciful tales had brought Coronado to the ultimate station of his quest, the Kansas valley that is virtually the geographical center of continental United States.[14]

This work of justice performed, and leaving the honest guide Sopete installed among his relatives according to the bargain, Coronado and his thirty men took the road back.

On the way they paused at one of the settlements to pick fruit and corn for the journey. There guides were obtained who promised to lead them directly to the flat-roofed villages of Tiguex, for it seemed that there was a straight trail much better than the circuitous southern route by which they had come. This "good road," which turned to the right—that is, west—after the crossing of the Arkansas below modern Fort Dodge, was an old and well-known trade route between Quivira and Pueblo Land, following the Cimarrón River upstream and cutting across the northwest corner of Oklahoma. It is today better known by the historic name of the Santa Fe Trail.

The army under Arellano, provided with large stores of jerked meat, departed from their camp in the ravines of the Brazos about the middle of June, in stifling heat. They started back to the pueblos over a direct route which was shown them by the friendly Teya guides, who were accustomed to travel to Cicuyé to pass the winters and trade robes, hides, meat, rabbits, and salt for the products of the towns.

Their route lay almost due west, and in spite of stopping on the way to hunt more buffalo they made the

return in twenty-five days, whereas the outward journey had consumed thirty-seven days. The Teyas used on
this trip a means they had devised for keeping a steady
course over the unmarked plains. In the morning they
would note the direction of the sun's rising, from this
determine the compass point that they wished to follow, and shoot an arrow in that direction. They would
then march toward the arrow, but before reaching it
they would shoot another arrow ahead in the same line,
and so follow forward as a woodsman takes compass
sights from one landmark to another.

On the way, probably in Texas just east of the New
Mexico boundary, in the southern section of the panhandle, the Spaniards came to some lakes of crystallized
salt. "There were thick pieces of it on top of the water
bigger than tables, as thick as four or five fingers. Two
or three spans down under water there was salt in grains
which tasted better than that in the floating pieces, because this was rather bitter."[15] These lakes and a number
of prairie dogs, descried sitting by their holes in the
ground, were the only objects of note encountered on
the return trip across the Llano Estacado.

The guides led them to the Pecos somewhere north
of modern Roswell, thirty leagues below the locality
where the bridge was built. The way from this point
was now plain; they ascended the stream, crossed the
bridge, and followed the west bank up toward Cicuyé.
The banks of the river were covered with a sort of rosebush with leaves like parsley and fruit tasting like mus-
catel grapes, growing at about the height of a man.

Unripe grapes, wine grapes, and wild marjoram were also found in this uninhabited country. The guides said that the river flowed into the Río de Tiguex (the Río Grande) about twenty days' travel downstream, and that its course was toward the east.[16]

At this time, in July, 1541, the two great expeditions that in the years 1539–1543 first explored the southern United States almost from ocean to ocean were as close as they were to come to each other. As early as the end of May, 1539, when Fray Marcos was hastening through Sonora back to Mexico with the burning news of Cíbola, Hernando de Soto and his party were landing at Tampa Bay to begin their wanderings through ten southern states. When Coronado was leaving Culiacán for the north, De Soto was on the Savannah River; when Coronado was wintering at Tiguex, De Soto was camped in the Chickasaw towns on the Mississippi; and when Coronado entered the Texas plains De Soto had but shortly before crossed the middle course of the mighty stream whose waters were to roll above his tomb. In the year 1541 the two armies were steadily drawing toward each other. An exploring party sent by De Soto to "Caluça" heard about the buffalo plains where the animals were in such plenty that they devoured all the maize fields; this party may have reached the lower Kansas River. In the early autumn, De Soto's army was on the Neosho River of northeastern Oklahoma at a time when Coronado was cutting across the western end of that state on his return from Quivira.

During all these years De Soto's attorney in Spain was

making out an impressive claim for his client, maintaining that he should be allowed a free hand in the new lands for fear lest a clash between the two forces should cause great scandal and bloodshed. This much feared meeting, although it might easily have taken place, did not occur. The only link between the two expeditions is to be found not in events in Kansas or Oklahoma but, surprising to say, in an incident that took place in New Mexico while Arellano was leading his men back to Tiguex.

Going up the Pecos, a Painted Indian woman of one of the Plains tribes, who had been accompanying the troop of Juan de Zaldívar, recognized the country they were approaching as leading to Tiguex, where she had once lived as a slave. She ran away and hid in the arroyos of the river until the army had passed on, and then went back to the eastward.

The following May, Hernando de Soto died and was buried in the bed of the Mississippi, and his men under Luis de Moscoso started for Mexico overland. They fought their way as far south as the middle Brazos River, on the upper branches of which the men of Coronado had camped. There, by chance, they encountered the same Indian woman who had fled from Zaldívar the previous July!

According to the chronicler of the De Soto party, some natives of the Brazos admitted under torture that farther up the river some Christians had arrived and then had gone back toward the west, whence they had come. Moscoso went up to this place, "and took some women, among whom was one who said that she had seen Christians, and, having been in their hands, had made her escape from them. The Governor sent a captain with fifteen cavalry to where she said they were seen, to discover if there were any marks of horses, or signs of any Christians having been there; and after travelling three or four leagues, she who was the guide declared that all she had said was false; and so it was deemed of everything else the Indians had told of having seen Christians in Florida."" Had this woman not changed her story, Moscoso and his men, instead of making a stormy Gulf voyage in crude boats, might have returned to Mexico by the Coronado Trail.

As the army of Arellano approached the walls of Cicuyé, the natives looked glumly out upon the strangers whom they had hoped would by now be lying dead of starvation on the plains.

But in the event of just such a return, the Cicuyans had spent the intervening time making preparations for war. They promptly barricaded themselves in their town, which they had fortified so well that Arellano, unable to get food or even to discuss peace with them, was forced to march on to take up his old headquarters at Tiguex, which he reached about the middle of July.

A few of the Tiguas had returned to their homes during the early summer, hoping like the Pecos people that they would see the deluded white men no more; but as soon as the helmeted Spaniards appeared, they slunk away to hide once again in their hill fastnesses.

Arellano quickly set about collecting provisions not only for the immediate needs of the men, but for the coming winter. The Tigua villages had been almost swept clean of foodstuffs, and therefore several captains were sent to outlying pueblo settlements north and south to hunt for provisions.

Francisco Barrionuevo—directed, perhaps, by a guide from friendly Sía—with one detachment went north and west from the Río Grande and visited the "seven" villages of Hemes (or Jemez) in the wilds of the Valle Mountains. On the way, passing through the San Diego and Guadalupe canyons of the Jemez River, he saw three small villages which he named Aguas Calientes or Hot Springs, because of the remarkable thermal springs of the San Diego gorge. The inhabitants of these towns came out peaceably and supplied provender for the Spaniards, although they were closely related by blood to the warriors of Cicuyé and might well have been hostile.

Swinging to the northeast over the high volcanic mesas and down the Santa Clara Canyon, thus avoiding the seventy-mile White Rock gorge that makes the Río Grande impassable below Española, Barrionuevo returned to the river through a region that is now thick with pueblos—Santa Clara, Nambé, Tesuque, San Ildefonso, and Puyé. There the soldiers came upon the two villages of "Yuqueyunque,"[18] whose Tehua inhabitants fled at the approach of the white men and retreated to some mountain hamlets in rough country where they could not be followed.

In the empty villages the Spaniards found large quantities of food, as well as some beautiful, highly polished earthenware jars and bowls of diverse shapes. "Here also they found many bowls full of a carefully selected shining metal with which they glazed the earthenware. This shows that mines of silver would be found in that country if anyone should hunt them."[19]

Apparently no attempt was made to go eastward to visit the Santa Fe region; there was little to attract interest in the district for, although claimed by the Tanos and once settled by them, it had been abandoned for at least half a century. Instead, the men of Barrionuevo crossed to the east bank opposite Chamita and ascended the brawling Río Grande through its narrow canyon. They probably visited the pueblo of Picuris, which they called Acha. Twenty leagues upstream from their crossing, the food gatherers came to the most northern of the pueblos, a fine, large town which they understood was named Braba or Yuraba, and which, "because of its pleasant seat," they promptly christened Valladolid. It was old Taos.

Taos, with Picuris, formed the northern province of the Pueblo Indians, and Castañeda asserted, although it is hardly possible, that some of Alvarado's men had seen the place a year before on a scouting trip out from Cicuyé.[20] Taos is situated in a "high and cold" country, between an arid plateau on the west and the towering, snow-capped crags of the Taos Range on the east, which rise six thousand feet above the pretty valley. The town contained eighteen *barrios* or wards, and in customary

Pueblo style was built on both banks of its stream, the little Río de Taos, which was arched by some fine native bridges of long, squared pine timbers brought down from the high mountain forests. Such bridges were very necessary, for there was no ford and the river when fresh could be rough and swift.

At Taos the finest of the pillared underground *estufas* was discovered and admired. "The houses," according to one account, "are very close together, and have five or six stories, three of them with mud walls and two or three with thin wooden walls, which become smaller as they go up, and each one has its little balcony outside of the mud walls, one above the other, all around, of wood."[21] This description gives a clear picture of the pyramiding terraces of this most symmetrical of all the pueblos; and its appearance might well have reminded a homesick Spaniard of lovely Valladolid. Barrionuevo was received peacefully, and after all his travels was able to return to Tiguex with a good supply of corn.

Another captain was sent south to explore the downstream settlements on the Río Grande which Coronado had heard about on his Tutahaco visit. Some distance below the Tigua towns of Tutahaco around Isleta, four large villages were visited by the unnamed captain, whose men were greeted peaceably by the Piro inhabitants. They were the southernmost of the town builders, of Tanoan stock like all their more northerly river neighbors.[22]

The Piro villages did not greatly impress the men coming from Tiguex, and the captain pushed on down the river "until he found that it sank into the earth, like the Guadiana in Extremadura." The place he reached, near Mesilla below the Jornada del Muerto, was a sink where in the dry season the waters of the Río Grande smothered in the sand.[28] The Indian guides said that farther down the river emerged much larger, but the orders were to turn back after the party had covered eighty leagues, and the squadron was no doubt glad to return to more comfortable regions.

The Coronado men, therefore, did not explore the Río Grande south of the great *bolsón* where the waters sank into the earth; nor did they depart far from the riverbank. But somewhat to the east of the river, in some of the most desolate and accursed desert in North America, is a region that later, through an unfortunate confusion of names, came to be called the Gran Quivira, and was to prove a greater delusion to white treasure seekers than any rainbow vision that Francisco Coronado ever chased. The story of the "Great" Quivira deserves a prominent page in the history of human folly.

In this Manzano wilderness east of modern Socorro lived the Tompiros, nicknamed the Salineros because they worked the salt lakes of that forbidding region. They had three small stone towns: Abó, Cuaráy, and Tabirá at the foot of the Mesa de los Jumanos. Francisco Sánchez de Chamuscado visited them in 1581, and before the end of the century white priests were performing their rites in the three towns and dreaming of the great churches that were later to be built in them.

In those far-off days, no one who had ever heard the name of Quivira was innocent enough to confuse it with Tabirá in the Manzano desert. He would know that not a man of Coronado's army had seen Tabirá, that the golden storehouse of The Turk's tales was eight hundred miles to the northeast, and that the grass lodges of the Wichitas were dwellings very different from the tall stone homes of the Tompiros.

But history was forgotten, the inhabitants of the salines were swept out by the Apache whirlwind, and later comers to the pueblo country knew only that there had been a Quivira and that there was supposed to be gold there. Could it be the same place as the ruined town in the waterless, ashen wilds to the east of Socorro? Thus through a misreading of the old chronicles Tabirá became the Gran Quivira, and the forgotten Tompiro town became a Mecca for all the treasure chasers of the Southwest. The sandstone walls of Tabirá were riddled and pulled down and undermined by tunnels and prospect holes by American trove hunters.[24]

Today the Gran Quivira is a national monument. It is also a memorial to the triumph of greedy dreaming over the sober facts of history. Many lives have been squandered in the foolish search; even at this moment, somewhere, a credulous seeker may be setting out, armed with a pick and some mystic map or rumored "dying confession," to look for cartloads of Indian gold at the Gran Quivira—whose only mystery is that anyone should have found it mysterious.

Coronado Has a Fall

September, 1541–April, 1542

Now it was September. The scouting parties had all rejoined the army at Tiguex, and the time had come when Tristán de Arellano could expect the return of Coronado from his Quivira quest. But when the general did not appear, Arellano took forty men and, leaving the army in the command of Francisco de Barrionuevo, set out toward the east to look for the Quivira party.

Reaching Cicuyé, Arellano found the people of the town more bellicose than ever. They came out in force to bar his passage of the Pecos. It began to look as if the Spaniards would have another siege on their hands.

With the two remaining field guns, Arellano's gunners put a few shots into the village, and happened to kill two of the chief men. This somewhat damped the opposition of the Indians; but Arellano remained before the walls a full four days trying to force the inhabitants to capitulate.

Then a messenger dashed into camp. The joyous

cry was raised: "The general is coming!" The soldiers, in high spirits, sallied forth on the river plain to welcome him. Now they would hear the great news from Quivira!

Foremost among the laughing crowd was the young Pawnee guide, Xabe. Seeming greatly pleased, he remarked knowingly: "Now when the general comes, you'll see that there is gold and silver in Quivira, although not so much as The Turk said." When the Quivira contingent arrived among the tents, having spent forty days on the road, no one appeared more dejected than Xabe to find that their horses were not loaded with sacks of nuggets and shining plate.

He seemed to be astounded that no treasure had been found, and muttered that something was wrong. Perhaps the general had not dared to enter the country of Quivira, because his force was so small. Or he had returned to the pueblos to escape the season of storms, and must be planning to bring the army to the conquest of the Quiviras in the spring. It could not be anything else that had kept him from filling his hands with treasure, for the gold was there!

Many a man in the army was deeply impressed by these dark words, and fully believed that if one could only penetrate far enough into Xabe's home country the gold would be found. Did not the natives know what the stuff was, giving it the name of *acochis?*

Listening to the stories of Coronado's thirty regarding the country of large rivers and shady glens, so much like the Spain of their birth, the men of the army soon came to a comforting conclusion. When spring came again, all of them would go to this Quivira, ransack its green hills, and find fortune at last. Gold had not been discovered in any other part of the new lands, but it could be found if only they would look long enough and far enough. Beyond Quivira, then, it would be found. It must be found.

That second winter the Coronado expedition spent in Tiguex was a dull time, and the Spaniards lived upon the shaky hope that Xabe was right, and that somewhere in the Quivira country, or beyond, the glimmering plunder would yet be discovered.

It was a hope that Coronado in his inmost mind suspected to be baseless, and this thought ate secretly at his heart. He was growing weary of the snows of high New Mexico and dreaded to traverse again the gloomy, shadeless plains. The attractions of his pleasant estate at Tlapa and the charms of his lovely wife were pulling him southward. The petty squabbles of the army, the vain attempts to get the Tiguas to return to their villages, and boresome administrative duties annoyed him more and more.

The Cicuyans, who had fought with Arellano, had come out peaceably to speak with Coronado, and with good promises he had smoothed over their hostility. Upon reaching his old headquarters at Tiguex, he had found the reinforcements that Don Pedro de Tovar had brought from the Sonora River town.

These men were the best half of the garrison of San Gerónimo, and had come with high expectations that

they would be able to go at once to Quivira and fill
their hands with the loot that Tovar had told them the
general was seeking there. They now consoled themselves with the thought that in the spring they would
be able to make the journey with the rest of the army.
It would have been better for everyone if the Sonora
detachment had stayed at Suya, for those remaining
there were the scum of the army, the weakest and the
most recalcitrant men, who under the lax command
of Diego de Alcaraz were almost sure to get into trouble
with the natives.

A terrible Indian war had broken out in Coronado's
province of New Galicia and the Spaniards had suffered a crushing defeat at the hill town of Nochistlán,
but Tovar had received no news of this war.[1] He did,
however, bring back to Tiguex with him a bundle of
letters from New Spain, written by the viceroy and by
friends of men in the army.

One of these messages was addressed to García López
de Cárdenas, giving him the news that his brother in
Spain had died, leaving the army-master the inheritor
of the entailed estates. As his arm, broken in a fall on
the Texas plains, was still paining him, Cárdenas received permission from Coronado to resign his command and return to enjoy a fortune greater than any
his comrades had so far gained for themselves by their
military efforts.

Ten or twelve other men, who were sick or wounded
and in no shape to carry on their soldierly duties, were

---

[1] For notes to chap. 14, see pp. 361–364.

allowed to depart with him. "There were many others," wrote Castañeda, "who would have liked to go, but did not, in order not to appear faint-hearted."² Many men besides the general were wearying of the quest, and were held to their posts almost solely by a sense of pride.

Coronado took occasion to send back with Cárdenas another letter to his sovereign, to whom he had already written on April 20. Now, at Tiguex, under date of October 20, he told of his march to Quivira and described the country that he had claimed in the royal name. Reading between the lines one may sense the anxiety and growing despair of the explorer lest his failure to find things of material value might tarnish his prospects in the service of the Crown.

Now that The Turk's yarns had turned out to be false, Coronado was inclined to deprecate his earlier enthusiasm. He said regarding the Indian story of Quivira that, "although, as I wrote Your Majesty, I did not believe it before I had set eyes on it, because it was the report of Indians and given for the most part by means of signs, yet as the report appeared to me to be very fine and it was important that it should be investigated for Your Majesty's service, I determined to go and see it." But now he was disillusioned: "What I am sure of is that there is not any gold nor any other metal in all that country, and the other things of which they had told me are nothing but little villages, and in many of these they do not plant anything and do not have any houses except of skins and sticks, and they wander about after the cows. . . . I have done all that I possibly could to serve Your Majesty and to discover a country where God Our Lord might be served and the royal patrimony of Your Majesty increased, as your loyal servant and vassal. For since I reached the province of Cíbola, to which the viceroy of New Spain sent me in the name of Your Majesty, seeing that there were none of the things there of which Friar Marcos had told, I have managed to explore this country for two hundred leagues and more around Cíbola, and the best place I have found is this river of Tiguex where I am now, and the settlements here."[3]

Coronado's greatest disappointment was that he had found no gold; and to find gold—a fifth of which would have gone to the king—had been one of the chief purposes of the expedition all along.

Francisco Vásquez Coronado has been censured by some writers for failing to establish a permanent settlement in the northern lands; but it does not appear that he was ordered to colonize anywhere there. The main endeavors laid upon Coronado, aside from seeking gold, were to conquer the country and to convert the natives to Christianity.

The expedition from the outset was primarily a military force, and at most Mendoza could only have expected the soldiers to subdue the lands to the north and hold tenure until colonists could arrive to settle them. The expedition was unprepared for a lengthy stay, and had to live off the country at all times. No mention is made that tools or building materials or seeds were taken; the flocks of animals driven along were for provisions, and few of the beasts were left uneaten at the end of two years of marching. The heavier baggage of the party, which might have included some equipment for the use of settlers, had been shipped with the sea forces; and the failure of Alarcón's fleet to find the land party must have prepared the viceroy for the realization that no permanent colony could be established by a band of soldiers traveling lightly equipped at all times. Many other large expeditions in the Indies had set out provided with complete outfits for colonization; but from the start the Coronado force was burdened merely with trinkets to trade with the Indians.

The chief reason why one may suspect that no immediate colonization was contemplated was the fact that few women were taken along. With Narváez to Florida, for instance, and with Ayllón to Georgia, many women had sailed; but so far as is known, only one Spanish woman accompanied the Coronado expedition.[4]

Nonetheless, there may have been some general understanding that the country was to be held through a permanent post.[5] Later, when there was agitation for the return of the whole force to Mexico, those in favor of a return behaved as though they guiltily felt that such a course would be contrary to Mendoza's expectations. And in his letter Coronado was at pains to present arguments showing why colonization was out of the question. He stated outright that it would be impossible to establish a settlement at Tiguex, "for besides being four hundred leagues from the North Sea and more than two hundred from the South Sea, with which it is impossible to have any sort of communication, the country is so cold, as I have written to Your Majesty, that apparently the winter could not possibly be spent here, because there is no wood, nor clothing with which to protect the men, except the skins which the natives wear and a small amount of cotton cloaks."[6]

Providing clothing for the army was one of Coronado's most troublesome tasks during the winter. The soldiers had returned from the plains almost naked, and covered with lice of which they seemed unable to rid themselves. The captains who were charged with collecting and distributing the garments obtained from the Indians were partial to their own needs—"necessity knows no law," observed Castañeda the realist—and they and their friends fared much better than many of the other shivering soldiers.

Some of the men complained that a few favorites were spared the more irksome labors of the camp, that they did not stand watches with the rest, and that they received better portions of the food—which was not too plentiful that winter.

All of this caused a certain amount of sordid backbiting that reflected upon the discretion of the weary general, who until then had been "beloved and obeyed by his captains and soldiers as heartily as any of those who have ever started out in the Indies."[7] The dull winter days were passed in such bickerings, and more than one opportunity arose for a disgruntled veteran to remark that they were all fools to have come, that there was nothing of value to be found in Quivira, and that all would be far better off if they returned to Mexico, which none of them had seen now for almost two years.

One of the chief duties of the men as spring came on was to exercise the horses in preparation for the return march to Quivira, which had now been announced. It was while thus engaged that Francisco Vásquez Coronado suffered a mishap that was to have its effect upon the future course of the expedition he commanded.

One feast day Coronado, astride a powerful horse, was out galloping on the Río Grande plain, practicing in company with Don Rodrigo Maldonado the knightly feat of "riding at the ring." Coronado's servants had changed the saddle girth that morning and apparently the new one was rotten, for when he was in full career it broke, throwing him to the ground directly in the path of the mount of Don Rodrigo.

The animal trampled him, giving him a nasty hoof blow on the head, an injury that brought him to the point of death. His recovery was to be doubtful and slow, and the mental and physical prostration accompanying his illness were to make him do strange things.

While the general was confined to his bed, his life still in the balance, García López de Cárdenas, who had departed several months before and who by this time might have been well on his way to Spain, came galloping into camp. He had a terrible story to tell. On his way to the Sonora he had come to the town of San Gerónimo in the Suya Valley and had found it deserted, with soldiers and horses lying massacred in the road!

The general's condition was so grave that it was decided to keep the ghastly news of the destruction of the army's southern base from him until his crisis had passed. When he at last rose and was told that the Indians to the south had revolted, he straightway suffered a relapse and took once more to his couch.

Lying thus, it seemed to him that his misfortunes were shattering. Now he recalled a prophecy which a friend of his in past years, a noted astrologer, had made to him in his native town of Salamanca. This *matemático* had foretold that Francisco Vásquez would become a powerful lord in distant lands, but that one day he would have a fall from which he would never recover. The oracle, in one respect, had spoken truly, for when Coronado took that ill-fated tumble from his horse at Tiguex his high repute for courage and perseverance tumbled with him, never to be restored.

But the general took the old prophecy literally. In the full expectation of death, he yearned to see his wife and children before his eyes should close forever. To him now, the effort of getting back to Mexico seemed the only one worth making.

In order to get his way, he pretended to be more sick than in reality he was. A severe illness would offer an excellent excuse for returning from the long and arduous campaign. So seriously had the injury affected his mind that he was anxious now to abandon at any cost the new lands he had so valiantly subdued.

In this unworthy malingering he had the connivance of the army physician who attended him. The doctor also desired to return; playing the rôle of talebearer he reported to Coronado that many of the soldiers wanted to retreat to New Spain, but neglected to tell him that there were also many who still courageously wished to push on to Quivira, land of hope.

With the doctor as go-between, those of the captains who were intent on returning formulated a plot to make it appear that Coronado was ordering the abandonment of the country in response to the unanimous request of the soldiery. The general was apparently to be persuaded by all his men to do what he had every intention of doing at all costs.

There was opposition. Jaramillo said later that he and ten or twelve of the others strongly attempted to dissuade Coronado. Obregón stated that some of the captains wished to make a last effort to find the Northwest Passage.[8] But Coronado sympathizers among the officers set the soldiers to talking in little gatherings and holding solemn consultations on the desirability of returning while they could. Since many of the men were honestly persuaded that this would be the wise course, in a short time a petition with a number of signatures was presented to Coronado, requesting the return to New Spain "because they had not found any riches, nor had they discovered any settled country out of which estates could be formed for all the army."[9]

Coronado at first pretended that he was unwilling to give in; but publicly urged by his captains and his staff he acceded to the demands with a show of reluctance, and gave the order to abandon the country.

It was soon realized, however, that this had been the general's secret intent from the first, for he had made much of the common soldiers who most strongly favored his purpose. The announcement of the return set up fresh doubts in the minds of those who had signed the petition unwillingly or without full consideration, and some of these now felt that it had been a shameful act to sign.

Foreseeing that the signers might repent, Coronado took unusual precautions. Making his illness serve as the excuse, he never left his room, kept guards about his person at all times, and at night had faithful servants sleeping at his bedside. In spite of all this, the determined dupes got away with his chest of papers; however, they failed to find the petition among them because the general had cannily hid the document in a corner of his mattress.

In a final effort, the discontented soldiers who still dreamed of marching to Quivira made one more plea. They proposed that the general pick sixty of the best and most resolute men to stay in the country and hold it until the viceroy should either send them support or order them to abandon the territory; or, as an alternative, that Coronado take sixty men to escort him back to Mexico, leaving the rest of the army in the new country.

But at once a stiff question arose: Who would be named commander of the forces left in the country should Coronado depart? Change in command of expeditions in the Indies had nearly always resulted in quarreling and insubordination, and sometimes in blood-shed. Every officer could foresee the danger if that question had to be met. Besides, even the most venturesome of the men were now thinking with more and more longing of the attractions that Mexico had to offer, and it is doubtful if as many as sixty volunteers could have been found willing to remain among the pueblos once their companions had departed toward the comforts of home. No, the forces must not be divided!

So Coronado won out in the matter, although at the cost of the loyalty and devotion which had formerly been given him by all his free captains; now his influence over them was weakened as his command over his own spirit was sapped by the dominating desire to give up the struggle. "The gentlemen, I do not know whether because they had sworn fidelity or because they feared that the soldiers would not support them, did what had been decided on, although with an ill will, and from this time on they did not obey the general as readily as formerly, and they did not show any affection for him."[10] Coronado had indeed taken a fall.

There was now nothing to do but to pack up the few belongings left to the army and to make ready for the retreat from Tiguex, which was to start, appropriately enough, on All Fool's Day, 1542. At this very time, many leagues to the eastward, Hernando de Soto was also turning back from his weary quest, his mind filled with thoughts of a Mexico that he would never see again, for he was destined to die before another month had passed, shattered in spirit.

During these preparations, Fray Juan de Padilla found that the memory of the cross that had been erected among the Quivira towns was much in his mind, and he thought often of the gentle people he had instructed in the worship of that cross. Fray Juan, from fiery Andalusia, the Spanish southland, who had been *hombre belicoso* in his youth, had been an equally ardent warrior in the service of Christ; now his zealous spirit would not suffer him to turn back even when an army might decide to retreat. He determined to return to Quivira, alone if need be, to devote his life and labor to the enlightenment of the heathen Wichita tribes of Kansas.

This intention he sermonized at one of the Sunday services during Lent, justifying his mission on the authority of Holy Scripture. He declared his zeal for the conversion of those peoples and his desire to draw them to the faith, and stated that he had received permission from the father-provincial to do so, although this was not necessary for one who was touched by a strong call.

Coronado and his captains demurred—but it is useless to argue with the martyr marked. Fray Juan replied simply that he would not desert the Quivira cross even though its service should cost him his life.

Fired by this example, the lay brothers Fray Luis de Escalona and Fray Juan de la Cruz also announced their desire to remain as apostles to the Indians, Fray Luis at Cicuyé and Fray Juan de la Cruz at Tiguex. Thus began the first unarmed mission of the Church upon the soil of the United States. The faith and bravery of these three men lighted a torch of zeal that served as a beacon for centuries to the missionary bands of their own and other brotherhoods.

Nothing certain was ever again heard of the two lay brothers after the departure of the army from the pueblos. Fray Juan de la Cruz, a Gascon who like Padilla had been a missionary in Jalisco, elected to devote his life to the Tiguas. According to tradition, he did not live long to convert and instruct his charges, for before the year was out he was slain by the arrows of those who refused to be weaned away from their barbarous customs, although he was highly esteemed by most of the chiefs and the lowly natives, who had seen the veneration with which Coronado and his captains had treated the priest.[11] Curiously, this friar is never mentioned in any of the contemporary documents of the Coronado journey.

Fray Luis de Escalona, an older man who may have come from the Spanish town of Ubeda, dwelt in Cicuyé in a hut where his converts supplied all his needs—a little *atole,* a few tortillas and beans. With him stayed two negroes of Mexico—one with a wife and children— and a slave of Captain Jaramillo's called Christopher. With adze and chisel they helped Fray Luis to raise some little wooden crosses in the pyramidal town.

Before the army finally departed, a squad of men drove to Cicuyé a small flock of sheep, remnant of the herds that had been brought north for provisions, for the pastor to keep with him. These men met the friar and a band of his converts, on the way to visit some other villages in the eastern pueblo country. "He felt," wrote Castañeda, "very hopeful that he was liked at the village and that his teachings would bear fruit, although he complained that the old men were falling away from him and, he believed, would finally kill him. I for my part believe that as he was a man of such good and holy life, Our Lord will protect him and give him grace to convert many of those people, and leave someone, when his days are over, to administer to them in the faith. We do not need to believe otherwise, for the people in those parts are pious and not at all cruel."[12]

Castañeda's hopes are hard to justify, for after these soldiers returned to Tiguex nothing more is definitely known of Fray Luis. The "old men," the wizards and medicine makers who clung tenaciously to the old gods and the old ways, would not let much time pass before stirring up the villages. There can be little doubt that Fray Luis soon met his fate, possibly before the end of the year. The sheep of his flock, the first livestock introduced into the United States, very likely were killed at the same time he met death and were eaten by his murderers.

Thus were the passings, known only from legend, of the first martyrs of Christianity in the American Southwest. The sad fate of Juan de Padilla is better known, through the stories of eyewitnesses whose survival and subsequent wanderings rival and in some ways surpass the adventures of Cabeza de Vaca and his three companions. The narrator of this escape from death was Andrés de Campo, a "Portuguese Spaniard" who had been gardener to one of the old conquerors of Mexico before joining the ranks of the Coronado party.

De Campo was the only white companion of Fray Juan de Padilla on his last journey to Quivira. Also in the group that bade farewell to Fray Luis in Cicuyé and set off on their long pilgrimage were two Mexican Indian *donados,* or lay brothers, named Lucas and Sebastián, from Michoacán; two other Indians who had served as sacristans in the army; a young half-breed; and a negro servant. Guided by some of the natives that Coronado had brought back with him from Quivira, they set out with a few sheep and mules (De Campo rode a mare, the only horse in the party) to cover the long leagues between the pueblos and the Wichita settlements on the Arkansas River. They vanished from the ken of man, and nothing more was heard of them until many years had passed.

About nine years later,[13] De Campo and the two *donados* turned up in Pánuco, the old northeastern province of New Spain. They had spent some years in their flight from Quivira, serving many months as slaves to the Indian tribes of the Mississippi basin, circling and cutting back, always striving to make their way to Mexico and their own people. Their tale of the death of Fray Juan de Padilla, protomartyr of the United States, is well worthy of a place in the calendar of saints.

Arrived at Quivira, they related, Fray Juan found the wooden cross where it had been erected, and the place about it swept and kept clear as he had charged the natives to do. He was overjoyed; and having been

presented by Coronado with the holy vestments and
the sacramental flour and wine, as well as with trinkets
to help in winning the favor of the natives, the rev-
erend father began to exercise the duties of holy apostle
to the Quiviras.

He found them docile and of good will, and in time
all had come into the fold. Yet, because it seemed to the
friar that even this was but a small number of souls to
win for God, he desired to open the haven of Mother
Church to other tribes. In spite of the protests of the
Wichitas, who cherished him as a father, he determined
to make a mission to the province of the Guas—the
Kansa or Kaw tribe of the lower Kansas River.

This was a dangerous step, for the Wichitas might
readily become jealous of sharing with their enemies
the fame and good fortune which they believed the
great medicine-making Fray Juan had brought them.
If he ventured into the country of their foes, he could
not expect to retain their protection. They refused to
go with him.

Accompanied, then, by only his few staunch followers from Mexico, Fray Juan set forth stoutly into the
unknown country. After only a single day's journey, a
pack of hostile warriors drew down upon them.

Their deadly intentions were evident at once, and,
knowing their barbarity, the priest commanded De
Campo to take the others of the group and ride away
as far as he could, so that no lives would be lost need-
lessly. Protests were vain; the friar who had incited the
attack on Tusayán and was one of the first to see the

buffalo plains and Quivira was now determined to embrace martyrdom at the outpost of Spanish exploration in North America. He was as one inspired to press the crown of thorns upon his forehead, to accept torture as a blessed felicity.

While the obedient retinue fled, the Kaw band had their way with the friar. Forgetting the fighting days of his youth, he knelt to offer up his ardent soul as their arrows transfixed him. The savages stole the holy vestments and threw the body of the martyr into a pit, heaping rocks upon it.[14]

The followers of Fray Juan, although frightened, had turned to watch the martyrdom from a distance; shortly after the killers left, they crept back to give their holy master Christian burial.[15] They then went back to Quivira with the sad tale, at which the Indians grieved greatly because of their love for Juan de Padilla; they "would have regretted it even more if they had fully understood the evil that had been done."[16]

The Portuguese and the Mexican Indians set out soon after to make their way to Mexico; they traveled for many years, until at last they reached New Spain. Although De Campo got to the capital, where he arrived, according to Gómara, "with his hair straggling and his beard done up in braids," his name never appeared in history again. Had he put his full story in writing, we might have had another great narrative to add to the world's collection of travel tales.

Sebastián died soon after the return, worn by his sufferings; Lucas, who became a missionary among the natives of Zacatecas, died of an illness during the conquest of the Chichimecs. These men, as Jaramillo suggested at the end of his account of the Coronado expedition, would have served excellently as guides had it been the viceroy's desire to explore and settle the country north of the Gulf of Mexico. But many years were to pass before another effort was made to penetrate the mysterious lands toward Quivira, and the venturesome men who finally made that effort had to do it without a De Campo to show them the way.

15

The Inglorious Journey
April–September, 1542

EARLY IN APRIL, the army began the long retreat from Tiguex. Their general ordered that all natives of the pueblos who were with the soldiers as servants should be allowed to depart to their homes, as he feared that violence might be done to the friars remaining in the country if any Indians were abducted and taken south with the Spaniards. There was many a tearful farewell, for some of the pueblo women had learned to cherish the embraces of the white invaders. Leaving the friars in the land alone, "like lambs among wolves," the army set out on the march toward Cíbola.

Misfortune dogged the dejected force from the start. The horses, smitten by some mysterious disease which struck swiftly, or which until now had lain dormant, began to die one after another. Although they were apparently in good condition when they started out, fat and sleek, on the ten-day journey from the Río Grande to Zuñi some were stricken each day, until the toll was no less than thirty. The malady, which may have been caused by browsing upon the maddening "loco weed," harassed the army as far as Culiacán. More than one proud cavalier who had ridden dashingly into the new country returned afoot with his saddle on the shoulders of a burdened native servant.

At Cíbola the army rested for several days and then started on the first southward stage of the long return journey. Some of the Mexican Indians preferred to remain among the Seven Cities.[1] The men of Zuñi desired that many more should stay with them, hoping perhaps to learn from them the arts that had made the white strangers triumphant in battle. Although the province of Cíbola was left in peace, the Zuñis followed the army for several days, to pick up any abandoned baggage and especially to importune the Indian allies of the Spaniards to settle at Cíbola. "Altogether, they carried off several people besides those who had remained of their own accord," observed Castañeda, "among whom good interpreters could be found today."[2]

In the White Mountain wilderness, two days before they reached Chichilticalli, the army was met by Captain Juan Gallego, who had come at a record-breaking pace from Mexico through hostile country with twenty-two able-bodied men to reinforce the expedition.

Gallego, Coronado's galloping despatch bearer, now on his fifth journey between New Spain and the pueblos, was much chagrined to find that the army had deserted the provinces which they had discovered. He and the reinforcements had expected to meet Coronado in

---

[1] For notes to chap. 15, see pp. 364–367.

Quivira, surrounded by heaps of golden loot; and when he came face to face with the general, Gallego's greeting, as Castañeda put it, was not: "I am glad you are turning back!"[3]

When he had conversed with Coronado and his staff, Gallego liked the situation little better. His coming awakened the old feeling of guilt among some of the officers. A new proposal was made that the army should retrace its steps and hold the country until the viceroy could be heard from; but by now the soldiers would agree to nothing except the return to New Spain.

Several of the men in Gallego's band were survivors of the terrible massacre at Suya, or had earlier deserted the garrison there, but these had been promised safe-conduct by Gallego. Coronado could not have punished them if he had wished, for already there was much disobedience in the army and he had lost the full respect of his men. After hearing the story of the Suya disaster and the adventures of Gallego in rebellious Sonora, terror came upon the general once more, and he pretended again to be ill, staying most of the time in his guarded tent.

The news of the Sonora war, as told by those who had lived through it, was in truth dismaying. The town of San Gerónimo at Suya had needed a Melchor Díaz in command, not a Diego de Alcaraz. Alcaraz had at last paid the penalty for his witless leadership and his brutal mishandling of the Indians of his district; and the men of his San Gerónimo garrison had all been killed or been scattered to the winds.

The post in the Suya Valley had been reduced by the Tovar draft to a mere forty men, the feeblest and most mutinous of all the army. Because they distrusted their officers, and with some reason, the men held daily councils and seditious conclaves. Before long they convinced themselves that they had been betrayed and were not going to be rescued, that the army was going to give the town a wide berth and go home by another route—which turned out to be true.

In growing fear, a party of these mutineers, led by one Pedro de Avila, decamped one night and sneaked back to Culiacán, ruthlessly killing any Indians they met on the way. Hernando de Saavedra, who had been left in charge at Culiacán by Governor Coronado, detained these men with promises—he had no wish to stir up a fight in the streets of the coastal town—in order to hand them over to Juan Gallego, who was known to be coming soon with reinforcements for the army. Some of these mutineers, fearing that they would thus be dragged back to their abandoned posts, fled once more in the night and got away to New Spain.

The craven deserters had left San Gerónimo in a desperate plight, garrisoned only by a few sick men and wretched indolents. Alcaraz did not have enough sound men even to stand a full watch. Now was the time to regret old follies: the levying of heavy tribute and the demands for wearisome body-service by the natives, the seizure of food and belongings paid for with sneers, the rape of Indian wives and daughters, the infection of Indian bodies with bone-rotting Spanish diseases. But these derelicts did not know the meaning of remorse, and were too besotted even to think of protecting themselves. No more would the Opata inhabitants of the district hail white men as "gods of the thunder and lightning."

With perception sharpened by grievances old and new, the red men soon noted that the force at San Gerónimo was destitute of strength. They ceased trading with the soldiers, thus shutting off the garrison's supply of provisions. "Veins of gold" had been discovered in the hills, but even had there been any hale men in the Spanish camp they could not have mined, for the hostility of the Indians was creating an effective barrier around the fated Villa de San Gerónimo.

One night the hill Indians gathered by their fires, threw on the ground an effigy of the despised Alcaraz and shot it full of arrows, and with great whoops celebrated a prophetic dance of victory over the hated invader. When the Spaniards, from the banks of their river site, saw the war fires, they put every available man on guard; but as the night dragged on and nothing sinister developed, the weary men relaxed their vigilance. At dawn the foe entered the village so silently that before their presence was known the killing and plundering were in full tide.

The aroused Spaniards snatched up their arms and laid about them, too late, however, to prevent the destruction of the town. They were without leadership, for their captain, former crony of Nuño de Guzmán and old slave trader, lay in a stupor, aftermath of a night's carousal. Obregón in his account⁴ told where Alcaraz was to be found in the moment of attack: "Those who were there have assured me that when the enemies fell upon the village, the captain was couched with two Indian women, who helped him to put on his *escuaguipil* or armor of quilted cotton; and between the edges and lacings of the *escuaguipil* they gave him two stabs of which he died in a short time."

It was a horrible death—a retribution for the captain's blind ignorance and failure to set a Christian example, concluded the chronicler—for the knives of the two Indian Jaels had been poisoned. Three other Spaniards of San Gerónimo and many servants also died in agony from poisoned weapons.⁵

The attacking Opatas were soon in full command of the town. A few of the soldiers rallied on the plain, mounted their horses, and went back in an attempt to regain control. But this small band, fighting separately, were soon scattered and forced to flee, leaving their dead behind, while the Indians made off with everything abandoned by the soldiers.

Some of the Spaniards fled south, on foot—for more than twenty horses had been killed—and with no food until they reached the friendly natives of Corazones. When at last they came to Culiacán, the survivors were held, like the earlier fugitives, by Saavedra. Others of the garrison scattered toward the north, hoping to get through to Cíbola and join their general. These had been shortly met on the road by García López de Cárdenas, who, horrified by the catastrophe, could do nothing but push on to the plundered and ruined town, bury the swollen dead, and return to give Coronado the fateful news that the road southward was barred by hostiles.

When Juan Gallego, returning from Mexico with a hopeful heart, reached Culiacán and learned the tragic story from the survivors there, a fury seized him. From among the soundest refugees from San Gerónimo he made up a squadron and headed north through the rebellious country, cutting a retaliatory swath of death and destruction that the Indians would not soon forget. The usually matter-of-fact Castañeda extolled Gallego's march as if it were something out of the *Iliad,* or an episode from one of the romantic fables of chivalry. Indeed, "if the deadly strength which the authors of those times attributed to their heroes and the brilliant and resplendent arms with which they adorned them are fully considered, and compared with the small stature of the men of our time and the few and poor weapons which they have in these parts, the remarkable things which our people have undertaken and accomplished with such weapons today are more to be wondered at than those of which the ancients write."[8] Gallego, a living Roland, whose force, including the Suya survivors, came to no more than twenty-two men, crossed two hundred leagues of a country aflame with rebellion, having brushes with the enemy almost every day.

Supported by six or seven Spaniards, leaving the rest of the men with the Indian allies to bring up the baggage, Gallego set out. With this handful of men, in a cold Achillean fury he swept ahead from one village to another, killing and destroying and firing the thatch, "coming upon the enemy so suddenly and with such quickness and boldness that they did not have a chance to gather or even to do anything at all, until they became so afraid of him that there was not a tribe that dared wait for him, but they fled before him as from a powerful army; so much so, that for ten days, while he was passing through the settlements, they did not have an hour's rest."[7]

When the rear party came up, there was little to do except plunder the villages, for Gallego and his executioners slew all that did not flee at once. Especially in the Suya region, where the town of San Gerónimo had been situated, wholesale hangings were ordered.

During all these forays, not a Spaniard was killed, and only one was injured. He was a soldier who was wounded in the eyelid as he was bending over to despoil a native whom he thought dead. The weapon was poisoned, and although the wound was a mere scratch the Spaniard lost his eye and would have died had he not applied the native remedy to the wound—the juice of a fruit like the quince. This antidote, which was carefully noted by the men of Coronado when they heard the story, was later to prove useful in the army's southward flight through the rebel country.

Whenever, in later years, Castañeda got together with fellow veterans who like him had settled in Culiacán, some of whom had been in Gallego's squadron of vengeance, their old-time feats were a favorite recollection.

"These deeds of theirs were such that I know those people will remember them as long as they live, and especially four or five friendly Indians who went with them from Corazones, who thought that they were so wonderful that they held them to be something divine rather than human. If he [Gallego] had not fallen in with our army as he did, they would have reached the country of the Indian called The Turk, which they expected to march to, and they would have arrived there without danger on account of their good order and the skill with which he was leading them, and their knowledge and ample practice in war."[8] Yes, Gallego, the Spanish thunderbolt, would long be remembered in the Sonora country.

The army of Coronado, reinforced by the paladins of Gallego, pushed southward through the rebellious land. Often the night rang with hideous savage yells as the Indians skirmished about the camp, working havoc among the horses.

Following one of these brushes, the life of a Spaniard named Mesa, who had been shot in the wrist with a poisoned arrow, was saved by the application of the "quince juice" remedy. Although the fresh poison was supposed to be fatal, and two hours passed before the juice could be found, he did not die. But the poison reached the shoulder, and left its mark on him; "the skin rotted and fell off until it left the bones and sinews bare, with a horrible smell."[9]

Although the army avoided the valley of the Sonora, the aroused natives dogged their footsteps as far as Batuco.[10] There the Indians of Corazones came out to greet the general and his men. These natives, since Cabeza de Vaca's day, had always been well treated by the white men and had been paid for their offerings of food. Now they were friends in need and supplied Coronado with the provisions he sadly lacked.

The soldiers stayed only a few days in Corazones, for the Indians, no matter how good their intentions, could not long continue to feed an army. Moreover, the country to the south was bare of provisions, and the natives there, recently lashed by the scourge of Gallego, were not likely to come with offerings. Several forays for food were made into the hill country about the Fuerte and the Mayo, but not until Petatlán was reached did the army find any quantity of food or get relief from the repeated harassing of the natives with their venomous arrows.

Governor Coronado's loyal town of San Miguel de Culiacán was now only thirty leagues away, but even as the army marched toward it desertions among officers and men began to be frequent. The valley was very attractive after the deserts and plains of the north; why not drift from the straggling ranks and rest for a while in cool shade? Only fools would be so rash as to hasten along to Mexico with the dejected army, merely to win a tongue-lashing or worse from the disappointed viceroy. The tatterdemalion column was strung out along the plain for leagues, and discipline went by the board as one band of soldiers after another drifted away on private forays of their own.[11]

Coronado, still keeping up the pretense of illness, knew that even his authority as governor of New Galicia was not sufficient to hold the disintegrating force together. In an attempt to keep up appearances, he issued orders to the laggard captains to gather food and meat from the stores in the coast villages, thus giving their desertions some semblance of obedience to orders. His friends were kept busy going back and forth between his tent and their stations among the men, where under his orders they offered every inducement to the soldiers to stay with the army until the city of Mexico was reached. Hoping to persuade them, Coronado promised preferment in his province of New Galicia and said that he would recommend the loyal ones to the viceroy for special favors.

But such promises were not enough to hold together a dog-weary and shamefaced force who, although never defeated in battle, were nonetheless in retreat and who dreaded to meet the jeers of the stay-at-homes in Mexico. They could imagine what would be said to them: "What, Don Fulano, you who started out so hopefully in borrowed armor, have you not brought back with you cartwheels of gold or sacks of pearls, not even a patent of nobility from Quivira?"

Moreover, conditions of travel were almost impossible. By the time Coronado set out from Culiacán, around St. John's Day, June 24, the traditional date for the beginning of the rainy season on the west coast, the daily torrents had begun to fall and the roads were quagmires. The uninhabited country north of Compostela was sheeted by flooding rivers; in crossing one of these, a soldier was carried off by an alligator in full sight of the whole army.

It was a bedraggled and beggarly crew of not more than a hundred men that General Francisco Vásquez Coronado brought at last across the mountains of Michoacán to the Mexican capital in the early autumn of 1542, there to be disbanded by Viceroy Mendoza and to drink the bitter medicine of defeat. The great expedition was over.

For weeks thereafter, footsore adventurers clad in shaggy hides and rusty corselets came drifting into the city. It was hard to believe that this was the same army that had set out so bravely, with banners flying high, almost three years before. All were marked by their hardships, many with arrow scars, and burnt by the desert sun. To them for months to come, Cíbola and Quivira would be words of affront.[12]

Sad-faced and haggard came Coronado to kiss the hand of the viceroy and to confess that the venture was lost. Sixty thousand golden ducats had been spent by Mendoza and another fifty thousand by Coronado himself, with nothing to redeem these sums except a much battered suit of gilded mail.

True, the three Franciscan friars had remained in the country, and Mendoza might derive what comfort he could from that. But indeed the viceroy, who had lost much of his personal estate and had to account for large borrowings from the royal treasury as advances to the soldiery, had some cause for giving his captain general a cold reception. His faith in the capabilities of Coronado was still unshattered, however, for the weary explorer continued in his governorship of New Galicia for two years longer.

The return of the expedition emptyhanded was felt keenly by the whole city, as there was hardly a resident who was not directly touched by it. Suárez de Peralta, a young lad at the time, recorded in his memoirs the sad disappointment.

"The country had been very joyous when the news of the discovery of the Seven Cities spread abroad," he wrote,[13] "and this was now supplanted by the greatest sadness on the part of all, for many had lost their friends and their fortunes, since those who remained behind had entered into partnerships with those who went, mortgaging their estates and their property in order to procure a share in what was to be gained, and drawing up papers so that those who were to be present should have power to take possession of mines and enter claims in the name of those who were left behind, in accordance with the custom and the ordinances which the viceroy had made for New Spain. Many sent their slaves also, since there were many of these in the country at this time. Thus the loss and the grief were general; but the viceroy felt it most of all, for two reasons: because this was the outcome of something about which he had felt so sure, which he thought would make him more powerful than the greatest lord in Spain; and because his estates were ruined, for he had labored hard and spent much in sending off the army. Finally, as things go, he succeeded in forgetting about it, and devoted himself to the government of his province, and in this he became the best of governors, being trusted by the king and loved by all his subjects."

The exploits of Coronado and his companion adventurers, little appreciated as these were in their own time, were of far-reaching consequence.

To his contemporaries, Coronado's quest was merely a costly incident in the greatest gold rush of history, the armed Spanish stampede that led to the first exploration of the American hemisphere. Gold had been one chief object of the search, a search that had been begun in 1535 when Fernando Cortés set out to found the colony of Santa Cruz on the Californian gulf. During the following eight years, until Ferrelo[14] returned from his survey of the Pacific coast line and the survivors of the De Soto expedition found their way to Pánuco in 1543, gold had been sought persistently, resulting in the first ocean-to-ocean reconnaissance of that section of the North American continent which lies roughly south of the fortieth parallel—a region comprising more than half of the present United States. From Cape Mendocino to Cape San Lucas, from the Colorado Canyon to the lower Missouri, from the Río Grande to the Savannah, from Galveston Bay to Tampa Bay, eager men had searched but had found no peoples exhibiting a superior civilization or possessing great stores of mineral wealth. The first result of this exploration was therefore the disappointing negative discovery that gold was not easily to be found in this imperial slice of the continent; consequently, Destiny had to bide her time while the frontier settled down to a more orderly and gradual advance.

But Coronado had accomplished much. True, he had found no gold; but he and his men had missed few of the features of the country that lay along their routes of travel. They had opened intercourse with the Mexican northwest and founded in the fertile valley of the Sonora River its first Spanish town. They had ascended the mighty Colorado in boats, and had clambered down the awful precipices that line its mile-deep gorge. They had visited all the villages of the Pueblo Indians and had reported on the arts and customs of these town builders. They had been likewise the first white men to hold speech with a dozen other great tribes, among them the Yuma, Papago, Apache, Caddo, Wichita, Pawnee, and Kaw. Following Indian guides along Indian trails, they had laid out the great overland routes from Mexico north to California, New Mexico, Arizona, Texas, and Kansas. Their mounted fighters had pursued the buffalo on the midland prairies and had known the life of hunter and scout. They had been the first Europeans to gaze on waving acres of corn growing along the Kansas and Arkansas rivers.

To these new-found tribes of the red race, the band of Coronado had brought Christian precept if not high Christian example, and had left among them their most devout and resolute teachers, the Gray Robes, who in meeting the martyr's fate planted in the pagan wastes the seed of the Church. They had given to these Indians

over a vast area their first knowledge of white civilization, both in the rugged clash of arms and in the peaceable exchange of goods and amenities. The Indians had
seen new sorts of weapons, clothing, and tools, and had
gained possession of several kinds of domestic animals.
For the first time in these parts, European blood had
been mingled with the dark aboriginal stream; in the
year following the retreat of Coronado from the pueblos, tawny-skinned babies were born and were called
Children of the Moon in memory of their bearded,
gruff fathers, the Children of the Sun.

Returning to Mexico, the Coronado brigade brought
with them a store of fresh knowledge that was one day
to be worth a thousand times the ransom of Atahualpa.
In 1540, when they had set out, nothing, not a scrap
of fact, was known even in New Spain of the location or extent of the northern lands. Four years later,
Sebastian Cabot in Europe published a map on which
the coasts of the Gulf of California and its jagged peninsula were shown and named. Thenceforward the car-
tographers of the civilized world began placing Cíbola,
Quivira, and Cicuyé on their charts; and many as were
the errors on these maps, they pale to insignificance before the fact that the known world had been greatly
enlarged by the inclusion of the spreading Coronado
country. The geographers had learned that there was
a great continent north of Mexico, and had come to
know more than a little about the peoples and beasts
that inhabited it. The debt of all later explorers to
Coronado and his hardy marchers is measureless.

Although the amazing journey was forgotten for a time by the high ruling powers that had sent out the first great explorations, many other humbler people did not forget that Spain had laid claim to those vast northern territories. No attempt was made within the lifetime of Coronado to hold and settle the country he had discovered—but one may remember that the discoveries of De Soto were neglected for a century and a half! When the time was ripe, after forty years of gradual colonial development, the pioneers living on the marches of the Southwest remembered the exploits of Cabeza de Vaca and Coronado, and began planning to settle the Indian countries where the flag of Hispania had previously flown. Thus the army of Coronado had taken the first steps in the establishment of the great Province of New Mexico at the century's end. This was fulfilled by men of pioneer breed; but if they were the pioneers, the men of Coronado were the pathfinders.

What is failure? Humankind advances only by a great wasteful process of trial and error, seeking and seeking again until the way is found. The first bold attack on the northern mystery had to be made, and it was made, and the foundation for all the future was laid down. To have been first in the great quest, even though the laurels of the day were few; to have dreamed highly, even though the awakening was rude; to have known achievement, even though stay-at-homes laughed or sneered—if that was failure, then it was failure at its most glorious.

One of Coronado's soldiers could even be philosoph-

ical about the expedition's lack of material success. Castañeda, the veteran, full of regret as he was that the
country had been abandoned, saw in this a manifest of
a higher ordination: "It was God's pleasure that these
discoveries should remain for other peoples and that
we who had gone there should content ourselves with
saying that we were the first who discovered it and
brought word of it. . . . It is the will of Almighty God to
please Himself in all things, for it is true that if it had
not been His will, Francisco Vásquez Coronado would
not have returned to New Spain without any reason or
cause, nor would the followers of Hernando de Soto
have failed to settle such a large, fair, and well-inhab-
ited country as they found, especially when they had
news about our expedition." And he concluded his stirring chronicle with the portentous words: "For the rest,
everything lies at the disposal of the Lord of All Things,
God Omnipotent, Who knows how and when those
lands will be disclosed, and for whom is destined this
great fortune."[15] All Americans who dwell in the southwestern states are heirs of Francisco Vásquez Coronado.

16

Farewell to Conquest
October, 1542–November, 1554

CORONADO THE EXPLORER had won his wish. He had returned at last to his family and his estates, and was soon to embrace the life of a minor official and country squire.

He attended a meeting of the *cabildo* of Mexico City on October 13, after an absence of precisely three years. Shortly thereafter he returned to New Galicia to pick up the threads of government from the capable hands of Cristóbal de Oñate. The lieutenant governor still continued to carry on much of the administrative work while Coronado was visiting in Mexico, however, and was more popular with the citizens of the province than was the actual governor, who was still distraught by his failure to find gold in the north and who grew more and more careless of the calls of justice and duty.[1]

On May 15, 1544, after a long leave, presumably to take care of his duties in New Galicia, Coronado again attended a meeting of the town council in Mexico.

[1] For notes to chap. 16, see pp. 367–370.

There were rumors in the wind, and he noted that men did not defer to him as they had formerly done.

He was back in Guadalajara for the summer, and there, two years after the fateful return to New Spain, he was summoned by a royal official, Lorenzo de Tejada, who bore full powers to take a secret *residencia* on the acts of Governor Francisco Vásquez Coronado and his subordinates. On August 8, 1544, Tejada proclaimed his right as special judge to hold hearings, and all the officials of the province were deprived of their wands of office until the inquiry should be concluded. During the days that followed until September 5 Tejada, *oidor* of the *audiencia* of New Spain, took the depositions of twenty-nine witnesses at Guadalajara and other towns of New Galicia.

Things looked black for Coronado. As a result of the hearings, Tejada filed thirty-four charges of misgovernment and slackness against him—general neglect of duty, favoritism in appointments, short accounts, acceptance of bribes, inhumane treatment of natives, setting a bad example by openly dicing and gambling in his house. He was accused of driving a draft of Indian porters to Mexico City and back without pay, all so heavily laden that a good number died on the way and many others died afterward in hospital. On other occasions, it was asserted, he had taken natives from their villages, separating families and making them work without compensation. In one instance he was said to have forced the town council of Guadalajara to accept his own appointee in place of the duly elected representative. It was also declared that he had departed for Cíbola leaving a considerable part of his province in revolt, and had drawn his salary as governor all the while he was absent.[2]

Coronado was given a week in which to reply to these accusations; in a few days he submitted his answers, denying a number of the charges and pleading extenuations for others. A few horses had been presented to him by one man or another, but the animals had died or else he had attempted to pay for them or had returned them to the owners. He had at first refused the gift of a gold chain from his friend Villareal but after some insistence had accepted it, paying three silver marks for it. He admitted accepting fowl and fish from the natives, but only as a necessary preliminary to the transaction of official business. He had used thirty Indians as carriers to Mexico City, but some had refused payment; he was not aware that any had died on the way. Some Indian girls had been sent from their villages on the advice of Fray Antonio de Castilblanco to be instructed in the faith by Doña Beatriz, and he, the governor, had not realized the distance involved. He had protected the Indians and kept order; when he had first come to New Galicia to take the *residencia* of Diego de la Torre, his predecessor, he had punished Melchor Díaz, mayor of Culiacán, for having mistreated the Indians and thus caused a revolt which he, Coronado, had put down. He had not realized the seriousness of the revolt at Zacatlán and had been unwilling to destroy the region by leading his large expedition through that district. He had played cards and diced, but not in a manner that would set an evil example.

So damaging were many of his admissions, however, that his response was taken almost as a confession of guilt; the document bears on the margin, in another's hand, the notation: *"Confesante."*

The expeditious Tejada on September 17 judged the case. Although he absolved Coronado of some charges and referred others to the Council for the Indies, he found the governor guilty of crimes and negligences for which Coronado was fined six hundred gold pesos. In addition, for his part in oppressing the natives of New Galicia during the preparation of the great expedition—a charge that was to be brought also against Viceroy Mendoza at his own *visita* three years later—Coronado was arrested and confined to the house of his judge. Moreover, as it appeared that Coronado's holdings of Indians were not clear in title, and that some were actually fraudulent, all the revenues from these grants were taken from him and returned to the Crown.

In disgrace, Coronado returned under bond to Mexico City in October, but continued to serve there on the *cabildo*. He appealed his case to the Council for the Indies, but apparently the judgment was sustained, for he was nevermore to hold the title of governor. He was the last governor of New Galicia, for his duties were taken over by Baltasar de Gallegos as *alcalde mayor;* as a result of the recommendations of Tejada, the province, under a royal decree of February 13, 1548, was governed thenceforward by an *audiencia* at Compostela (later transferred to Guadalajara) subordinate to that of Mexico.

The remaining decade of Coronado's life was spent in the Mexican capital, with occasional visits to his country estates, where he indulged his hobby of breeding fine merino sheep, introduced from Castile by the viceroy. In town he dwelt at the former home of his wife's parents, the Estradas, a large castellated stone house at the east end of the block bordering the south edge of the Municipal Plaza. Almost next door to him, at the west end of the block and separated from his house only by a group of shops that Estrada had built, was the town hall, and there Coronado attended the meetings of the council with great regularity.

The conqueror of Cíbola at first found it irritating to settle down to the petty round of municipal affairs. Through a misunderstanding, he was reprimanded in the minutes of the council for December 11, 1544, and suspended for two months on the grounds that, although he had been back from New Galicia for some weeks, he had not turned up at the meeting. This order was revoked on New Year's Day when the porter of the building affirmed that Coronado had in fact appeared but had been told by mistake that there was to be no meeting on the given date.

But the breach of amity was widened further by another incident. On April 27 Coronado was notified that it was his turn to carry the banner of St. Hippolytus in the coming procession to commemorate the capture of the city from the Aztecs, since he had not been at hand to do so when his turn had come previously. On May 11 he refused on the ground that he had been absent then on the viceroy's business, and that by rights he should not be called again until the rounds of the other councilmen had been made. At the meeting of June 22 his colleagues declared that he had invented the business as an excuse to evade his duty, and had maliciously lingered on the road to delay his return. It was a heated session, for his failure to colonize Cíbola was thrown in his face, and the badgered conquistador retorted "with more passion than good sense or understanding." Although threatened with fines and punishment, he did not submit until July 3, when he who had borne the royal banner of possession to the far valleys of Quivira at last tamely agreed to carry the flag of a minor saint at a city fiesta.[3]

In time, Coronado learned to swallow his pride and carry on his duties with the diligence expected of a city father. A few small municipal honors even came to him. In 1549 he was chosen by the council with another member to represent it in two official visits to the viceroy, who was recovering from a severe illness at Guastepeque. On the following January 1 he was elected *procurador mayor* of the city, and as part of his task of keeping public order erected a pillory in the central plaza.

Although Coronado had lost the full confidence of Mendoza as a result of his poor record as governor of New Galicia, he continued on friendly terms with the viceroy and was a staunch advocate in the *cabildo* of the policies of the administration. He had an excellent opportunity to show this loyalty on January 18, 1547, when he was called before the powerful *visitador* Francisco Tello de Sandoval as a witness during a series of hearings that submitted all the viceroy's official acts to scrutiny and review.

During this *visita* Coronado, who affirmed on oath that he was "over thirty years of age" and not related to Mendoza, responded to the *interrogatorio* of more than three hundred questions, and on virtually every point upheld the claims of Mendoza. As a witness, Coronado was precise in his answers and even finicky about making sure that his public testimony did not contradict his exact words in the previous secret examination; undoubtedly his experience on the town council had taught him a certain verbal caution. Fourteen of the questions touched upon subjects relating to the expedition to Cíbola, and these gave Coronado a chance to affirm the wisdom of his acts in command of the army and to defend the venture as having brought large new territories into the possession of the Crown.[4]

About a year after this Coronado applied, "in recognition of his great services to His Majesty, the dignity of his employments, and his personal qualifications, as well as of the fact that he cannot subsist with the Indians which he has,"[5] for an increase in his allotment of native workers. Confident, perhaps, in the support of Mendoza, he boldly stood upon his record and stressed the expense and personal risk he had suffered as captain general of the great expedition, when he had "observed absolutely the instructions which His Majesty gives to those who hold similar positions, committing no abuse." The application made a favorable impression, apparently, for a royal grant adding a number of Indians to his *encomienda* was issued on November 9, 1549, as a reward from the Crown for his meritorious services in discovery and conquest.[6]

His holdings of land were also increased on July 17, 1551, by a small allotment at Tacubaya, a present from the *cabildo* of Mexico City for faithful service.[7] But his fitness ever again to hold high administrative positions was judged unfavorably by Mendoza and the *audiencia,* who in 1548 recommended against the royal grant of any such post.[8]

In June, 1553, Coronado was given a short leave of absence from the council because of illness, and in the following year he was away from the city four months in search of health. He returned to his duties some time in June, 1554, but on July 9 made his last appearance among the members of the *cabildo* of Mexico and scrawled his signature on the minutes for the last time. The decline of his latter days must have been slow, for his death is reported at the meeting of November 12 as a rather recent happening.

Peacefully on his own comfortable estates, surrounded by wife and children, the commander of the greatest exploring party of his time passed away, mourned by many friends and fellow officials. Fate was more kind to him than to most of the conquistadores, for Coronado died with his boots off, and still holding a respected office, even though a minor one, under the royal government he had served for twenty years. The failure to colonize the lands of Cíbola was long forgiven if not forgotten, and by diligent service he had retrieved much of the high repute in which he had begun his career in Mexico.

Francisco Vásquez Coronado was buried, in all likelihood, beneath the Shrine of the Crucifix on the left side of the high altar of the Church of Santo Domingo, the oldest church in Mexico City, in the family sepulcher of the Estradas, who had been the chief patrons of the Dominican order in the city.[9] His end may have been hastened by his unremitting labors and by the privations and injuries sustained on his famous quest, for he died before reaching middle age. He was not more than forty-four years old.

One of the greatest motives for conquest, a motive lacking in Francisco Vásquez Coronado, is the dream of dynasty. Although he was renowned for devotion to family, his hope for direct male descendants perished at the death of his only son in childhood.

The children of Coronado and his wife Beatriz, who came to be called "The Saint" because of her great virtues, were three: the son, Juan Vásquez, who bore the same name as his Spanish grandfather and his uncle in Costa Rica and who died very young; and two daughters, each named for a grandmother. The daughters married brothers belonging to an illustrious Spanish family in Mexico City. Doña Isabel de Luxán Vásquez

de Coronado married Don Bernardino Pacheco de Bocanegra y Córdova, who like his father-in-law became
one of the aldermen of Mexico. As they had no children, the inheritance passed to the younger sister, Doña
Marina Vásquez de Coronado, who married Don Nuño
de Chaves Pacheco de Córdova y Bocanegra. All the
ladies of the Estrada and Coronado families were devout patrons of the Dominican order, the religious
brotherhood charged with carrying on the Holy Inquisition in Mexico; and in recognition of the pious labors
of Doña Marina she was accorded the high honor of
being created Marquesa de Villamayor by royal order
of Philip III on May 27, 1617.

Her second son, Don Francisco Pacheco de Córdova
y Bocanegra Vásquez Coronado (the elder, Fernando
de Córdova y Bocanegra, became a monk and ~eded the
inheritance), had been given the inheritable title of
first Marqués de Villamayor de las Inviernas on March
6, 1610. A biography of Don Francisco, who bore the
name of his illustrious grandfather, the conqueror of
Quivira, was published by Fray Alonso Remón in 1617.
The marquis was married twice: at first to a Chavez
cousin, who bore him two daughters, and then to a
descendant of the renowned Christopher Columbus,
Doña Juana Colón de la Cueva y Toledo, who pretended to the dukedom of Veragua, an inheritance that
Columbus had thought to establish for his heirs forever. The six sons and one daughter born of this later
marriage thus united the blood of two great discoverers, Coronado and Columbus.

Although the direct descendants of Francisco Vásquez Coronado on the distaff side have been traced to the present day,[10] the male line of the Coronados of Mexico was extinguished in the conqueror's own generation by the death of his only son. Much of the wealth that Coronado had gained by his marriage and by the management of his estates went, through the hands of his widowed wife, "The Saint," into the building of the Church of St. Dominic in which the bones of the conqueror now lie.

Coronado, the last of the conquistadores, presents in the light of his lifelong achievements the picture of a man who was in most respects the opposite of that first paradigm of conquerors in the New World, Fernando Cortés, to whose dream of a rich northern land Coronado fell heir.

Coronado was not one of the old order of vainglorious personal adventurers like Cortés; he was rather a competent administrative officer who, under the instructions of the energetic and clever Viceroy Mendoza, carried out a difficult mission to the best of his conscientious, if limited, abilities. Cortés was of the brood of Caesar, and his ambitions threatened to overshadow even the throne of the Holy Roman Empire; Coronado was never anything more earth-shattering than an ardent lieutenant of that throne. But had Cortés been given the greatest desire of his later years and had he embarked upon the conquest of Cíbola as he fervently wished, it is very probable that he would have accomplished little more than Coronado was able to do.

The famous Cortés had broken his heart striving to find the country that Coronado's army not only entered and methodically occupied but even passed beyond, pushing on for three hundred leagues to discover the Staked Plains of Texas and the fertile hills of the lower Kansas. For three years, in command of a large force in unknown and often hostile country, Coronado carried out a careful reconnaissance of the land and studied its people and natural resources. The American Southwest was for the first time intensively explored, and all the Indian tribes and their chief towns were discovered and pacified. The commander set the pattern for future expeditions to those regions; later adventurers followed the paths he trod and pursued the strategy he had devised.[11]

On that journey his losses were few, especially when one considers the terrible losses sustained by other expeditions of his time, such as those of Narváez and De Soto. The Indian allies under Coronado's command were so well treated that none forsook him, and during the three years no more than thirty of the natives serving in the army perished. Nor, aside from the Tigua war provoked by the ill-judged act of a subordinate, was the bloodshed among the enemy tribes greater than was necessary to enforce compliance under his instructions from the Crown and to prevent endangering the safety of the whole expedition. Until almost the very end, when the poor prospects in the country seemed to make colonization impracticable, Coronado held the respect of all his free captains and volunteer followers, and kept his unruly gold seekers under his discipline and out of great mischief.

Coronado could not work miracles and find gold in Quivira where there was none; Cortés himself would have returned from that long quest with hands quite as empty. Although the expedition ended in disorganization and was considered unsuccessful, Coronado had accomplished much that was to become of great value to Spain. After marching and fighting for two years without finding a grain of gold or any richly fertile countries that could be easily settled from Mexico, he cannot be censured for failing, with almost no means of existence, to colonize the southwestern stretches that have never, even to the present day, presented a hospitable aspect to white settlers. Indeed, it was forty years before anyone else was daring enough even to go forth and see once more the fringes of the lands that Coronado had discovered.

Had Francisco Vásquez Coronado actually found the city of gold that everyone in New Spain dreamed of, he would have been hailed immediately as a second Cortés and a second Pizarro. When his explorations revealed that Eldorado was not to be found in the north, the universal disappointment vented itself upon him.

Gold was the lure that drew Coronado and his men to explore the great American plateau, as it had drawn many other Spaniards to their discoveries in the New World; and when no gold was found, several generations passed before anyone else thought of making a colony among the Zuñis and the Tiguas. Gold was the distant prize, and there was gold to be found—not, it is true, in Quivira, but much closer to the home settlements—for, by a curious irony seldom noted by the historians, Coronado traversed in Sonora some of the richest metal-bearing regions on the continent. For centuries, the mines that were later discovered in that section were to produce its chief wealth. But the fierce Yaquis did not know how to use gold, the sharp-eyed men of Coronado's band did not find it, and there is no reason to believe that even the shrewd Cortés would have known it was there. Few of the gold seekers in the army could recognize the virgin metal, for they were not rock miners and might not even have noticed the glints of dust in the riffles. The gold they sought was not in the earth, but in the shrines of barbarians or about the necks of furtive squaws. They looked for great worked sunbursts and chains of gold such as had been presented to Cortés by the Aztec emissaries; and the dull yellow sand that swirled about the hoofs of their mounts as they splashed up the Río Sonora was to them naught but sand.

So there was no gold for Coronado, no gold for Mendoza, and no fifth part of any gold for the king. The lack of gold in Cíbola was perhaps at the root of the disgrace into which Coronado fell. Had a few native beads or bracelets or fetishes of the shining metal been found by his men, it might have made all the difference between fortune and fiasco. The renewed hope that such a bit of luck could inspire would have brought new vigor and new courage to face the future with patience; supplies and reinforcements would have been showered upon the famished army, and Coronado would not have allowed the forebodings of failure to prostrate him in his quarters for months after he had fallen from a horse. The land would have been held for Spain, Coronado would have been permitted to resign and to return to the home he cherished, nor would the ghost of ill-fortune have distracted him from the proper care of any government position that he might have held. But there was no gold, and this fair picture vanishes back into the might-have-been.

The main traits of Coronado's character were personal valor, loyalty to his superiors, a power to inspire loyalty and even affection in his men, a careful capability in matters not too far beyond his depth, a high conscientiousness, a strong devotion to his home and family, and an assiduity in retrieving a blighted reputation. His greatest evidence of weakness was to retreat from a country where he had never been vanquished by arms, and afterward to allow himself to fall into carelessness and misrule when subjected to chagrin and ill-health and scorn.

These, it is clear, are neither the virtues nor the vices of the conquistador type. Coronado was thus by nature less the ravening, glory-seeking conqueror than he was the first of the new sort of Spanish leaders in North America—the captains who obeyed the laws rather than invented them, the pioneers who pacified the savages according to set rules, the advance guard of the builders rather than destroyers such as those who had torn down the Aztec capital city of Tenochtitlán stone by stone. Coronado, the heir of Cortés, was himself the forerunner of Juan de Oñate and Juan Bautista de Anza.

As soon as Coronado returned from the scene of his discoveries in the north, the mantle of darkness again descended over those lands; and Coronado had lain in his sepulcher for forty years before another captain entered the pueblo country, this time by an entirely different route.

The Coronado trail, in fact, was almost forgotten for many generations. As a result of the discovery of mines in the Sierra Madre, the slow tide of northern advance flowed instead up the inland plateau of Mexico. True, Francisco de Ibarra, governor of the province of New Biscay, led in 1565 and 1566 an armed exploring party which covered part of the Coronado route in Sonora and founded the Villa de San Juan de Sinaloa on the Río Fuerte. But later the town was abandoned and the frontier receded to the Petatlán River, where in 1584 the Villa de San Felipe was the Spanish outpost. The zone of occupation was now no farther north than it had been when Nuño de Guzmán founded Culiacán fifty years before; and across the trail to Cíbola spread the scrub thickets of the primeval *monte*.

One reason why the northward march of empire did not follow this ancient trail was that no traces of gold had been reported by Coronado in that region. This failure had involved Mendoza in personal losses and the greatest scandal of his administration; and his distrust of any proposals to colonize in that direction may have set a precedent for his viceregal successors, for it was a long time before any one of them interested himself in the harsh northwestern provinces.

Another bristling barrier to colonization, or even prospecting, in that region was the continued and stubborn hostility of the Yaqui and Mayo Indians, the Mexican Apaches, tribes that are largely unsubdued even to this day. The Mixton War had cleared the way for peaceful penetration of the Zacatecas country, where mines had been found; but in no skirmish that the Spaniards had fought with the Indians of Sonora, except during the march of Juan Gallego, had the white men been victorious. Both Coronado and Ibarra had fled the territories of these *bravos* or else had avoided them, and the experiences of both expeditions with the poisoned weapons of the northwestern tribes—the men of Ibarra were even more terrified of the "poison tree" of Sonora than were the survivors of Suya—tended to erect a barrier of fear about the unconquered coastal territories. Nor could the regions held by these raiding fighters be circled, for inland the way was blocked by high mountains and waterless deserts.

Again, the few reports of the Coronado explorations that were known to the people in power were highly unpromising,[12] and to hardheaded men must have offered no great rewards for enterprise. More startling discoveries of treasure might be made in Durango, or in many spots in South America. The general opinion held in Spain, and even in Mexico, was that nothing valuable was to be found in the regions now comprised in the United States.

A final bar to fresh achievements on the northwestern frontier of New Spain was the fact that the day of the conquistadores was ended, for their bold and startling efforts had on the whole led to little more than losses, bloodshed, and failure. The deathblow to private expeditions exploring under Crown patents was dealt by the royal "Ordinances of the King for the New Discoveries, Conquests, and Pacifications" issued on July 13, 1573, which strictly defined and prescribed the methods by which unknown or vacant lands might be discovered and occupied. Indeed, the very word "conquest" was banned; instead, one must use the word "pacification."[13] These ordinances, which formed the system under which ultimately all the Crown colonies within the present boundaries of the United States were brought into subjugation, seemed to penalize all personal initiative in exploration.[14] They likewise prohibited armed discoveries of the old sort. Thus Coronado may truly be termed the last of the conquistadores.

One loophole, however, was expressly provided: the countries beyond the frontier could be visited by small trading parties made up of Indian vassals of Spain, as well as by Spaniards whose sole purpose was peaceable trade and by Spanish priests. The Franciscan friars in particular, those later brothers of the adventurous Marcos and the martyred Juan de Padilla, were envisioned as the great pacifying and civilizing force for the advancement of Spanish culture and dominion; and it was beneath the shadow of the mission cross that all Spain's territories now comprised in the United States were first permanently occupied.

It is therefore not astonishing that the next great step in the exploration of the Coronado country was made by a party of priests accompanied only by a tiny squad of volunteer soldiers under the unlucky Captain Francisco Sánchez Chamuscado. The leading spirit in this expedition was the Franciscan friar Augustín Rodríguez, or Ruíz, who had read the narrative of Cabeza de Vaca and had heard, in the course of his missionary work among the Conchos Indians, of large kingdoms to the north—the pueblos discovered by the men of Coronado. Stirred by repeated news of fresh populations ripe for conversion, Ruíz and two fellow Franciscans and their small escort set out from Santa Bárbara in southern Chihuahua to descend the Conchos and ascend the Río Grande, to rediscover the pueblos of the "other Mexico"[15] and there to meet martyrdom.

With this venture opened the second act in the drama of the discovery and settlement of the Southwest. It was a noble and thrilling spectacle. Through its shifting vistas marched many a picturesque figure. Ruíz was avenged by the mine-hunting Mexican merchant Antonio de Espejo. Then appeared the impetuous Castaño de Sosa, the runaway adventurers Bonilla and Humaña, murdered while seeking far Harahey. At the century's end advanced the conqueror of the Pueblos, bold Juan de Oñate, whose valiant captains stormed the heights of Acoma and fought the cunning Kaws on the buffalo

QUIVIRA ON THE AMERICAN SHORE

Tiguex and Cicuyé, as well as Quivira, were curiously mislocated by map makers, frequently appearing as towns near the fortieth parallel on the Pacific coast. (From Ortelius atlas, Antwerp, 1574.)

plains. Sebastián Vizcaíno sailed in the track of Cabrillo and Ferrelo to smell out the secret ports of Francis Drake and to seek the elusive passage of Anian. New Quiviras arose in legend, and men dreamed of finding golden Teguayo and Copala over the northern horizon. The pueblos flamed with revolt, and stern Diego de Vargas came to teach them the meaning of reconquest. Juan Domínguez de Mendoza sought pearls on the plains of Texas. Father Kino, cattleman, explorer, and great baptizer, rode the thirsty sands of Papaguería. A great revolution was fought on the Atlantic seaboard; in the west, wagon wheels first rolled to California with Junípero Serra and Gaspar de Portolá and Juan Bautista de Anza; and Francisco Garcés and Silvestre Vélez de Escalante, those holy great walkers, pushed through the Colorado River country and the deserts beyond.

Men of God, warriors, silver diggers, traders, buffalo killers, scouts, and settlers—the long procession rises in the mind's eye, once more to march and fight and barter and hunt and pray and die. Out across the cloud-rimmed southwestern horizon they stream, over the dull wastes and beyond the painted mesas where cling the solid, square terraces of the red-skinned town builders. But far in the van, side by side with the gentle, unfaltering Cabeza de Vaca, the prancing black Esteban, and the voluble Fray Marcos de Niza, rides the gallant company of Coronado. A last glint of sunset touches the gilded, plumed helmet of the leader—Francisco Vásquez Coronado, crusader, gold-hunter, legend-chaser, finder of the American Southwest.

Notes

Prologue: The Northern Mystery

[1] "He [Sandoval] likewise brought me an account of the chiefs of the province of Ceguatán, who affirm that there is an island inhabited only by women without any men, and that, at given times, men from the mainland visit them; when they bore daughters they kept them, but the sons they put away. This island is ten days distant from the province [Ciguatán], and many persons have gone there from the province and seen them. I was also told that they were rich in pearls and in gold" (Fourth Letter of Cortés, October 15, 1524; see Cortés, *Letters* [MacNutt, ed. and trans.], II, 177).

[2] As late as 1590, when the map of Joannes Myritius (A. E. Nordenskiöld, *Facsimile Atlas* [Stockholm, 1889], pl. 49) was published, some geographers persisted in showing Mexico as a great peninsula attached to the continent of Asia.

[3] Cortés was the first of a long line of adventurers to attempt the discovery of the Northwest Passage; note his project in his Fourth Letter to Charles V (*op. cit.*, II, 207). The name "Strait of Anian," deriving from a typographical error in a passage from Marco Polo, was not in use until Gastaldi issued his map of 1562 (see Wagner, *Spanish Voyages*, p. 358).

[4] The island of Espíritu Santo, at the mouth of the bay of La Paz on the eastern coast of the peninsula of Lower California. This was probably the earliest site for the legendary island of the Amazons. As late as 1597, the boatswain of the ship under Sebastián Vizcaíno which put into the bay wrote: "We came upon a large haven which was called the Bay of La Paz . . . and an island at the mouth which was called the Island of Women, who were without men, none passing over to them except in summer on rafts made of reeds" (see I. B. Rich-

man, *California under Spain and Mexico* [Boston and New York, 1911], p. 364). The land of the Amazons was soon shifted by popular rumor to the mouth of the Río de Ciguatán, or San Lorenzo River, on the mainland coast opposite La Paz.

[5] The Gulf of California was for many years known as the Sea of Cortés, and also as the Mar Bermejo, or Vermilion Sea, because of the reddish color given to it by colonies of minute marine organisms floating on its surface.

[6] This name for the last province that Cortés was fated to add to the Spanish Empire was possibly in use previous to the voyage of Ulloa in 1539; however, Wagner (*Spanish Southwest*, I, 103) believed the name to have been interpolated by Ramusio into the Preciado account of the Ulloa voyage. It has been remarked that in all his writings Cortés himself disdained to use the name California.

[7] This typical romance of chivalry, published by Ordóñez de Montalvo in 1510, was popular reading in the New World.

[8] Alvar Núñez assumed this sobriquet in memory of the heroic deed of a shepherd ancestor of his mother's. Cabeza de Vaca's own account of his travels was first printed in Zamora in 1542.

[9] For accounts of the *entrada* of Guzmán, see the following Bibliography listings: Guzmán, "Carta"; "Segunda relación"; Mota Padilla; Bandelier, *Gilded Man;* and Sauer and Brand.

[10] Comparisons with known distances reveal that the league mentioned in the old chronicles may be assumed as roughly equal to three miles.

[11] The town of San Miguel was founded in 1531 on the coastal plain of Sinaloa at the junction of the mountain streams Humaya and Tamazula, which is the site of modern Culiacán. Guzmán's town was, however, shortly moved a few leagues south to the banks of the Río de Ciguatán, the present San Lorenzo; and it was from this place that Coronado later set out for the north. This location is shown on one of the earliest large-scale maps of the region (Ortelius, *Theatrum orbus terrarum* [Antwerp, 1570], pl. 7).

[12] The Cabeza de Vaca party descended the valley of the Sonora River, the age-old native highway between the New Mexico pueblos and the villages of the west coast (see Sauer, *Road to Cíbola,* pp. 16–18).

[13] An Opata settlement on the Río Sonora below the gorge near modern Ures. It was given the name of Corazones, or Hearts, because the inhabitants presented the traveling gods with six hundred dressed deer hearts.

[14] Probably malachite.

[15] The *residencia* was opened by Luis Ponce de León on July 4, 1526, and against the conqueror his many enemies, including Guzmán, lost

Notes 327

no time in bringing a hundred and eighty-five charges, alleging crimes ranging from strangling his wife to allowing dicing, card games, and swearing in his house.

[16] See William H. Babcock, *Legendary Islands of the Atlantic* (American Geographical Society Research Series, No. 8 [New York, 1922]), pp. 68–80.

[17] From his name, Tejo may have been a Teja or Teya Indian, belonging to a tribe which Coronado later found on the plains of Texas.

[18] The story was given by Pedro de Castañeda (see Winship, *The Coronado Expedition* [hereafter cited as Winship], pp. 472–473).

[19] The chronicler Baltazar de Obregón wrote, about 1584: "The principal reason why the discovery of, and expedition to, the provinces of Cíbola and the original home of the Mexicans was desired was that the marquis [Cortés] had found, among the tribute, possessions, and treasures of the powerful king Montezuma, some chronicles, drawings, and paintings which revealed the origin, spread, and arrival from those regions of the Culguas and the ancient Mexicans" (Obregón, p. 15).

[20] The route of the Cabeza de Vaca party west of the Río Grande may have brought them north of the present international boundary (see Sauer, "Discovery of New Mexico Reconsidered," p. 276). But the account given by Cabeza de Vaca is so vague that it will probably never be possible to prove that these white men did enter the present states of Arizona and New Mexico.

Chapter 1: Fledgling Conquistador

[1] Sometimes "Vázquez"; sometimes "De Coronado." Unfortunately, no contemporary portrait exists to give an idea of his features.

[2] Remón.

[3] See Aiton and Rey, p. 289. Francisco's father was the son of Berenguela Vásquez and Juan Vásquez *"el viejo,"* who married a second time. The second wife, María Fernández, had several children, in whose names the suit was brought.

[4] See Castañeda's statement, in Winship, p. 474.

[5] Joaquín García Icazbalceta, *Tipografía Mexicana* (1894), p. 194.

[6] "Cortés complained that the income from this estate was worth more than three thousand ducados, and that it had been unduly and inconsiderately alienated from the Crown" (Winship, p. 379).

[7] García Icazbalceta, *Colección*, II, 95.

[8] Winship, p. 477.

[9] The royal confirmation, signed at Toledo on March 21, 1539, reached the town council on October 13 of that year.

[10] Orozco, *Actos de cabildo*, June 14, 1538.

[11] This would indicate that Coronado was married previous to the traditional date of 1537.

[12] Winship, p. 380.

[13] Aiton, "Coronado's First Report," p. 308.

[14] It is not clear whether Coronado was first sent to New Galicia as governor, or merely as *juez de residencia* with full powers to take over the administration of the province. Royal confirmation of his governorship was signed in Spain on April 18, 1539.

[15] See Mendoza, "Carta al emperador," December 10, 1537. Dorantes had started for Spain with Cabeza de Vaca, but had been turned back by storms and had then settled in Mexico to make a wealthy marriage.

[16] "Lettere" (undated). In an earlier letter Coronado was mentioned as a promising young man. "Who he is, what he has already done, and his personal qualities and abilities, which may be made useful in the various affairs which arise in these parts of the Indies, I have already written to Your Majesty" (Mendoza, "Carta al emperador," December 10, 1537). Unfortunately, the earlier document referring to Coronado has not been discovered.

[17] According to Gonzaga (*Origine Seraphicae Religionis* [Rome, 1587]), he was born in Aquitaine (see also Wagner, "Fray Marcos," p. 185).

[18] Las Casas, *Brevissima Relación* (Seville, 1552).

[19] At any rate, several titles were given by Velasco.

[20] He was in Guatemala on September 25, 1536, when he was called as a witness at an investigation of the illicit expedition of Alvarado to Peru.

[21] Cuevas, p. 83.

[22] The assertion has been made that Marcos was sent at the instance of Mendoza's friend Las Casas; but Las Casas was not in Mexico in 1538.

[23] See Mendoza, "Instrucción."

[24] These were the Pimas, who had come south as Cabeza de Vaca's escort and had later settled at Bamoa; some of them, through the forethought of the viceroy, had been taken to Mexico City and had been trained to serve as linguists.

[25] Translation by Baldwin, p. 200.

[26] Dorantes, grieved at the thought of separating from his slave comrade of the wilderness, refused to part with him for five hundred pesos on a plate of silver, but freely lent him to the viceroy "because of the good that might accrue to the souls of the natives of those provinces" (Obregón, pp. 13–14).

[27] Mendoza, "Lettere."

[28] The district of Topía in Durango, later noted for its rich mines.

[29] Coronado, "Svmario di lettere."

[30] *Ibid.*

[31] In the Italian of Ramusio, "a thousand leagues" (*milla legua*)—presumably a slip of the pen.

[32] Mendoza, "Lettere."

[33] The grant was given at Madrid on November 8, 1539 (see García Icazbalceta, *Colección*, II, 371).

Chapter 2: Coronado's Forerunners

[1] On July 15 (see Sauer, "Discovery of New Mexico Reconsidered," p. 278). Sauer has suggested that the letter may have actually been written in Mexico City.

[2] Because a Franciscan historian wrote in 1540 an account of an expedition to the northward by two friars in 1538, and failed to name these friars, Bandelier (*Contributions,* pp. 84–105) and others have assumed that there was a discovery of Arizona one year earlier than the journey of Fray Marcos and Esteban. No other contemporary mentioned this previous discovery; and recently Sauer (*The Road to Cíbola,* pp. 21–24) has shown that the misleading account given in 1540 by Motolinia (in García Icazbalceta, *Colección,* I, 171–172) is actually a description of the Fray Marcos *entrada.* In his account Motolinia stated that in 1538 two friars were sent north by way of Jalisco and New Galicia in company with a captain—also unnamed—who was going on a journey of discovery. The captain followed a road inland, but encountered a wall of mountains so rugged that he was forced to turn back. Of the two friars, one fell ill, but the other pushed northward for more than three hundred leagues and was welcomed by the Indians of the country, who greeted him as a messenger of heaven. The Motolinia account contains every important particular regarding the incursion of Marcos and Honorato. The date, 1538, is correct, as Marcos left Mexico City late in that year. The "captain" was Coronado. Apparently the historian wrote just after Marcos had returned to Mexico and before Coronado had been appointed to head his famous expedition, and therefore Motolinia could not anticipate that the names of these figures would become renowned. Later, the historian Mendieta, copying his predecessor's account almost word for word, failed apparently to realize that Motolinia might speak of the notorious Marcos without mentioning his name, and thus inserted the unfounded statement that Marcos hurried forth on his noted journey in order to confirm the report that the unnamed friars had given. Other writers, such as Mota Padilla and Mange, added to Mendieta's fabric with circumstantial details, and even gave names to the apocryphal friars!

[3] This Fray Honorato was still alive in 1551, attached to the convent of Jalisco (Bandelier, *Contributions*, p. 108).

[4] Marcos asserted in his report that twenty or thirty leagues beyond Petatlán some Indians from "the island visited by the Marqués del Valle" came to him and informed him that it was really an island, "and not, as some think, part of the mainland. I saw that they passed to and from the mainland on rafts and that the distance between the island and the mainland might be half a sea league, rather more or less." It is doubtful if anyone could have crammed more improbabilities into a few words. Any Indians he may have met could not have made the rough voyage from Lower California, nor were the coast tribes able to cover any great distances in their *balsa* canoes. Neither could these people have been the wolfish Seri Indians of Tiburón Island, as Bandelier suggested, for Tiburón was much farther to the north and its dwellers had little intercourse with the mainland. Marcos may have seen a few uninhabited islands of mud at the mouth of the Río Fuerte; he could not have been much farther up the coast at this time, for he had been on the road less than a week.

[5] All translations from the report of Marcos in this chapter are from Baldwin.

[6] This debatable town has been located by Sauer ("Discovery of New Mexico Reconsidered," p. 282) as lying on the old coast trail midway between the Fuerte and Mayo rivers. This location was some twenty leagues from the sea—half the distance given by Marcos.

[7] See Castañeda's statements in Winship, pp. 474-475.

[8] Bandelier (*Contributions*, p. 131) suggested that Cíbola is derived from "Shi-uo-na," the Zuñi name for their tribal range, and hence was used correctly to indicate the whole territory inhabited by the Zuñi Indians.

[9] Marcos said that after talking to these coastal Indians he put down on a separate paper the names of thirty-four islands off the coast, which here trended, he asserted, almost directly toward the north. This paper is not known to exist.

[10] These may have been wandering Jumanos from the plains of the Río Grande; this tribe was first seen by Cabeza de Vaca on the lower Conchos.

[11] The valley of the Río Yaqui.

[12] Perhaps the Indians were attempting to describe the blanket garments of jack-rabbit fur, wound about yucca fiber, that the Hopi tribesmen still know how to weave.

[13] Probably the fertile land around Mátape, headquarters of the hard-working Opata tribe, who lived in compact villages, practiced irrigation, and traded with the pueblo dwellers to the north.

[14] The valley of the Sonora River.

[15] The coast was then two hundred miles away; the time at the friar's disposal could not have permitted any such wearisome round trip; there is no marked westward trend to the Sonora coast south of Adair Bay; and for a man with his reputed skill in navigation, Marcos was absurdly wrong in his estimate of the latitude he had reached—three and a half degrees in error.

[16] It was later learned by Coronado that these were actual places. Ahacus was the Zuñi pueblo of Hawikuh; Marata, to the southeast of Zuñi, was a group of towns which, unknown to the Opatas, had recently been destroyed in the warfare of which they had told; Totonteac was an abandoned settlement near the Hopi towns of the Painted Desert of Arizona; and Acus was the citadel rock of Acoma in central New Mexico.

[17] These Indians brought Marcos a curiosity, a long-haired pelt "half as big again as that of a large cow, and told me that it was from an animal which has only one horn on its forehead and that this horn is curved toward its chest and then there sticks out a straight point."

[18] This *despoblado* was probably the grassy Cananea plain extending to the headwaters of the San Pedro River in Arizona. The "last village" would be Arispe, or more likely Bacoachi, on the upper Sonora. Esteban and those who followed him probably crossed the present international boundary somewhere in the vicinity of Naco.

[19] The old trail to the pueblos led through the heart of the White Mountains of eastern Arizona, a region of rugged peaks and dense forest that is still virtually a wilderness. It should be noted that Marcos gave no description in his report of the type of country through which he traveled from the time the messenger from Cíbola reached him until the time he first viewed the "city." He made no written mention of the ruined landmark of Chichilticalli, although he later led Coronado to believe that this ruin was something wondrous. (The Aztec name of this ruin, meaning "red house," may have been given to it, however, by Marcos or one of his Indians from Mexico.) Most curious is the omission of any mention of the Gila River, which was brimming with snow waters at the time of his journey. It seems hardly possible that Marcos, had he reached this great desert stream, would have failed to mention it.

[20] See Castañeda's account in Winship, p. 475.

[21] Cushing, quoted by Lowery, pp. 281–282.

[22] The inaccuracies that modern students have found in the report seem to spring from self-delusion on the part of Fray Marcos and from calculated reticence and misstatement (perhaps to serve the political needs of the viceroy). They could not have been due to a failure of

memory, as the account was written directly after the return of Marcos; nor should they have resulted from failure to observe, for he was apparently a skilled cosmographer and had received strict orders to make frequent surveys, and yet, as Sauer has said (*The Road to Cíbola*, p. 30), his report is the "worst geographical document on this frontier."

The most dubious part of the report is that describing the friar's actions after the time when he "entered the wilderness." It is almost impossible to believe that he ever came within view of the first city of Cíbola. A survey of all the facts shows that he had opportunity to falsify this part of his report, and also that he had several good reasons for falsifying it. His contemporaries Cortés and Coronado maintained at the time that he was a lying imposter. Castañeda stated that the Indians escaping after the killing of Esteban "happened to come upon the friars in the desert sixty leagues from Cíbola, and told them the sad news, which frightened them so much that they would not even trust these folks who had been with the negro, but opened the packs they were carrying and gave away everything they had except the holy vestments for saying Mass. They returned from here by double marches, prepared for anything, without knowing any more of the country than what the Indians told them" (Winship, p. 475). Motolinia, in his version, did not assert that Marcos knew the pueblos except by hearsay; Mota Padilla (*Historia*, p. 111) said only that Marcos "had news" of Cíbola. Although Bandelier in 1890 (*Contributions*, p. 108) attempted to prove that Marcos was the "worst slandered man known in history," present-day authorities using internal evidence in his own report have shown how incredible it is that Marcos came within two or three hundred miles of Cíbola or Zuñi. Perhaps he did not get much farther than the desert country of southern Arizona.

By a calculation using the few dates given by Marcos in his report (the dates of his departure from Culiacán and arrival at Compostela are verified by other sources), and by using the traveling times that Coronado was later to achieve over the same trail, Sauer (*The Road to Cíbola*, pp. 28–32; "Discovery of New Mexico Reconsidered," pp. 284–287) and Wagner ("Fray Marcos," pp. 214–216) have agreed that Marcos could not have penetrated farther north than the Gila River at best.

It is interesting, taking the report of Marcos at its face value, to compare the time required by Esteban to go from Vacapa to Cíbola with the time consumed by Fray Marcos himself in supposedly covering the same distance. It is true that Esteban was well in advance and was in a hurry; however, he is stated to have had three hundred people in his party, a number probably exceeding that in the friar's party. Esteban left Vacapa on Passion Sunday, March 23 (Julian Calendar). On May 21, almost two months later, an Indian fleeing from Cíbola with news of the capture of the negro met Marcos in the *despoblado*. If it is assumed that this spot was three days from Cíbola (the Indians asserted that the *despoblado* took fifteen days to cross), then it would have taken Esteban fifty-six days from Vacapa to Cíbola. Marcos left Vacapa on April 8. If there is no deduction for the time required for his impossible trip to the sea or for the time consumed by him in talking with the natives and examining the country, and three days are deducted for the delay at the village where the "thirty chiefs" joined him, he would on May 21 have been on the northern road a maximum of forty-one days. Adding three days to continue on to Cíbola (it could not have been more, for he declared he overtook the main body of fugitives on the return journey in two days), his time from Vacapa would be almost *two weeks less* than the time made by Esteban. The schedule which Marcos allegedly maintained as far as Cíbola therefore seems impossible.

[23] "The noble viceroy arranged with the friars of the Order of St. Francis so that Friar Marcos was made father-provincial" (Castañeda; see Winship, p. 476). There must have been some strong pressure to gain him this important office, especially at a time when he was expecting to leave the country again for an indefinite period; moreover, he was a comparative newcomer to Mexico, and many of the revered original missionaries were still alive and must have been candidates for such an honor.

Although Marcos got his wish to accompany the expedition that soon set out for Cíbola, he was to return from there in a few months in disgrace, with the curses of Coronado's soldiers, who maintained that he had cheated them, ringing in his ears.

Throughout the remainder of his years Marcos was branded by the collapse of his dream. He took part in the Mixton War of 1541 against the rebellious natives of New Galicia, counseling the severest measures against the Indians (see Mota Padilla, p. 149). Crippled by the hardships through which he had passed, he retired to pleasant Jalapa, where Mendieta spoke with him in 1554. His latter years were spent in more than Franciscan poverty, and he was forced to beg of his old friend Zumárraga a little monthly donation of wine, "of which I am in great need, as my sickness is of lack of blood and natural heat." The bishop, one is happy to know, ordered that each month an *arroba* of wine was to be delivered to the aging explorer by Indian messenger (see Wagner, "Fray Marcos," p. 226). To Mexico City, thinking that the hour of his death was drawing near, Marcos retired to be interred among the ancient holy ones, and died on March 25, 1558, twenty years after he had left that city to march northward with great hopes in his heart.

Chapter 3: Coronado, Captain General

[1] Juan de Zumárraga, Letter of August 23, 1539 (in Joaquín García Icazbalceta, *Nueva colección de documentos para la historia de Mexico* [5 vols.; Mexico, 1886–1892], II, 283).

[2] Letter from Fray Gerónimo Jiménez de San Esteban to Santo Tomás de Villanueva, Mexico, October 9, 1539 (*ibid.*, I, 194).

[3] "Proceso," p. 397.

[4] Aiton and Rey, p. 302.

[5] Cortés, "Memorial que dió."

[6] As will be seen, the De Soto forces were at one time to come very close to the route of Coronado's army in the region of Oklahoma.

[7] Mendoza's decree of August 26 forbade any shipmaster sailing from the Mexican mainland to touch at any port in the New World on his way to Spain. In spite of this precaution one captain, who maintained under oath that there was sickness on board and that his stock of food and water were so low that he dared not venture to cross the Atlantic, in November put in at San Cristóbal de la Havana. It could hardly have been a coincidence that the father in law of Fray Marcos' barber, a sailor named Andrés García (perhaps one of those suddenly seized with the sickness that made the stop necessary), had some letters in his pocket which he had been asked to deliver to Governor De Soto in Havana (see "Proceso," p. 397). The letters apparently went on to De Soto's man of business in Spain.

[8] Indeed, the question of the Cíbola expedition was brought up during the *visita* held at the expiration of Mendoza's term of office (Aiton and Rey, p. 302), and proved to be the most embarrassing of all the charges he had to answer. In reply, the viceroy asserted that all his expeditions by land and sea were dispatched with the license and consent of His Majesty. This consent, however, may merely have been implied, for there is no record of any specific license having been issued.

[9] Mota Padilla, p. 111.

[10] The voluminous mass of petitions and testimony was turned over by the Council for the Indies to its fiscal, Juan de Villalobos, who on May 25, 1540, some months after the expedition organized by Mendoza had departed, submitted a report which virtually decided the whole matter. His recommendation was that, since the Cíbola region was unexplored country not included in any previous license, none of the petitioners should be recognized. The Crown was therefore free, as always, to license anyone it chose to explore the new country. The effect of this report, which was undoubtedly accepted by the Council,

was to sanction the efforts of Mendoza, who as viceroy was the personal representative of the king in New Spain. Both Cortés and De Soto's attorney appealed the action, which dragged on until 1544, long after the bone of contention was clearly seen to have no meat on it.

[11] Winship, p. 476.

[12] See Aiton, "Coronado's Commission." The document, issued at Michoacán on January 6, 1540, appointing him "anew" as captain general of the expedition, had the form of a royal writ, but was signed by Antonio de Almaguer, the viceroy's secretary, and cited as warranty Mendoza's own commission as viceroy dated at Barcelona on April 17, 1535. Separate written instructions concerning the lawful treatment of natives that might be met in the course of exploration on behalf of the Crown were also given Coronado at this time. The almost absolute powers bestowed upon Coronado in this commission included the right to defend the new lands, in the royal name, against "other persons who may enter those lands and take possession of them, saying that the government of the said new land belongs to them"—a clear command that might well lead to bloodshed in any encounter with the rival De Soto expedition, which also held a royal warrant!

[13] Aiton and Rey, Question 201.

[14] Suárez de Peralta, p. 144; see also Winship, p. 364.

[15] The *Actos de cabildo* (Orozco, ed.) show Coronado to be absent from all meetings after October 13, 1539, and up to October 13, 1542.

[16] In the *visita* of 1546 (Aiton and Rey, Question 127) Mendoza was charged with permitting injury to the people of Michoacán through the passage of his expeditions. Coronado as a witness for the defense testified that he had been ordered not to allow his party to cause any offense or ill-treatment to any of the natives of Michoacán or to take anything from them, and that these orders were fulfilled exactly.

[17] Among other duties, he proclaimed on January 9 the royal order of December 20, 1538, to the effect that the colonists should build no houses not of stone, brick, or adobe, as protection against the frequent fires that wiped out their thatched dwellings, and that they should model their homes after those of Spain for the adornment of His Majesty's new city (see Mota Padilla, p. 109).

[18] The request is dated February 21, 1540; see "Información," p. 373.

[19] This *testimonio* (Pacheco, XIV, 373–384; abstract in Winship, pp. 596–598) makes amusing reading. It was probably prepared to provide a formal protection against charges that might arise if a serious Indian war broke out in New Galicia—as actually happened not long after Coronado had left the province for the north.

[20] Winship, p. 477. It has been assumed that Castañeda did not join the expedition until it reached San Miguel de Culiacán. However,

it is very likely that he was the "Pedro de Najera" listed on the muster (Aiton, "Coronado's Muster Roll," p. 563), and that his description of the review is therefore, as it would sound, an eyewitness account. For a note on this most important chronicler of the Coronado expedition, see introduction to Bibliography below.

[21] The muster roll lists a minimum of 558 horses and a lone mule (see Aiton, "Coronado's Muster Roll," p. 557).

[22] "Only a few of the soldiers reported a full European equipment of armor, though nearly all had one or two pieces of Spanish armor, for example, a pair of kneepieces, a coat of mail, a helmet, a corselet, a bevor, or gauntlets. The great majority wore native buckskin suits of armor, *cueras de anta*, which were much more comfortable on the march and quite effective against Indian weapons. European armor must either have been at a premium, or else the men had learned from their sojourn in America the superiority of the lighter armor for fighting in the New World" (*ibid.*, p. 558).

[23] "The horsemen, according to the muster roll, were equipped in the majority of cases with lances and swords, and some carried extra daggers. The foot soldiers were armed with twenty-two harquebuses, the primitive ancestor of the musket, fifteen crossbows, and a variety of swords, daggers, and native weapons from Mexico" (*ibid.*).

The crossbow used was of the medieval type mounted on a stock, which helped in aiming. With its thick cord it threw a short bolt tipped with feathers or leather vanes. The bow was cocked by a hinged lever, or else wound up with a small windlass while the archer kept his foot in a sort of stirrup at the end of the stock.

The sixteenth-century harquebus was an even weightier weapon and was usually fired from a tripod. Loading and firing this forerunner of the modern carbine was a serious business. It was loaded from the muzzle, and often half a dozen bullets were rammed in as a charge. A pan at the right side of the breech was primed with powder, which was jarred into the flash-passage by a slap of the hand. The matchlock was fired by pulling a trigger, but the reaction was far from instantaneous. The release allowed a glowing slow match or fuse to descend to the pan, and the explosion might occur at any time within fifteen seconds thereafter. Before going into action the musketeer lighted his fuse, the long end of which was carried in his left hand or wrapped around the gunstock. The twenty-two harquebuses in the Coronado army were valuable more for impressing the natives than for use as superior offensive weapons; actually the Spaniards did most of their fighting with the same sort of arms as were used by their Indian opponents.

[24] Ten thousand Indians of New Spain had volunteered to go, but the viceroy limited the corps to a tenth of this number.

[25] Castañeda; see Winship, p. 478.

[26] See H. I. Priestley, *The Luna Papers* (Publications of Florida State Historical Society, No. 8, De Land, Florida, 1928). Arellano was a cousin to Mendoza.

[27] Castañeda called him "Pedro"; see Winship, p. 477.

[28] Winship, p. 477.

[29] Bandelier ("Discovery of New Mexico," p. 32) has faultily identified him with the Juan Jaramillo who married Marina, heroine of the Conquest and former mistress of Cortés, during the march through Honduras in 1524; this Jaramillo was in Mexico during the Cíbola expedition (see Andrés Cavo, *Los tres siglos de Mexico* [Mexico, 1836–1838; Jalapa, 1870], I, 28). Juan Jaramillo *"el mozo"* (Icaza, No. 867), who had two uncles who served in the Conquest (perhaps Marina was his aunt), later wrote a valuable account of his experiences in Cíbola and Quivira; see introduction to Bibliography below.

[30] Icaza, No. 1298.

[31] See Aiton, "Coronado's Muster Roll," p. 557. With this escort, or among those who had not yet arrived from Mexico City, were a number of soldiers who are not listed on the muster. Among these may have been the Scottish soldier of fortune "Tomás Blaque" (Icaza, No. 738), who stated in a petition made some years later that he had served in the pacification of New Granada in 1532 before coming to Mexico in 1534 or 1535, and that he had enlisted with Coronado and served with the army until its return three years later. His true name was Thomas Blake, the son of William and Agnes Mowat Blake. For twenty years he was the only man of British blood who was allowed to reside in Mexico; if he went with Coronado (and he would hardly have dared to lie about his service with this famous expedition), he was likewise the only British Islander, so far as is known, to take part in any of the Spanish explorations in what is now the United States. Shrewd and experienced as this Scotsman undoubtedly was, he was fated to gain little silver or gold through his service with Coronado. Shortly after his return he married Francisca de Ribera, widow of a prosperous "old conqueror" who had been a nuncio and fiscal of the Holy Inquisition in Mexico; but about 1550, like many another veteran of Coronado, he applied for aid from the Crown because he "suffered great need." Blake was alive and residing in Mexico in 1556, when he befriended Robert Tomson, an Englishman whose remarkable account of travels in Mexico and the West Indies appears in Hakluyt.

Chapter 4: Misadventures of the Road

[1] Winship, pp. 479–480.

[2] In the last days of his governorship, Coronado was to be punished for practicing the frequent custom of impressing natives as carriers (see Tejada, *Carta*, p. 189).

[3] Aiton and Rey, Question 203.

[4] Mendoza testified that there were more than a thousand animals—horses, mules, and stock; Coronado said that he ordered these to be counted at a certain narrow pass, and found them to be more than fifteen hundred (Aiton and Rey, Question 199 and note).

[5] Díaz must have misunderstood some of the gestures of his informants, for he brought back the tale that the pueblo people were cannibals and kept prisoners of war as slaves (Mendoza, "Carta," April 17, 1540; see Winship, p. 548).

[6] Zaldívar found the viceroy near Jacona on March 20, recovering from the effects of a fever he had caught in Colima. The news was relayed by Mendoza to the king in a letter written on April 17, by which time Zaldívar was once more with the Coronado force moving northward. In his report, Díaz had also remarked that the people he found along the way did not have any settlements at all, except for one in a valley a hundred and fifty leagues from Culiacán (probably Cabeza de Vaca's town of Hearts), and that all the natives he had seen were not good for anything except to make Christians of them—"as if," Mendoza piously observed to His Majesty, "this was of small account!" The viceroy's faith in the ultimate success of the expedition was still little dimmed.

[7] Winship, p. 481.

[8] Two men named Trugillo—Rodrigo (a horseman) and Pedro (a foot soldier)—are listed on the muster (Aiton, "Coronado's Muster Roll," pp. 566 and 569). For the story of the Devil at Culiacán, see Winship, pp. 481–482.

Chapter 5: The Hungry Journey

[1] This friar may have remained in New Galicia, for he was not mentioned again by the members of the expedition.

[2] Now the Río Mocorito.

[3] Winship, p. 515.

[4] The modern Fuerte.

[5] This "Ravine of the Cedars," still so called, undoubtedly got its

name from the many Mexican cypress trees to be found along its banks; it meets the Mayo at the town of Conicarit.

⁶ Coronado, "Relatione"; see Winship, p. 553.

⁷ The river was probably forded in the vicinity of Soyopa.

⁸ These were the Eudeve branch of Opatas living in the Mátape Valley, later to become an important mission center.

⁹ Coronado, "Relatione"; see Winship, p. 554.

¹⁰ So spelled by Jaramillo (see Winship, p. 585); Castañeda (see Winship, p. 515) called it Arispa, from the Indian dialect Huc-aritz-pa. This was the town of Arispe, now somnolent, but formerly a thriving place with a population that at one time reached thirty-five thousand. The Spanish town, founded in 1648, was selected in 1780 as the colonial capital of the Internal Provinces, embracing the provinces of Sonora, Sinaloa, New Biscay, Coahuila, Texas, Arizona, New Mexico, and the two Californias, all under the dominion of the military governor, Caballero de Croix. It has been in its time a prominent mining and agricultural center, but nowadays is not mentioned in the guidebooks.

¹¹ This base for the Coronado expedition was at the last of the Opata towns south of the Cananea plain, probably at or near the present village of Bacoachi on the east fork of the Sonora headwaters.

¹² Winship, pp. 515–516.

¹³ The San Pedro, desert tributary of the sprawling Gila.

¹⁴ These were the now extinct Sobaípuri branch of the upper Pimas.

¹⁵ Jaramillo; see Winship, p. 585. Two possible routes might answer to this meager description. Sauer (*The Road to Cibola*, pp. 36–37) believed that they descended the San Pedro to a point somewhere north of modern Benson, then swung off around the Galiuro Mountains into the upper basin of Arivaipa Creek, and thence through Eagle Pass between the Pinaleño and Santa Teresa ranges to the Gila River somewhere above San Carlos. Hodge (Winship, 1932 ed., Introduction) believed that they turned east much earlier and crossed the Pinaleño Mountains, reaching the Gila by way of Railroad Pass and the San Simeon Valley to the vicinity of Solomonsville. Either route seems possible, and either would have landed them on the Gila somewhere south of the present White Mountain Apache Reservation.

¹⁶ The mention of Chichilticalli by Jaramillo might indicate that the site of this never-identified ruin would be found in the Arivaipa Valley, but everything Castañeda has said of it would favor a location on the Gila. He wrote: "At Chichilticalli the country changes its character and the spiky vegetation ceases.... Here they had to cross and pass through the mountains [of the Colorado Plateau] in order to get into the level country" (Winship, p. 516). A number of pueblo ruins in the Gila Valley were listed by Hough (*Antiquities of the Upper Gila and*

Salt River Valleys in Arizona and New Mexico [*Bulletin of Bureau of Ethnology*, No. 35, Washington, 1907]). He stated (p. 37) that not far from Old Camp Grant is one that may be that identified as Chichilti-calli by Bandelier. If the Coronado route led through the neighbor-hood of Solomonsville, a more likely site for Chichilticalli is the one described by Hough on pages 34–35, called Buena Vista. Another pos-sible site is that mentioned by Sauer and Brand (*Pueblo Sites in South-eastern Arizona* [*University of California Publications in Geology*, vol. 3, no. 7, Berkeley, 1930], pp. 423 and 450) as lying on a bluff about one mile north of the town of Geronimo. However, at this late date it will probably never be possible to identify the site of Chichilticalli indis-putably.

[17] Winship, p. 482.

[18] Coronado, "Relatione"; see Winship, p. 555.

[19] One Francisco de Espinosa appears on the muster as a harque-busier (see Aiton, "Coronado's Muster Roll," p. 567).

[20] Coronado, "Relatione"; see Winship, p. 556.

Chapter 6: The Conquest of Cíbola

[1] The ruins of Old Zuñi lie thirty-five miles south of Gallup, New Mexico, just inside the edge of the present reservation.

[2] Winship, p. 586.

[3] Many proofs of the identity of Cíbola with Zuñi may be cited. Words of the native language given in the accounts can be linked with those in the Zuñi dialect; for example, Castañeda stated that the people of Cíbola had priests whom they called *papas*, and this word in Zuñi-talk means "elder brother," in the sense of either actual or ceremonial relationship. Jaramillo (Winship, p. 587) gave another clue which is probably more exact geographically than he could have known when he said that all streams as far as and including the Río Vermejo flowed into the South Sea (the Pacific), and those encountered beyond flowed into the North Sea; this is a precise description, for the Zuñi River, rising just west of the Continental Divide, flows into the Colorado Chi-quito, thence into the Colorado proper, and so to the Gulf of Califor-nia, whereas beyond the Zuñi Mountains the drainage is eastward. If more proof were needed of the identification of Cíbola with Zuñi, it could be found in the stories of later explorers such as the Espejo party, who in 1583 heard of the deeds of Coronado's men in the Zuñi villages through the inhabitants, found some Mexican Indians of Guadalajara still resident in Zuñi, and in one village, Mátsaki, uncovered a book and a small trunk left by Coronado (Hodge, Introduction to Winship, 1932 ed.).

[4] Coronado, "Relatione"; see Winship, p. 558.

[5] Winship, p. 483.

[6] See "Requerimiento."

[7] Coronado, "Relatione"; see Winship, p. 557.

[8] "Traslado"; see Winship, p. 565.

[9] These were turkeys, kept by the Zuñis not for food but for the feathers, which they prized for headdresses.

[10] During the Pueblo Revolt of 1680 the town of Mátsaki was abandoned and its people took refuge on the almost inaccessible mountaintop, where they built homes and lived for some years thereafter.

[11] Coronado, "Relatione"; see Winship, p. 563.

[12] Castañeda hazarded the guess that "they must have come from that part of Greater India whose coast lies to the west of this country, for they could have come down from that region, crossing the mountain chains and following down the river [the Río Grande], settling in what seemed to them the best place" (Winship, p. 525). In this the chronicler was wiser than he knew, for the accepted origin of the American Indian is Asiatic. The primitive ancestors of the Indians, according to the theory, crossed into America by the Aleutian "land bridge" or by Bering Strait about 8000 B.C. and in successive waves of migration peopled the two empty continents. The ancestors of the Pueblos very likely drifted down the east side of the Rockies and settled in the regions now known as the Land of the Cliff Dwellers. The history of this group shows that they emerged into a fairly high state of culture at least two thousand years ago, and developed one of the most satisfying civilizations in all the Americas, comparable to that of the Mayas of Yucatán or the Incas of Peru.

The peak of their achievement came from the tenth to the fifteenth century, at a time when most of Europe was sunk in medieval darkness. But a great shrinkage in numbers, probably because of climatic conditions, had set in several hundred years before the arrival of Coronado, whose men discovered more than seventy towns (including the six at Cíbola and the seven found by Tovar at Tusayán) in what is now northern Arizona and New Mexico, having in all a population of some twenty thousand souls. But for every town inhabited in 1540 there were hundreds of abandoned villages, scattered over the length and breadth of the Southwest. Some of this abandonment was a result of wars or of drought, but the pueblo dwellers have always been remarkably prone to desert their towns bodily and move to new locations for what might seem the flimsiest of reasons—such as unfavorable omens from their gods—and once they had departed they were little disposed to return. Coronado saw several towns that had recently been deserted. Since his day, the number of sites occupied by the Pueblos has dwindled to twenty-six, with a population totaling about ten thousand descendants of those Indians who welcomed him or fought against his army; not more than two or three of these towns are situated exactly as they were in 1540, and some have been moved several times (much of the shifting, of course, occurred in the devastating Pueblo Revolt of 1680). Although in the sixteenth century the pueblo dwellers had fallen somewhat from their earlier high estate, had forgotten some of their former skills, had shrunk in numbers, and had been driven by nomad enemies from many of their old ranges, they still clung to their ancient customs, and in spite of the heavy dominion of the white man struggled resolutely to realize their free destinies. Today, under a wise governmental policy of encouragement without domination, these intelligent tribes are holding their own and practicing their native arts and ways of living as hardily as any Indian group in the United States.

[13] Probably the most extensive early communities of these tillers of the soil—places long deserted even in 1540—were those found in the Mesa Verde and in the Chaco Canyon, two regions near the "four corners of the Southwest," where the states of Utah, Colorado, New Mexico, and Arizona intersect at the valley of the San Juan River. The Mesa Verde people dwelt in stone rooms and towers under swelling overhangs of rock high on the walls of deep-cut gorges, whereas the Chaco people lived in enormous community houses like spreading wasps' nests on the valley floors or on the tops of high mesas. Other ancient centers of population were the Colorado Chiquito and Gila valleys in Arizona (although the Coronado party left no record of having seen any ruins except the famous Chichilticalli) and the Chihuahua basin region of Casas Grandes in north-central Mexico. It is likely that the pueblos discovered by Coronado and his men were founded by emigrants from these abandoned ancient cradle-cities.

[14] Winship, p. 518.

[15] An odd omission from the list of plants cultivated by the Pueblos as given in the Coronado chronicles may be noted. Nowhere is mention made of the tobacco weed (although the Pimas and Yaquis to the south of them grew tobacco), nor of the custom of smoking. This may be surprising to those who appreciate the ritual importance of smoking among Indian tribes, where the act is one of high religious and social significance. Lummis asserted (*Mesa, Cañon, and Pueblo*, p. 384) that the Pueblos did smoke at the time of the conquest, puffing the dried leaves of certain mountain herbs in a holder made of a pithed reed, forerunner of the now universal cigarette of tobacco rolled in brown cornhusk. It is no wonder that the Spaniards failed to note the custom, for the young native dared not smoke until he was twenty-five, and then never in the presence of his elders. Smoking was the seal on a

truce or friendship, a magical spell to ensure good hunting, an act of reverence, a rain prayer, a medical treatment, and a fraternal ceremony performed in the underground *kiva*. Such a sacred observance would never have been revealed to the eyes of the white strangers, even had they been on the watch for it—which they were not, for the use of tobacco was not common to the Spanish colonists even at this late date after the discovery of America.

[16] The Zuñis who later dwelt on the summit of Towayalane had a curious method of storage. Whenever there was snow on the ground, the villagers would all turn out and roll up huge snowballs which were deposited in stone reservoirs, so that the melting snow would provide them with a continuous source of water.

[17] Winship, p. 518.

[18] Coronado, "Relatione"; see Winship, p. 559.

[19] There were no beasts of burden before the Spaniards came, and even today the most agile burro would be unable to negotiate many of the mesa paths.

[20] These pre-Columbian apartment houses were often of immense size; one cluster in the old pueblo of Cicuyé, or Pecos, had 517 rooms, and another 585.

[21] It is often asserted that the wild horses of the western plains were descended from those lost by the explorer De Soto, but this is impossible, as all his animals died during his journey. Nor is it very likely that the American mustang had for his ancestors the wiry breed ridden by the men of Coronado. Although, as will be seen, a number of the army's horses were stolen during a raid on the garrison at Tiguex, the muster roll lists only two mares owned by members of the expedition (see Aiton, "Coronado's Muster Roll," p. 557 and note).

Chapter 7: The Desert and the Canyon

[1] The name of Tusayán derives, according to Bandelier (*Contributions*, p. 115), from the Zuñi name Usaya-kue, or "people of Usaya."

[2] This tribe, the earliest known and the most famous of all the Indians of Arizona, seems doomed to be named variously, and even today it is possible to start a lively debate over whether they should properly be called "Hopi" or "Moqui." The tribesmen called themselves Hópituh Shínumu, or "people of peace," but certainly not "Hopi" for short. Most other Indians knew them as "Moqui," a Tusayán term meaning "dead." Neither appellation is especially apt, but as a result of the disagreement of the partisans every passing reference to the tribe, whose annual Snake Dance brings hundreds of spectators to their villages, needs must include mention of both "Hopi" and "Moqui."

[3] Bandelier asserted that Totonteac was a corruption of a Zuñi term applied to a cluster of twelve pueblos lying in the direction of Tusayán but already abandoned in the sixteenth century. "It is interesting to note," he said (*Final Report*, I, 114 n.), "how the reports which Fray Marcos gathered in Sonora concerning the northern Pueblos frequently relate to events which had occurred some time previous to his coming. Tribes were mentioned to him, like 'Marata' and 'Totonteac,' who had ceased to exist, though the distant southern Indians had no knowledge of their disappearance."

[4] Mendoza, "Carta," April 17, 1540; see Winship, p. 550.

[5] See Winship, p. 488.

[6] The names of none of the Hopi villages are given in the Coronado chronicles, but through the studies of archaeologists we know that five towns were occupied at the time of Tovar's visit. On the East Mesa were Walpi and Awatobi, the latter probably the first village entered by Tovar; on the Middle Mesa were Shongopovi and Mishongnovi; and on the West Mesa was Oraibi. This town is the only one still occupying the same site; the rest have been moved, and only ruins of the ancient villages remain.

[7] Their language was of the branch called Shoshonean, which includes the nomad Utes and Comanches, as well as the Aztecs of the Mexican Plateau. The Hopis of Tusayán were the only northern tribe of this lingual stock to form the habits of dwelling in towns and consistently cultivating the soil.

[8] Luxán, who was with the Espejo party in 1583, asserted in his journal (pp. 95–96) that Coronado had destroyed one of the towns of Hopi: "We halted in the province of Moji [Moqui or Hopi], at a pueblo that had been attacked and destroyed by Coronado because they had killed five of the nine men he had sent to discover this province of Mojose while he remained in the province of Sumi [Zuñi]. When Coronado heard the news he fell upon it with his men and devastated and destroyed it. It was and is situated a league from the pueblo of Aguato [Awatobi]." There is no other hint that such an attack occurred; Luxán may have inferred much of it from an examination of the ruined town of Kawaioku, which was probably abandoned around 1540 for some other reason.

[9] He appears on the muster roll (see Aiton, "Coronado's Muster Roll," p. 561) as a trooper. Said Castañeda: "They gave the general a written account of what they had seen, because one Pedro de Sotomayor had gone with Don García López as chronicler for the army" (Winship, p. 490).

[10] Winship, p. 489.

[11] Castañeda's statement that they did not reach the Canyon until

they had journeyed twenty days from Hopi was made from hearsay. The airline distance from Hopi to Grand Canyon station is less than a hundred miles, and a brisk walker could reach Marble Canyon from Hopi in three or four days. It is possible that, in order to find water, the guides may have led Cárdenas in a wide southern loop around the Painted Desert before striking north to the Canyon, in which event the journey would have been about two or three times as long. However, the trail due west may have been taken, crossing the Colorado Chiquito somewhere south of Cameron, possibly on the old Hopi salt trail at Tanner Crossing a few miles below Black Falls. Along this stretch the Chiquito runs through a deep-cut ravine which is steep and dangerous, but fordable; and the fact that this river and its canyon were not mentioned in the accounts might well be because the difficulties they presented to the travelers were completely overshadowed by their breath-taking experiences on the heights of the Grand Canyon itself. In the "Relación del suceso" (see Winship, p. 574) there is no mention of the twenty-day journey, but the statement was made that the distance from Tusayán to the rim was fifty leagues, which would be a close estimate for the Black Falls route. In this document also mention was made of the fact that the party struck the Colorado River gorge at a place where "it came from the northeast and turned to the south-southwest." The only place where the river takes this course between the sheer walls that the adventurers tried to descend is below the Kanab Rapids at the mouth of Kanab Creek.

[12] Winship, p. 490.

[13] The water supply at the Grand Canyon is even today so limited that water must be shipped in daily by tank cars on the railway.

[14] The first mention of this tribe in documentary history occurs as late as 1626, when they were called "Apaches de Navaju" (Hodge, *Handbook*, II, 41). These warlike wanderers were inveterate foes of the sedentary pueblo dwellers, for the Zuñi name for the Navajo was *ápachu*, meaning "enemy," a term applied likewise to the Querechos, fierce Apaches of the Texas plains.

[15] The date is fixed by the clever deductions of A. E. Douglass, Arizona astronomer, from comparisons of tree rings found in ancient building timbers. See Douglass, "Dating Our Prehistoric Ruins," *Natural History*, XXI (January–February, 1921), 27–30.

Chapter 8: Discoveries East and West

[1] A truncated account of what they discovered is given in the document which later was erroneously labeled "Account of What Hernando de Alvarado and Fray Juan de Padilla Discovered in Search of the South Sea, August, 1540" (see Hernando de Alvarado). The misleading title—Alvarado went eastward, not toward the Pacific—was added by a clerk some years afterward, and the lack of date and regional names in the original document led to a curious misconception among historians. The account begins, "We set out from Granada .. ."; by confusing Hawikuh under the guise of its newer name Granada with the town of Granada situated on the north shore of Lake Nicaragua, one of H. H. Bancroft's collaborators was led to insert into the early history of Central America an account of a completely mythical excursion by an equally nebulous Alvarado (Bancroft, *Central America*, II, 185).

[2] Hernando de Alvarado; see Winship, p. 594.

[3] This monument, which was a well-known camping place, is of great interest because its smooth rock wall is a sort of stone autograph album, on which may be found the inscriptions of many travelers. One of the oldest is the carved signature of the first Spanish governor of New Mexico, Juan de Oñate, who passed that way in 1605.

[4] The name derives from Akóme, meaning "people of the white rock", and the pueblo, in the Queres tongue of the inhabitants, is called Ako. This famous *peñol* lies about seventy miles west of the Río Grande and about sixty miles east of Zuñi. In the middle of a cliff-lined valley, the mesa on which the town is built towers three hundred and fifty-seven feet above the surrounding plain. In many places the rock sides of this sandstone Gibraltar of the desert are not merely perpendicular, but actually overhanging. On the summit, which is seventy acres in extent, perches the village, little changed today from what it was four hundred years ago, and holding the distinction of being the oldest continuously occupied town in the United States.

[5] The ascent described here seems more arduous than the Ladder Trail on the northwest side of the rock, an ancient trail much in use today. There are toe holds cut in the rock which show generations of wear. However, even in 1540 it is likely that there was more than one trail up to Acoma. Perhaps the conquerors were taken up the very steep ascent on the northeast, and were not shown the Ladder Trail, which would have provided an easier climb than they apparently had to make.

[6] Winship, p. 491. Some fields were tended at Acomita on the plain

some distance from the base of the rock, but a few plants were also grown on the summit, even though all the soil in which the corn was planted had had to be carried up the dizzy cliff path on the backs of Indians. Firewood, timbers, and even the adobe clay to make the buildings likewise had to be brought from the plain. Cisterns to catch rain water were hollowed out of the rock on the summit, but much of the water needed by the villagers was borne up the cliff in jars on the heads of women. The jars were made by the Acoma women, who were then and are today among the most expert of the Pueblo potters.

[7] "Relación del suceso"; see Winship, p. 575.

[8] Winship, p. 491.

[9] One of the most bitter and heroic battles in American border history was fought in 1599 when part of Juan de Oñate's army was sent to Acoma to avenge the massacre of a party of soldiers (led by Juan de Zaldívar, one of Coronado's captains) who had all been killed except five; these five jumped from the top of the rock, and four miraculously survived and escaped. The avengers, commanded by Juan de Zaldívar's brother Vicente, gained access to the village by scaling an undefended outlying pinnacle; but the warriors held out for two days as house after house was battered down around them by cannon balls. In 1696 Diego de Vargas, leader in the reconquest of New Mexico, was unable to breach the defenses of the rebellious Acomans.

[10] Spanish for "lake." The pueblo was settled by the Queres tribe in 1699, some time after the Spanish occupation of New Mexico.

[11] Cabeza de Vaca and his party had discovered this river and ascended some of its lower stretches, but had not given it a name. Jaramillo astutely observed that "this river comes from the northwest and flows about southeast, which shows that it certainly flows into the North Sea [the Gulf of Mexico]" (see Winship, p. 587).

[12] Some writers have maintained that the towns of Tiguex were on the west side of the Río Grande, since it was stated that in the spring the army, which had settled in the villages, had to cross the river when leaving for Pecos. However, excavators have found old ruins scattered more profusely on the east bank. That controversy on this detail is pointless is shown by a more careful reading of the documents. Castañeda stated (Winship, p. 519): "Tiguex is a province with twelve villages on the banks of a large, torrential river, *some villages on one side and some on the other.*" He made a similar statement elsewhere (Winship, p. 495): "... and as there were twelve villages, some of them went on one side of the river and some on the other." Obregón, writing much later, said (p. 20): "On this river of Tiguex they found a number of pueblos with houses of lesser height, built and grouped on both banks of the said river."

[13] Jaramillo; see Winship, p. 587.

[14] These towns were probably on the sites of modern San Lázaro and Galisteo.

[15] Cicuyé was the Tigua name; the Pecos people called themselves Pe-kúsh. By 1540 the ancient settlement on the upper Pecos had grown to be the largest Indian town within the present United States, having a population of more than two thousand. This easternmost of the pueblos was built on an elevated rocky outcrop a few miles south of the modern town of Pecos and a mile or so west of the Pecos River, which at this point changes from a brawling trout brook to a wide, pleasant, willow-lined stream. In the cupping high valley, seven thousand feet in elevation and completely surrounded by mountains—to the north, the bare summit of Pecos Baldy and its companion peaks; to the east, the chain of the Tecolote; and to the west, the red cliffs of the Pecos Mesa—the mound on which the Indian town was built rises like a boss on a shield. From the roofs of the two great pyramids of buildings, each containing more than five hundred rooms, the inhabitants had an expansive view in all directions. The pueblo was perfectly fitted for defense; the blank outer faces of the houses were skirted by a circle of stone walls, and on each side a deep arroyo, containing never-failing cool springs, served as a sort of moat.

[16] The raising of cotton is doubtful, as in the "Relación del suceso" (see Winship, p. 575) the statement is made that they did not do so.

[17] Obregón, p. 21. He wrote about 1584, and had probably talked with veterans of the Coronado expedition.

[18] Winship, p. 523.

[19] These stones were plentiful in Cicuyé, for most of the turquoise supply of the ancient Southwest was mined at a place that the Spaniards must have passed midway between Tiguex and Cicuyé, near the modern town of Los Cerrillos. But the Indians were careful not to reveal their diggings to the white men, who had already shown themselves to be greedy collectors of the sky-blue stones.

[20] "Relación del suceso"; see Winship, p. 576.

[21] It is true that the narrative of Cabeza de Vaca gives a description of the bison. But Wagner believed that this was interpolated, possibly by a bookseller, into the narrative just before printing, on the basis of facts given in Coronado's letter of October 20, 1541, or in the "Relación postrera," or in some other early report from the Coronado expedition. Wagner doubted that Cabeza de Vaca saw even one buffalo (see Wagner, *Spanish Southwest*, I, 46–48).

[22] It was on a branch of the Río Yaqui and is not to be identified with the Vacapa of the Marcos report.

[23] "I myself saw and followed them," wrote Castañeda, in one of the

few references to his own acts. "They had extremely large bodies and long wool; their horns were very thick and large, and when they ran they threw back their heads and put their horns on the ridge of their backs. They are used to rough country, so that we could not catch them and had to leave them" (Winship, p. 487).

²⁴ Nothing more than this is reported in the chronicles regarding his route to the Colorado, but the shortage of water in coastal Sonora would have precluded travel along the sandy Gulf, and no assertion is made anywhere that his route took him along this shore. It is likely, as Sauer (*Road to Cíbola*, pp. 37–38; "Communication") has suggested, that the Indians led him through Papaguería by an old trail up the valley of the Río Altar and thence by one way or another to Sonoita, the desert gateway on the present international border. He would then have followed the old way that came to be called the Camino del Diablo, the Devil's Highway, the main road from Sonora to California in colonial days.

²⁵ Winship, p. 485.

²⁶ Castañeda; see Winship, p. 486.

²⁷ The tribe that opposed the crossing by Díaz may have been the hitherto friendly Yumas. The men with Díaz made no mention of the Gila River; also, they reached the quicksands of the delta in only four days' march downstream after the crossing was made.

²⁸ Winship, p. 486.

²⁹ Obregón, p. 25.

³⁰ Castañeda; see Winship, p. 501.

³¹ Mota Padilla, p. 158.

Chapter 9: The Secret of the Gulf

¹ The author of the "Segunda relación" described it in curious terms: "The place that we sought when we went forth to discover this river was the Seven Cities, because the governor, Nuño de Guzmán, had news of them, and of a river that came out at the South Sea, which was four or five leagues wide and across which the Indians, who were very warlike, put up an iron chain to hold back canoes and *balsas* that might try to ascend it" ("Segunda relación," p. 303).

² The ships that these men built and sailed were oared galleys, brigantines, lateen-rigged launches, and caravels. In all probability the ships of Alarcón were of the caravel type, a vessel almost universally used by the Spaniards in their great voyages of exploration from the time of Columbus well through the sixteenth century. (The galleon of romance did not come into use until later, and was a lumbering, roomy ship designed for service as an armed merchantman.) The caravel, the

type of vessel that was used in the first circumnavigation of the globe, had a design remarkably suited to the demands of blue-water exploration. These ships were somewhat round in hull with rather high bulwarks, and had a bowsprit and square fighting castles at bow and stern. The usual Spanish type had three or four masts, all lateen-rigged like a Venetian galley except the foremast, which was square-rigged. They may or may not have been decked. The caravels were light in draft, were more easily maneuvered than earlier types of ship, and were fairly fast sailers for their time, with maximum speeds of from eight to fifteen miles an hour.

[3] "The mariner is bound in all things which pertain to the ship, to go to the forest and fetch wood, to saw and to make planks, to make spars and ropes, to bake, to man the boat with the boatswain, to stow goods and unstow them; and at every hour when the mate shall send him to go and fetch spars and ropes, to carry planks, and to put on board all the victuals of the merchants, to heave the vessel over, and to aid to repair the vessel, and he is bound to do everything to improve the conditions of the ship and of all which belongs to the ship while he shall be engaged to the ship." So runs a part of the *Consulado del Mare*, the Spanish common-law code of the sea which was compiled as early as the thirteenth century (see Taylor, pp. 632–633).

[4] In the *Consulado del Mare* it is expressly stated that "a mariner ought not to undress himself if he is not in a port for wintering. And if he does so, for each time he ought to be plunged into the sea with a rope from the yard-arm three times; and after three times offending, he ought to lose his salary and the goods which he has in the ship" (see Taylor, p. 633).

[5] By one of the curious accidents of time, one may read Hernando de Alarcón's report of his voyage in Italian, French, or Elizabethan English, but not in the Spanish in which the report was first written. The original manuscript has been lost, but it was fortunately at hand when Ramusio's collection was prepared. The Italian version agrees at most points with the account given by Herrera, who used the original while writing his early general history.

[6] Alarcón, "Relatione," p. 363.

[7] Now San Blas in the state of Nayarit.

[8] On the choked delta lands of this immense river system draining the Southwest, the turbid, silt-laden waters are never still; the ebb tide clashes with the incoming flood and forms a great thundering "bore" or wall of water which sweeps up the winding channel for miles, in some places attaining a height of twelve feet.

[9] Not only Alarcón, but Cabeza de Vaca, Fray Marcos, Coronado, De Soto, and after them such leaders as Francisco Chamuscado, were all

given the title of Children of the Sun by the natives. Sun worship was universal among the various tribes that received these discoverers, and to welcome white-skinned strangers under this title does not seem unnatural. Among the Pueblo tribes there are many myths dealing with twin boys, the Children of the Sun, who were given knowledge and dominion over men. To these natives, creation and also life after death were always associated with the underworld, which was properly the house of the Sun, to which returned the spirits of the dead. W. J. Perry (*The Children of the Sun* [New York, 1923]) developed at length a theory that the first settlers of the Pueblo region were led by Children of the Sun who were members of a ruling caste from Mexico who came there to work the turquoise, gold, and other deposits. The reception of the first white men in the Southwest as emissaries of the god is paralleled by Montezuma's superstitious fear that Cortés and his men were sent by the blond Aztec culture god, Quetzalcoatl.

[10] The cross as a symbolic design is almost universally found among the American Indians, and usually represents the Evening Star, an important deity in their heavenly pantheon.

[11] Alarcón was told that the river people lived in communal huts of wood, plastered outside with earth, and that they stayed by the riverside only during the growing season. The people were monogamous, the maidens were chaste before marriage, widowers remained six months or a year unmarried, and adulterers were put to death. Kinsmen or members of the same clan could not marry. The dead were burned, and the sick were treated by medicine men with charms and by breathing upon the patient. These people, who were of the Yuma and Mojave tribes, were more civilized than those lower down the river. They also used tobacco; they ate fish, maize, squash, and a sort of millet which they ground on stones and cooked in earthen pots.

[12] He said also that beyond Cíbola was a great river which had "crocodiles" from whose hides shields were made. Possibly this was a reference to the alligators of the lower Mississippi.

[13] Regarding the manner of the negro's death, the old man reported: "The lord of Cíbola inquired of him whether he [Esteban] had other brethren. He answered that he had an infinite number, and that they had a great store of weapons with them, and that they were not very far from there. When the lord heard this, many of the chiefs consulted together, and they resolved to kill him, so that he might not give news to his brethren where they dwelt, and for this cause they slew him, and cut him into many pieces, which were divided among all those chief lords, that they might know assuredly that he was dead."

[14] Probably a chief of the Mojave tribe.

[15] This personage was nobly arrayed in "a garment closed before and

behind and open at the sides, fastened with buttons, wrought with white and black checkerwork; it was very soft and well made, being of the skins of certain delicate fishes called sea breams."

[16] It is likely that the cross erected by Alarcón to mark his upper limit of exploration was not at the point where Melchor Díaz discovered the message from him (see chap. 8). The differences in the two accounts are marked: the point given by Alarcón in his account was eighty-five leagues up the river, and that by Díaz only fifteen; Alarcón carved his message on a cross, but did not mention any letters; Díaz found the letters under a tree, not under a cross; the messages he found made mention of the ships, not of the boat party, and stated that Alarcón had gone back with the ships to New Spain. Even considering that Castañeda's account of the Díaz discovery is secondhand, these differences are great enough to indicate that Alarcón left at least two messages in widely separated places, and that the cross he erected was never found.

[17] Alarcón himself said that it was eighty-five river leagues; fifty-five were made on the first trip, and thirty beyond this on the second. Fifty-five leagues is equal to about a hundred and sixty-five miles, which would have brought him close to the junction of the Gila River and the Colorado. Thirty leagues more would have brought him above the Gila about a hundred miles. Here he would have encountered the Chocolate Range, the first mountains of any considerable height to be found lining the river on an ascent from the mouth, and it was probably here that the Cumana sorcerer tried to bar their passage with the magical reeds. Some writers argue, since no mention was made by Alarcón of passing the mouth of the Gila, that he never reached it and the distance he assertedly covered is exaggerated; but this is negative evidence, and as Alarcón wrote his report in a great hurry he might easily have forgotten to mention that river. Also, as Bandelier pointed out, "at the time of the year when Alarcón made his exploring expedition the Gila is so low that it would scarcely attract attention from anyone who, like Alarcón, was ascending the main stream in boats" (*Final Report*, I, 108 n.).

[18] Indeed, Mendoza issued orders to Alarcón to make a second voyage in a determined new attempt to communicate with Coronado and Melchor Díaz—who was known to have left San Gerónimo in search of the fleet (see Mendoza, "Instrucción"). In these instructions, written May 31, 1541, the viceroy gave Alarcón full credit for discovering the Río de Buena Guía: "you are the discoverer of that river and the people there hold you in good will." In other documents it is stated that three vessels were made ready for this second voyage to settle the Buena Guía country and to reinforce Coronado, but when they were

Notes

on the point of sailing the Mixtón War broke out in New Galicia, and Alarcón was placed on duty with thirty men at Autlán to garrison the town against the rebellious Indians (see Wagner, *Spanish Voyages*, pp. 57–63; n. 46, p. 316).

[10] During the lifetime of Alarcón and for long after his time, it was general knowledge among the Spaniards that Baja California was a peninsula; Obregón (p. 197) clearly stated that it was part of the mainland and communicated with the countries of Quivira, Cíbola, New Mexico, and Florida. It appeared on all the maps as a peninsula until the Briggs map of 1625 introduced the idea, which had been a hazy theory steadily gaining credence, that the Gulf did not end at the mouth of the Colorado but extended northward beyond until it joined the Strait of Anian. Thereafter, for some time, the misled geographers again showed the Amazonian land of Cortés as a great island, until at last the famous Jesuit explorer, Father Eusebio Kino, took the trail in 1701 and repeated the forgotten demonstration (see Wagner, *Spanish Voyages*, p. 388).

Chapter 10: The Winter of War

[1] There is no mention that he passed by Acoma on the usual Indian trail to the east. His party may have swung through Cebolleta and followed the course of the San José River.

[2] Possibly Mount Taylor (11,389 ft.) in the San Mateo Range.

[3] Winship, p. 492.

[4] These were the early Tigua towns in the vicinity of Isleta. The present pueblo, with a population of more than a thousand, is one of the largest of the surviving Indian villages. Isleta lies on the west bank of the Río Grande, fifteen miles south of Albuquerque, and may once, as its Spanish name suggests, have been an island settlement.

[5] They were probably the Piro settlements northeast from modern Socorro. Ten or more ruined ancient towns have been located, some of them near the salt lakes east of the forbidding Manzano Mountains. One of Coronado's captains visited some of these towns the following year (see chap. 13).

[6] See Gómara, *Historia*, p. 288.

[7] See Winship, p. 493. The word he used was probably *hakwichis,* the Wichita Indian word for "metal."

[8] De Soto's chronicler, in telling of the coming of a Mississippi River chieftain named Aquixo with a colorful armada of two hundred canoes, said that "the barge in which the *cacique* came had an awning at the poop, under which he sat, and the barges of the other chiefs had the like" (see Hodge and Hays, p. 203).

[9] Winship, p. 493.

[10] *Ibid.*, p. 494.

[11] This headquarters town of the Spaniards at Tiguex was referred to by Mota Padilla (p. 160) under the odd name of "Coofer." This may be a corruption of Alcanfor—the Spanish word for "camphor"—which seems to have been applied to the town by the occupying army of Coronado.

[12] He was probably the Juan Alemán, or "German John," whose petition is given in A. F. and F. Bandelier, *Historical Documents* (Hackett, ed.), I, 33.

[13] Castañeda; see Winship, p. 495.

[14] *Ibid.*, p. 497.

[15] Mota Padilla, p. 162.

[16] Mota Padilla recorded (p. 162) that the other men who were killed were named Carbajal, Benítez, and Alonso de Castañeda; see Aiton, "Coronado's Muster Roll," which lists one Francisco de Caraujal (p. 564) and one Mathin de Castañeda (p. 566).

Chapter 11: The Devil in the Jug

[1] The tribe was to suffer a similar chastisement by the Spaniards some years later, for in 1583 Antonio de Espejo, angered by the murder of two friars and by the refusal of the Tigua town of Puala, or Puaray, to supply him with food, laid siege to the town and burned it. The Pueblo Revolt of 1680 was led by Popé, an Indian of San Juan on the Río Grande.

[2] Winship, p. 520.

[3] Later, at Taos.

[4] There are various traditional explanations for the construction of the *estufa* underground. One is that it is excavated in imitation of the primordial cave in the center of the earth where the human family was created, and whence the people climbed up a pine ladder to the daylight through an orifice called *Sipapu*, an opening like the hatchway entrance to the *estufa*. The ladder always rested on a low platform, not on the bare earth. The walls of the chamber were decorated with sacred symbols, the thunderbird or animals of the chase, or perhaps legendary heroes or historic scenes, all in magnificent color.

[5] Winship, pp. 520–522. Tigua women prepared the corn for eating in a way different from that of other Indians. Their method was more fully described by Mota Padilla (see Day, "Mota Padilla," p. 97).

[6] Mota Padilla, p. 160.

[7] Winship, p. 521.

[8] *Ibid.*, p. 522.

[9] They evidently never saw any of the doll-like personal fetishes, or *katcinas,* revered by the Indians.

[10] "We regarded them as witches," wrote Alvarado in his report (Winship, p. 595), "because they say that they go up into the sky and other things of the same sort." The medicine men of the pueblos, whose conjuring tricks are equal to any performed by the fakirs of India, are able to exercise a power of levitation which might have impressed Alvarado in this way.

[11] Winship, p. 544.

[12] The only reference to cremation among the Pueblos is found in Mota Padilla (p. 160): "On one occasion the Spaniards, when an Indian had died, saw erected a large pyre of firewood upon which they put the body covered with a blanket, and then all the people of the pueblo, men and women, went and put on the bed of firewood cornmeal, squashes, beans, *atole* [a sort of corn-meal gruel], roast corn, and whatever else they are accustomed to eat, and set fire to it all over, so that shortly all was turned to ashes with the body." Alarcón, however, reported that the Indians of the lower Colorado also burned their dead.

[13] Had the white men stumbled upon the excavations made by the Pueblo miners, they would have been astounded at the extent of the operations. Immense pits had been cut in the solid rock of the mountain, and tens of thousands of tons of ore had been broken out and moved almost barehanded, the work having been done with the crudest of stone tools. From the level of the largest pit a number of tunnels and stopes had been run into the rock heart of the hill. In these "caves" have been found numerous veins of turquoise, from an eighth of an inch to two inches in thickness, as well as strips of gold-bearing quartz. It is almost inconceivable that entire mountains were honeycombed by these Indian toilers, working without powder or machinery.

[14] The Queres tribe survives today in the Río Grande towns of Santo Domingo, San Felipe, and Cochití, as well as at Santa Ana on the Jemez River and at Acoma.

[15] Probably on the site of modern Galisteo, about twenty miles east of Santa Fe. The other Tano towns may have been on the sites of San Cristóbal, San Lázaro, and San Marcos.

[16] Little else that Coronado said can be surely known, however, for the letter, which was in answer to one written by Charles V from Madrid on June 11, 1540, and probably delivered to Coronado by his courier Juan Gallego, has not been found.

[17] Castañeda; see Winship, p. 502.

[18] Probably at or near Bacoachi.

Chapter 12: Astray in the Buffalo Plains

[1] Coronado, "Letter to the King, October 20, 1541" (see Winship, p. 580); according to Castañeda (see Winship, p. 503), it was May 5.

[2] The Pecos River was the immemorial Indian road from the pueblos to the buffalo plains, and in later years was called the Río de las Vacas, or River of the Cows. Wrote Jaramillo (see Winship, pp. 587–588): "It seems to me that we went rather toward the northeast [an obvious slip for 'southeast'] to reach this river where we crossed it, and after crossing this, we turned more to the left hand, which would be more to the northeast, and began to enter the plains where the cows are."

[3] Probably in the vicinity of Puerto de Luna, New Mexico.

[4] "Letter to the King, October 20, 1541" (see Winship, p. 581).

[5] Winship, p. 542.

[6] That is, like those of Spain.

[7] Winship, p. 542.

[8] *Ibid.* The quantity of buffalo bones dotting the prairies in early days was so great, according to a statement by Colonel Inman, that in Kansas alone, between 1863 and 1881, two and a half million dollars was paid by fertilizer manufacturers for bones collected along the railways, representing, at eight dollars a ton, the skeletons of thirty-one million bison.

[9] "Relación del suceso" (see Winship, p. 576). The temper and fighting qualities of the buffalo were later so highly prized that, as Mota Padilla related (p. 165), at the time of the fiestas celebrating the accession of King Luis I of Spain the Count of San Mateo de Valparaiso arranged to have a female buffalo brought to Mexico City to fight in the ring, an attraction which proved to be so great a drawing card that almost all the people of the region came to see it, "to the great profit of the scaffold-maker that day."

[10] The name, meaning "buffalo eaters," is the old Comanche name for the Tonkawa tribe of west-central Texas, early progenitors of the Apache warriors of later centuries (see Hodge, *Handbook*, II, 339). They or a similar tribe had already been encountered by Coronado living in huts on the upper Gila near Chichilticalli.

[11] The word *tejas* or *texas* ("friends") was used by the Hasínai (to whom it later came to be applied) to indicate a large group of Caddoan and other stock who were their allies (see Hodge, *op. cit.*, II, 738). Guzmán's guide Tejo, as suggested by his name, may have been one of the Teyas. One can readily imagine that the word was attached to the plains wanderers by the men of Coronado who, when asking the

name of the tribe, received the amicable greeting of "Friends, friends!" But Castañeda, in describing the havoc wrought by the Teyas in the ruined villages west of Cicuyé, said that they were called Teyas by the Pueblo Indians because they were "brave men," just as the name of the savage Chichimec tribe of northern Mexico was used generally to designate any extremely warlike and wild native race (see Winship, p. 524).

[12] Winship, p. 527.

[13] See p. 23.

[14] Winship, p. 588.

[15] On the journey one Teya was seen to shoot a buffalo through both shoulders with an arrow, "which would be a good shot with an harquebus" (Castañeda; see Winship, p. 507).

[16] "Relación postrera"; see Winship, p. 570. According to Mota Padilla (p. 164), the flesh of the female was thought to be insipid and tasteless, "which is the providence of the Almighty, so that the Indians will kill the males and leave the females to multiply."

[17] Mota Padilla, p. 165.

[18] Winship, p. 527.

[19] Haxa was not the Pawnee province of Harahey, according to Hodge (Benavides, XIV, 145 n.), but was Aixaos, or Aish, the home of a tribe of the Caddo confederacy which lived in eastern Texas. Haxa has often been identified with Harahey or Arache in southeastern Nebraska.

[20] Because it is highly improbable that Cabeza de Vaca got this far to the north on his way to the Sonora with his three companions, the Indians of the upper Brazos must have heard only indirectly of this rite in honor of the Children of the Sun. Doubtless they had learned of it from an old blind, bearded man—possibly a Jumano—whom Coronado later found living among them. This old man indicated to the Spaniards by signs that many suns before, off in the direction of New Spain, he had seen four men like them—clearly Cabeza de Vaca and his three friends (Jaramillo; see Winship, pp. 588–589).

[21] Castañeda; see Winship, p. 506.

[22] The Teyas may have been early Comanches, or they may have been a tribe of Caddoan or other stock like the Hasínai (to whom the Spanish much later attached the name of "Texas" Indians).

[23] The *sambenito* ("St. Benedict") was the long penitent garment worn by persons convicted by the Inquisition.

[24] See Winship, p. 507.

[25] "Letter to the King, October 20, 1541"; see Winship, p. 581.

Chapter 13: The Conquest of Quivira

[1] Castañeda; see Winship, p. 508.

[2] This stream was undoubtedly the Arkansas River in the vicinity of Ford, Kansas, near the old cow town of Dodge City—a crossing used earlier by the buffalo and the Indian, and later by the soldier, the trapper, the cowpuncher, and the settler. This is the only river in the region which runs northeast for anything like thirty leagues. No other stream is mentioned in the accounts of the trip, although several other good-sized rivers, notably the Red, the Canadian, and the Cimarrón, would have had to be crossed in their upper stretches. Perhaps Jaramillo mentioned only the River of Peter and Paul because Sopete, the guide, recognized it, asserting that the province of Quivira was not far beyond (see Winship, p. 589).

[3] Only passing reference need be made to the theory of Donoghue that Coronado's cavalry never left the Llano Estacado of the Texas panhandle, and that Quivira lay on the upper Canadian River. Donoghue developed this theory by depreciating the various testimonies on the distances traveled and by fitting a few selected contemporary descriptions of the country traversed to certain geological landmarks of Texas. Likewise, he assumed, rather dangerously, that the men of Coronado did not cross the Red, Canadian, or Cimarrón rivers, merely because these crossings were not mentioned in the somewhat brief accounts of the journey. Donoghue did not attempt to show that the valley of the Canadian River was inhabited at this time; nor did his theory take account of the fact that several of the chroniclers gave easily recognizable descriptions of the rolling river country of central Kansas, described the typical flora of the region, and in general presented a mass of evidence, linguistic and ethnological, that the maize-growing tribes which they encountered living in grass lodges were almost certainly the Wichita and Pawnee known to have occupied the valleys of the Arkansas and Kansas rivers in the sixteenth century.

[4] See Winship, p. 590.

[5] The name Quivira is probably a Spanish derivation from *Kidikwius*, the name the Wichita Indians used for themselves, or from *Kirikuruks*, the Pawnee name for the Wichita (see Hodge, *Handbook*, II, 346–347).

[6] See Winship, p. 590.

[7] "Relación del suceso"; see Winship, p. 577.

[8] The name of the province of Harahey, between the Platte and Republican rivers in southern Nebraska, was derived from *Awáhi*, the Wichita name for the Skidi Pawnee (see Hodge, *op. cit.*, I, 532).

[9] He was little more than a degree wrong—not a bad estimate considering the crude instruments of the time.

[10] "Letter to the King, October 20, 1541"; see Winship, p. 582.

[11] It was certainly a rarity, since the chief must have obtained it from the Indians of the Lake Superior region through a long and indirect process of barter.

[12] Coronado said that he was never out of the plains country, and therefore he probably did not reach the forests of northeastern Kansas or the bluffs of the Missouri Valley. The chief discoveries in Quivira were geographical; as a result of the expeditions of Coronado and of Hernando de Soto (who was to spend the coming winter on the lower Arkansas just east of the Oklahoma-Arkansas line and whose scouts may have encountered the Kansa tribe) much information about the Mississippi basin was collected. At the time Castañeda wrote his recollections, he was able to describe with some assurance the configuration of the American midland. "The great river of Espíritu Santo [the Mississippi] which Don Hernando de Soto discovered in the country of Florida, flows through this country. It passes through a province called Arache [Harahey], according to the reliable accounts which were obtained here. The sources were not visited because, according to what they said, it [the Missouri] comes from a very distant country in the mountains of the South Sea, from the part that sheds its waters on to the plains. It flows across all the level country and breaks through the mountains of the North Sea [the Gulf of Mexico] and comes out where the people with Don Hernando de Soto navigated it. On account of this, and also because it has large tributaries, it is so mighty when it enters the sea [and here Castañeda was recalling a part of the narrative of Cabeza de Vaca] that they lost sight of the land before the water ceased to be fresh" (see Winship, p. 529). Unfortunately, the narrative of Castañeda was not available to the mapmakers of the sixteenth century.

[13] The daily travel records left by the various members of the Coronado expedition for the period of the Quivira excursion do not exactly agree, but a comparison of these with the salient dates appears to show that the party left Tiguex the third week in April, left the ravines the last week in May, reached the Arkansas River on June 29, reached the villages of Quivira the first week in July, left Quivira the first week in August, and were back again in Tiguex about the middle of September.

Coronado in his letter of October 20 to the king stated that he left Tiguex on April 23 and reached Quivira after seventy-seven days, traveling forty-two days from the ravines; this would leave thirty-five days for traveling from Tiguex to the ravines. Castañeda stated that they took thirty-seven days to reach the ravines, but he is probably in error in giving the date of departure as May 5. The date of the departure from the ravines according to Coronado's reckoning would be May 27, which agrees closely with Mota Padilla's statement that the council was held on Ascension Day (May 26) and with the statement in the "Relación del suceso" that the great river was reached in thirty days (for in order to do this the cavalry would have had to leave about May 30, since the river was discovered on June 29, the feast day of Saints Peter and Paul). Coronado stated that they reached Quivira in forty-two days, or about July 6, and remained in Quivira twenty-five days, which would bring him to August 1; Castañeda said that the riders took forty-eight days to reach Quivira and left there "early in August," whereas Jaramillo asserted that to the best of his memory it was "after the middle of August." Castañeda gave forty days as the time from Quivira back to Tiguex, which would put the return about the middle of September. According to Castañeda also, the army under Arellano remained in the ravines for a fortnight and then returned to Tiguex in twenty-five days; if the general separated from them around May 27, this would bring the army back to the settlements around July 5.

[14] If anything was justifiable to a man in Coronado's position, it was the execution of this Indian who all along had been his secret enemy. But Mota Padilla (p. 166), writing just two hundred years after the deed, found in it a curious moral. "It was a bad act, in truth, for in other circumstances he might have told them of other pueblos of New Mexico or Florida. In this province there is certain to be much copper, so that the poor Indian might thus have deceived himself; or he might have mistaken the road in going to find the quantities of gold with which he had promised to load the horses and even carts. It must have been the punishment of God that they did not find these riches on this expedition, because this ought to have been the secondary object of that journey and the first the conversion of all those heathen; but they pushed aside the first and coveted the second, and thus the misfortune is not so much that these labors should have come to naught, as that up to the present such a large number of souls have remained in their ignorance."

[15] Castañeda; see Winship, p. 510.

[16] Castañeda, putting together scraps of knowledge he later acquired regarding the explorations of Hernando de Soto, hazarded the erroneous guess that the Río de Tiguex, or Río Grande, joined the Mississippi (see Winship, p. 510).

[17] "Gentleman of Elvas," Smith translation (see Hodge and Lewis, p. 244). Castañeda also referred to this amazing chance (see Winship,

p. 510): "After I got back to New Spain I heard them [probably some men of the De Soto expedition] say that the Indian told them she had run away from other men like them for nine days, and she gave the names of some captains; from which we ought to believe that we were not far from the region they discovered, although they said they were more than two hundred leagues inland."

[18] The first of these two ancient towns was the forerunner of the present Chamita, site of the first Spanish church in New Mexico (its old name of Yugeuingge was changed to San Gabriel by Governor Juan de Oñate when he installed his capital there in 1600), on the west bank of the Río Grande some miles north of Santa Fe. The other was the present San Juan, across on the east bank; it is to be remembered as the second permanent settlement founded by Europeans within the borders of the United States.

[19] Castañeda; see Winship, p. 511. It is true that there was silver in New Mexico; but the shining metal, which the Indians used also for painting their faces, was probably antimony, galena, or mica ground with clay.

[20] See Winship, p. 511.

[21] "Relación del suceso"; see Winship, p. 575.

[22] The remains of ten of their villages, of which the largest and farthest downstream was Trenaquél, are known today, reaching south from Isleta to San Marcial, through the Socorro district; but these people were almost wiped out about 1675 by raiding Apaches, and today only a few Mexicanized families squat in the abandoned stone ruins.

[23] Above it today a vast reservoir of water is impounded by the Elephant Butte Dam.

[24] One syndicate in the 'eighties sank a shaft a hundred feet through undisturbed bedrock in search of "buried" gold.

Chapter 14: Coronado Has a Fall

[1] This bloody rebellion, commonly called the Mixton War, broke out in New Galicia at about the time Coronado was setting off with his army for Quivira. The fighting strength of Coronado's government in the province had been so reduced by his departure that barely two hundred men were left to defend the wide territories under his authority. It seemed a propitious time for the "devil-worshiping" natives of Zacatecas to declare a holy war against the white settlers, and these savages easily enlisted many lowland Indians, who had been receiving brutal treatment at the hands of the Spaniards since the days of Nuño de Guzmán.

Cristóbal de Oñate, the highly capable lieutenant governor, warned Mendoza as early as Christmas Day, 1540, that the natives were growing disobedient and were meeting secretly. In the spring of 1541, a force of seventeen horsemen sent by Oñate under Miguel de Ibarra fought a four-hour battle at the Indian stronghold of Tepestistaque. Ibarra evaded a trap and retreated to Tonalá, or Guadalajara, rescuing on the road a number of Spanish settlers and negro servants imperiled by the general uprising of thousands of Indians.

The almost impregnable fortified height of Mixton in the wilds of southern Zacatecas was besieged by Oñate on the eve of Palm Sunday, April 10, 1541. At about eight in the morning, during an eclipse of the sun, a horde of natives took the Spanish camp by surprise, killed some thirteen Spaniards and three hundred Indian allies, and drove the remainder in retreat to Guadalajara.

Nochistlán, another citadel of the "terrible Chichimecs," was stormed on Midsummer Day by a Spanish force led by the impetuous Pedro de Alvarado, governor of Guatemala and former companion of Cortés. In a driving rain, the bull-like tactics of Alvarado led to an overwhelming repulse by the Indians; in the following retreat Alvarado was fatally injured when a bolting horse reared and fell upon his body.

On September 28, Guadalajara was attacked by a triumphant throng of "fifty thousand" Indian braves, who destroyed most of the city; after a four-hour battle, however, they were beaten off as a result of a heavy cannonading and the miraculous intervention of St. Michael, whose feast day it was (see Mota Padilla, p. 135).

This disaster at last aroused Mendoza to set the full military strength of New Spain against the rebels. He raised an army of four hundred and fifty Spaniards and thousands of Aztec warriors, and led them personally in a hard-fought campaign culminating at the *peñol* of Mixton. After a siege of three weeks the Chichimecs, weakened by starvation and the defection of allies, surrendered during the last days of 1541. Early in 1542, a year after the first clash, the remotest regions of the province were brought to terms; the rebellion, which was the last concerted struggle of the natives of New Spain against their Spanish masters, had been followed by a plague of smallpox that killed five-sixths of the Indian population, making a renewal of the struggle out of the question.

The charge was made at the *visita* of Mendoza (see Aiton and Rey, Question 130) that the revolt had in fact been caused by the passage of the Coronado expedition through the province and the demands made by it upon the natives. Coronado in his testimony confirmed Mendoza's denial of the charge by pointing out that the army had passed along the coast at a place forty leagues from the hill of Tepestistaque where the first outbreak occurred. Coronado added further that Mendoza had purchased corn for the army from the towns of the province of Avalos, so that the natives and settlers along the route of the expedition should not suffer hunger or loss.

During the Mixton War the old complaint that the Coronado expedition had drained the province of its manpower was revived. However, none of his soldiers had been settlers in the regions that revolted; had the province of New Galicia remained at peace—as seemed likely at the time Coronado departed for the north—the restless cavaliers who went with him would have been a burden to the government, perhaps an active menace. But the withdrawal of the Coronado army to the north may have seemed to the mountain savages a promising opportunity for a successful rebellion.

[2] See Winship, p. 531.

[3] "Letter of October 20, 1541"; see Winship, p. 583.

[4] She was María Maldonado, wife of the *alguacil del campo,* Juan de Paladinas. She served the army as a sort of hospital corps (see A. F. and Fanny Bandelier, *Historical* [Hackett, ed.], p. 47): "She most kindly ministered to the sick of the army besides sewing and mending for them the best she could and doing many other good works for the soldiers in the field, where she on her part also suffered great hardships"—as well she might.

[5] Coronado's commission from the viceroy (see Aiton, "Coronado's Commission") was not mandatory on this point: "Regarding the said lands, you may hold them *(les tengays)* until other arrangements are provided and ordered by us or by the said viceroy of New Spain."

[6] "Letter of October 20, 1541"; see Winship, p. 583.

[7] Castañeda; see Winship, p. 531.

[8] "The gentlemen of Coronado's expedition were greatly chagrined at the return of their general because they wished to know and discover the secrets of that vast land and its termination on the sea, mainly because it was hinted and suspected that they had come near the great Salt Water River and the Northern Sea, where was thought certainly to lie the Strait of Newfoundland toward Ireland. The discovery of this coast and strait was desired so that they could travel by way of it to Spain and discover the nations of people in its environs and on its banks" (Obregón, p. 27).

[9] Castañeda; see Winship, p. 532.

[10] *Ibid.,* pp. 532–533.

[11] According to Mendieta, the Franciscan historian, Coronado had such a respect for Fray Juan de la Cruz that he ordered his men to bare their heads every time the friar's name was mentioned. The date of his death is given in the martyrologies as November 25, 1542.

[12] See Winship, p. 535.

[13] It was not more than nine, for the incident is mentioned in Gómara's *Historia general de las Indias,* published in 1552.

[14] Jaramillo had a different understanding of the friar's death: "Those who did it were the lay servants, or these same Indians whom he took back from Tiguex, in return for the good deeds which he had done" (see Winship, p. 592). "It was remembered," wrote Mota Padilla (p. 167), who gave the year of the friar's death as 1542, "that at his passing many prodigies took place; the land was flooded, comets and balls of fire were seen, and the sun was hidden." Vetancurt, who said in the *Menologio* that the friar set out on his mission after two years among the Quiviras, gave the date of his death as November 30, 1544.

[15] The town of Herington, Kansas, has erected a monument to Fray Padilla at a place marked by tradition as the site of his martyrdom.

[16] Mota Padilla, p. 167.

Chapter 15: The Inglorious Journey

[1] When Espejo came to New Mexico in 1583 he found three Christian Indians who had been left there by Coronado—Andrés of Cuyuacán, Gaspar of Mexico, and Anton of Guadalajara. These Indians had almost forgotten their native Mexican tongue (see Pacheco, XV, 180).

[2] Winship, p. 537.

[3] *Ibid.*

[4] Page 152. He had the story from a man named Ureña who escaped to Culiacán with five companions, one of them a priest who may have been Fray Antonio de Victoria.

[5] It was taken from a tree which Obregón (p. 155) called "the most terrible, strange, and venomous tree in the history of the whole world. . . . It is usually green, pretty, and full of flowers; it grows about twelve feet high, more or less; its leaf is something like that of the olive, although of a lighter green. Even those who merely sleep in its shade will swell up, and die of the swelling unless treated with antidotes and medicines. The juice and sap is white and curdled like well-soured milk, and is extremely deadly, poisonous, and diabolic in nature. With it they anoint their arrows, and the wound from these, even if tiny, causes such horrible and fearful agony that the victims die writhing." Obregón, who had traveled through this region, gave several pages of his narrative to a description of the fearful poison tree and its antidotes (a small herb and likewise "quince juice" used internally or as an application); and his wholesome horror of it had much to do with the avoidance of the Sonora Valley for many years by explorers.

[6] See Winship, p. 540.

[7] Castañeda; see Winship, p. 541.

[8] See Winship, p. 541. The exploits of Gallego were recalled in 1886 when on the headwaters of Pawnee Creek in Finney County in western Kansas a sword blade was found, on the corroded surface of which the finder was able to decipher the name "Juan Gallego" and the inscription *"No me saques sin razon   No me embaines sin honor* (Never draw me save with cause; never sheathe me save with honor)." Although it is likely that the name on this blade was that of a swordmaker Gallego, for a duplicate has been turned up in the National Museum of Mexico, it is more stirring to imagine that the sword of Juan Gallego the avenger, its red work done, had been found and carried among the southwestern Indians as an iron embodiment of Spanish fury, a grim relic to be passed reverently from hand to hand.

[9] Castañeda; see Winship, p. 538.

[10] There were two Sonora towns of this name, but the one meant by Castañeda was probably that on the Río Moctezuma not far above its junction with the Aros and about twenty-two miles east of Ures. It would therefore seem that Coronado avoided the Suya and Sonora valleys on his return route by descending the Moctezuma, the next watershed to the east.

[11] Castañeda was probably among the deserters, for he settled at Culiacán and it was there that he wrote his narrative many years later. In spite of his wearisome experience with Coronado, Castañeda was to volunteer for another exploration to the north (see introduction to Bibliography), from which he was not to return.

[12] "Like another Nimrod," wrote the fire-eating poet-historian Villagrá (p. 61, Espinosa translation), "seeking to conquer the very heavens, each went forth boasting that the world and all its glories would not suffice for him. And now they returned as confounded as the builders of the Tower of Babel when they were smitten by the hand of God. Some attempted to express regret that their depleted resources had made it necessary for them to return; others even denied that they had seen any cities or made any discoveries; others made many excuses for their conduct, asserting that they had been confronted with every imaginable adverse condition. Every one of the elements, hunger, thirst, freezing cold, burning heat, rain, and hail, were each in turn blamed for their failure, as if the exacting and cruel profession of the sanguinary Mars had promised them a life of ease and plenty instead of its natural and expected incidents!"

[13] Translation in Winship, p. 402.

[14] The Cabrillo-Ferrelo voyage up the Pacific coast was an outgrowth of Mendoza's plan to send out supporting fleets to accompany the Coronado expedition. Mendoza had decided to send Hernando de

Alarcón on a second voyage to the Colorado, in conjunction with another fleet that would follow the western side of the California peninsula in the track of Ulloa (see Mendoza, "Instrucción que debía observar"). Although the outbreak of the Mixton War prevented Alarcón from sailing, it was still considered advisable to send out at least three ships on the Pacific side of the peninsula in a last effort to make contact with Coronado.

By offering a share in the profits of the Coronado venture, Viceroy Mendoza obtained a partnership with Pedro de Alvarado (see Pedro de Alvarado, "Asiento"), who had assembled a large fleet for a voyage to the Spice Islands; and by the death of Alvarado's widow in 1542 Mendoza came into possession of all these ships. Five of these sailed in November, 1542, under the command of Ruy Gómez de Villalobos, Mendoza's brother-in-law, to colonize the Philippines. The other vessels of the Alvarado armada were used to carry out Mendoza's final efforts at exploring the northwest coast, efforts which were to lead to the discovery of Alta California by sea and to the pioneer mapping of its shores.

Francisco de Bolaños sailed from the port of Navidad on September 8, 1541. He was apparently charged with orders to get in touch with Coronado's men if possible, and particularly to look for a river emptying into the ocean which might be the Río de Nuestra Señora (the Río Grande); Hernando de Alvarado's report of the previous year had failed to mention in what direction the river flowed, and Mendoza presumably hoped that it might meet the Pacific and serve as a pathway to Tiguex, thus aiding colonists to sail there and make a permanent settlement.

But Bolaños did not get as far up the coast as Ulloa had done; somewhere to the south of Cedros Island the two largest ships were dismasted in a fierce December storm, and the fleet limped back to the mainland, reaching there in the spring of 1542 (see deposition of the aged Juan Fernández de Ladrillero in Wagner, *Spanish Voyages,* pp. 63–71; this man was pilot of Bolaños' ship the "San Gabriel," which was almost certainly the same vessel that had joined Alarcón's fleet at the Culiacán roadstead and made the rest of the voyage with him back to New Galicia).

As soon as Bolaños was well on his way, Mendoza started to outfit another small fleet that would follow the same route to the northwest coast. Conditions had now changed, for news from Coronado revealed that it was no longer possible to reach his forces in the new lands; indeed, at the time this expedition sailed Coronado was just leaving Culiacán on his march home to Mexico. The objectives of the new venture still included a search for the mouth of the Río de Nuestra

Señora, but chiefly it was hoped that the sailors could discover the elusive Northwest Passage and possibly even reach China.

Two ships—the flagship "San Salvador" with a gun deck, and the undecked "Victoria"—sailed from Navidad on June 27, 1542 (for an account of the voyage see Wagner, *Spanish Voyages*, pp. 79–93). The skillful and brave Juan Rodríguez Cabrillo was in command, but after his death at the Channel Island of San Miguel on January 3, 1543, the Levantine chief pilot, Bartolomé Ferrelo, or Ferrer, took charge. The Pacific coast was ascended as far north as the present California-Oregon boundary; off this point, on March 1, the ships almost foundered in a storm and were driven south. The fleet reached Navidad on April 14, 1543, after ten months of laborious discovery, during which only one man had been lost aside from the heroic Cabrillo.

The return of these two ships marked the beginning of one epoch but the end of another, for, although theirs was the first voyage of Spanish discovery to the western coast of what is now the United States, it was more than half a century before another expedition followed in its path. The Cabrillo voyage marked likewise the end of the first great period of Spanish discovery in the United States—the period of exploration which had had its inception in the exploits of Narváez in Florida in 1528, had reached its peak in 1541 and 1542 with the adventures of Coronado and De Soto in the continent's heart, and by 1543 had come abruptly to an end.

[15] Winship, p. 546.

Chapter 16: Farewell to Conquest

[1] The charge was later to be made against him that in 1543 he spent forty days at the town of Purificación at the expense of the inhabitants, which amounted to the worth of a gold peso a day in food for his horses and servants. The implication is clear that his presence there was not worth the cost. See Aiton, "The Later Career of Coronado," p. 300.

[2] See Coronado, "Residencia," *passim*. It may be noted that Coronado's commission as captain general (see Aiton, "Coronado's Commission") specified that he should continue to collect his salary as governor during his explorations, and also gave him the right to appoint lieutenants to govern New Galicia in his absence.

[3] Orozco, *Actos*, minutes under mentioned dates.

[4] See Aiton and Rey, *passim*.

[5] See A. F. and Fanny Bandelier, *Historical* (Hackett, ed.), p. 33.

[6] See Coronado, "Grant."

[7] Orozco, *Actos*, minutes of July 17, 1551.

[8] See Aiton, *Antonio de Mendoza*, p. 128, n. 24.

[9] In Béthencourt (IX, 500) it is stated, referring to Coronado's daughter Marina: "Shrouded in the robes of a Dominican nun she was buried in the convent of the said order in that city [Mexico] where her parents and grandparents were buried, in the renowned chapel of the crucifix beside her husband." The church is three blocks north of the central plaza of Mexico, in which is situated the great cathedral.

[10] See Barra.

[11] "In spite of what was said against Coronado in some of the accounts of those who went with him in that conquest, it is indubitable that without his ability and prudence, few would have returned from that sad expedition. He wisely divided the forces so that although they could not be beaten by the natives of the land, neither could they suffer the ravages of hunger and thirst as a consequence of massing all the soldiery in a single place." Thus, in an important history of Mexico, is tribute paid to Coronado's military skill; see Vicente Riva Palacio (ed.), *México a través de los siglos* (5 vols., Barcelona, 1888–1889), II, 261.

[12] The Castañeda manuscript, which gave the most complete account, was never published. Reference to Coronado is found in the papers concerning the offer made by Francisco Díaz de Vargas in 1584 to explore and settle New Mexico, but the name of the first discoverer of that land was not mentioned in a similar application by Juan Bautista Lomas de Colmenares in 1589. The documents pertaining to the proposal of Juan de Oñate for colonization briefly mentioned Cíbola, Tiguex, and Quivira, but placed the beginning of Coronado's expedition in 1538; and Oñate's versifying soldier-historian Villagrá treated the first discoveries of these towns with more poetry than truth. Indeed, the exploits of Coronado, when known at all, were misunderstood and undervalued even by the geographers who placed the magical names of the pueblos on their maps. For example, in the "Sumario de las Yndias tocante a la geografía" appearing in 1580, the following characteristic reason was given for neglect of these lands: "The provinces of Cíbola and Quivira are the last ones that have been reached from the Kingdom of Galicia. Cíbola is thirty [!] leagues from Culiacán toward the north, and Quivira two hundred from Cíbola to the east. Although of this there is little certainty, nor about the qualities of the country, except that it is cold from being in a high latitude, and therefore poor." Gómara's history gave a fairly accurate account, it is true, but his book was officially suppressed from 1553 to 1727. As late as 1619 the royal historiographer, Luis de Cabrera of Córdova, solemnly stated that Coronado penetrated toward the north but soon

returned, and that Fray Marcos de Niza went on and was killed by the Indians! Hence it is not surprising that the new explorations of the Southwest toward the end of the sixteenth century were carried out by men almost unaware of the first exploration of those lands by Coronado, and that their rediscovery at that time appealed to the minds of Spaniards as an original discovery. See Bandelier, *Documentary History of the Rio Grande Pueblos* (reprinted), pp. 253–255.

The location of Quivira on maps published after the middle of the sixteenth century was almost invariably shifted from the middle of the continent to the northwest coast. This curious error probably derives from a sentence in Gómara (chap. 15), following a description of Quivira: "They saw on the coast ships that had pelicans of gold and silver on the prows, bearing merchandise, and they believed these to be from Cathay and China, because they indicated they had sailed thirty days." The sentence seems to be an interpolation copied from the first volume of Ramusio's *Navigationi,* published in 1550. Ramusio made this identical statement on the authority of a gentleman who said that he had seen at the emperor's court in Flanders in 1541 a letter from Viceroy Mendoza stating that Coronado had discovered the Seven Cities and that beyond to the northwest after passing a great desert he had come to the sea, and there met the sailors in their merchant ships with golden prows. These golden-prowed ships existed only in the imagination of The Turk; but because of the statements of Gómara and Ramusio, mapmakers in Europe represented Quivira as being on the northwestern coast of America. Later, even Tiguex and Cicuyé were placed on this coast, in the general position of San Francisco Bay. For a survey of progress in mapping the Coronado discoveries, see Wagner, *Cartography.*

[13] "The discoveries shall not bear the name or title of conquests since, as they shall be made with all the peacefulness and charity we desire, we do not want the name to give occasion or pretext for violence and harm to the Indians" ("Ordenanzas," p. 152; translation by Bandelier).

[14] "No person, of whatever rank or condition he may be, shall by his own authority make new discoveries by land or by sea, nor incursion, nor new town, nor settlement, without license and writ from us or from whoever is empowered by us to give it, under pain of death and the loss of all his property for the benefit of our treasury ("Ordenanzas," p. 143; translation by Bandelier). This severe clause was actually invoked against the unlicensed venture of Antonio Gutiérrez de Humaña to Quivira in 1595 and that of Gaspar Castaño de Sosa to Cicuyé in 1590. Castaño was punished by exile to China, and was murdered at sea while trying to return to Mexico after the courts had

finally adjudged him innocent of the charge and he had been given the title of governor. But clearly the old days of personal conquest were over.

[15] Francisco de Ibarra had written on his return from his expedition to Sonora and Chihuahua, where he reached the famous ruins of Casas Grandes, that he had found a New Mexico as well as a New Biscay. The name of *"el otro Mexico"* was later shifted northward, perhaps because the piled terraces of the Pueblo Indians were thought to resemble the pyramids and terraced houses of the Aztecs of the "old" Mexico. "Nuevo Mexico" was first used to indicate the pueblo region of the Río Grande in the reports of the Ruíz party of 1582.

Chronology of the Discovery of the American Southwest

1527

June 17. Pánfilo de Narváez sails from Spain to explore and settle Florida.

December 13. Charles V decrees that an *audiencia* of five shall take over the government of New Spain.

1528

Nuño de Guzmán is made president of Pánuco, a province which had been detached from Fernando Cortés' domain of New Spain.

Spring. Cortés leaves Mexico for Spain to answer charges before Charles V.

April 14. Narváez party lands at Tampa Bay.

November. The boats of the Narváez expedition are wrecked on Misfortune Island near Galveston Bay and the expedition ends in failure.

1529

January 1. The *audiencia* headed by Guzmán takes over administration of New Spain from Alonso de Estrada.

November 5. Royal license is issued to Cortés in Spain to explore and conquer islands of the Pacific and unknown coasts of the mainland.

December 20. Guzmán leaves Mexico City with army of five hundred Spaniards and eight thousand Indians to conquer New Galicia.

1530

Death of Alonso de Estrada, royal treasurer of New Spain and father of Coronado's future wife.

Cortés returns from Spain with title of Marquis of the Valley of Oaxaca and begins to prepare new sea expeditions up the Pacific coast.

Guzmán conquers Jalisco and Nayarit.

1531

January 16. Guzmán writes to the king from Chametla that he has heard of the country of the Amazons and plans to go north up the coast in search of it as far as the fortieth parallel.

Summer. Town of San Miguel de Culiacán founded in Sinaloa by Guzmán. Later he leaves town and retires to Jalisco to consolidate his conquest.

Lope de Samaniego, Guzmán's lieutenant, discovers Río de Petatlán, the modern Sinaloa River.

1532

May or *June.* Two vessels are sent out by Cortés under Diego Hurtado de Mendoza and Juan de Mazuela; both vessels are lost, Hurtado is killed by Indians at the mouth of the Río Fuerte, and the only discovery made is the Tres Marias Islands.

1533

September. Diego de Guzmán discovers the Río Mayo and the Río Yaqui.

October. Two ships are sent out from Tehuántepec by Cortés, under Diego de Becerra and Hernando de Grijalva; Becerra is killed by mutineers under Ortuño Jiménez, who with most of the party is later massacred at the Bay of La Paz on the Gulf of California.

1535

Antonio de Mendoza comes to Mexico as viceroy of New Spain.

Spring. Cabeza de Vaca and three companions begin their overland journey from the lower Río Grande Valley.

May 3. Cortés founds a settlement at La Paz.

1536

March. Cabeza de Vaca and three other survivors of the Narváez expedition encounter Diego de Alcaraz about a hundred and thirty miles north of Culiacán.

March 17. Diego Pérez de la Torre is ordered by the king to assume governorship of New Galicia and take the *residencia* of Nuño de Guzmán.

April 1. Cabeza de Vaca and three companions reach Culiacán.

July 23. Cabeza de Vaca and companions reach Mexico City.

September 24. Outbreak of negro revolt in New Spain.

September 25. Marcos de Niza testifies in Guatemala concerning the Peruvian expedition of Pedro de Alvarado.

1537

Marriage of Coronado (or earlier).

Coronado subdues the rebel miners of Amatepeque.

February 11. Mendoza writes to the empress from Mexico stating that Cabeza de Vaca and Dorantes are on their way to Spain (Dorantes later turns back, to remain in Mexico).

April 4. Zumárraga, bishop of Mexico, mentions in a letter that Marcos de Niza is staying in his home.

April 20. De Soto as governor of Cuba receives a royal grant to conquer, pacify, and people the mainland from Florida to the Río de las Palmas.

August. Cabeza de Vaca talks with the emperor in Spain, but finds that De Soto has already been appointed to the coveted post of *adelantado* of Florida.

December 10. Mendoza writes to the king saying that he has obtained the negro Esteban, slave of Dorantes, to guide an expedition to the north. Coronado is mentioned as a promising and useful young man about whom Mendoza had previously written in detail.

1538

Governor De la Torre is killed fighting Zacatecas Indians.

Mendoza writes to the king saying that the expedition of fifty horsemen under Dorantes which he had planned had fallen through.

April 17. Charles V authorizes Mendoza to send out Fray Marcos de Niza, vice-commissary of the Franciscan order in New Spain, to discover new lands to the north.

June 14. Coronado takes office as *regidor* of Mexico City on Mendoza's nomination.

June 30. Guzmán is ordered to depart for Spain to answer charges of maladministration.

August. Coronado is called as a witness to formal notification of Cortés that De Soto has been appointed *adelantado* of Florida.

September 7. It is rumored that Coronado has been nominated governor of New Galicia; and as such he is called upon to acknowledge De Soto's appointment as *adelantado* of Florida.

October. Marcos de Niza is instructed by Mendoza to make a journey of exploration north of New Galicia. Marcos acknowledges receipt of written instructions at Tonalá, or Guadalajara, on November 20.

October 15. Coronado attends a *cabildo* meeting; thereafter he is absent, engaged in the administration of New Galicia and in the Topira expedition, until the following August.

November 19. Coronado in Guadalajara; he writes to the king from there on December 15, giving an account of his administrative labors in New Galicia.

1539

February 7. Fray Marcos and Esteban leave Culiacán to explore Topira; they soon return.

March 7. Marcos, accompanied by Fray Honorato and Esteban, starts from Culiacán to find the Seven Cities.

March 8. Coronado at Culiacán writes to Mendoza stating that he intends to set out for Topira on April 10.

March 21. Coronado's appointment as *regidor* of Mexico City confirmed by royal *cédula* signed at Toledo.

March 21. Fray Marcos arrives at Vacapa. Two days later Esteban is sent on ahead to scout. Four days after his departure, Marcos receives a cross as high as a man, and news that the negro has heard of Cíbola, "the greatest country in the world." Marcos does not leave Vacapa until April 8, two days after Easter.

April 18. The appointment of Coronado as governor of New Galicia is confirmed by royal *cédula* signed in Spain.

May 9. Marcos, on the road to Cíbola, enters the wilderness around the southern boundary of Arizona.

May 18. The De Soto expedition sails from Havana to settle Florida.

May 21. Marcos learns of the death of Esteban at Cíbola; a few days later he starts his return to Mexico.

May 30. De Soto lands on the coast of Florida near Tampa Bay.

July 8. Francisco de Ulloa, sent out by Cortés, sails from Acapulco on a voyage almost to the head of the Gulf of California; the commander is lost and discoveries are few, although one ship reaches Cedros Island on the Pacific coast of the peninsula.

July 15. Coronado writes to the king from Compostela, mentioning the discovery of Cíbola by Fray Marcos.

July 26. Cortés writes to Mendoza from Cuernavaca thanking him for advance news of the return of Marcos from the north, and asking to be kept further informed.

August 6. Cortés writes to Mendoza, again thanking him for news and hinting that he would be willing to collaborate on an expedition to follow up the discoveries of Marcos.

August 18. Coronado attends meeting of *cabildo* in Mexico City.

August 23. Bishop Zumárraga writes to a friend in Spain that Marcos has found a large country to the north, and many people are planning to go there.

August 26. Attestation of Marcos' report by Fray Antonio de Ciudad-Rodrigo in Mexico City.

August 26. Mendoza issues proclamation, aimed at Cortés, forbidding anyone to leave the country without his permission; nor shall any shipmaster sailing to Spain from New Spain put in at any port in the New World. This embargo on the news of Fray Marcos fails of its purpose.

September 2. Fray Marcos certifies on oath to the veracity of his report.

September 4. Cortés is refused permission by the *audiencia* to send a ship to the aid of Ulloa.

September 15. Pedro de Alvarado, on his return from Spain bearing license of April 16, 1538, to conquer the Spice Islands, reaches Guatemala and starts building fleet.

October 13. Royal confirmation, dated March 21, of Coronado's appointment as *regidor* reaches Mexico. Coronado attends *cabildo* meeting for last time previous to a three-year absence.

November 12. Depositions taken at Havana from crew of ship which, in spite of Mendoza's ban, put into Cuba with letters from Mexico for De Soto.

November 17. Melchor Díaz and Juan de Zaldívar leave Culiacán with small party to explore northward by order of Mendoza. They reach Chichilticalli, but are forced to turn back by cold weather.

November 18. Pedro de Alvarado writes to the king from Guatemala that he is willing to follow up discoveries of Fray Marcos by means of the fleet he is building.

1540

January 1. Mendoza celebrates the New Year at Pátzcuaro on his way to Compostela.

January 6. Commission issued at Michoacán and signed by Antonio de Almaguer, secretary to Mendoza, giving Coronado the privilege of conquering the new lands to the north in the king's name.

February 5. Cortés stops at Havana on his way to Spain, never to return to the New World.

February 22. Sunday review of the Coronado expedition at Compostela, where the army has gathered.

February 23. The army, under the command of Coronado and accompanied by Mendoza, starts on the march northward.

February 26. Mendoza returns to Compostela, having left the army two days before, and examines witnesses to discover how many citizens of Mexico have accompanied Coronado. He writes a letter to the king (this letter has been lost).

March. The army marches north to Culiacán. The army-master, Samaniego, is killed near Chametla. Melchor Díaz and Juan de Zaldívar, returning from Chichilticalli, meet the army at Chametla; Díaz takes command of his company, and Zaldívar carries report on to Mendoza.

March 1. Cortés in Spain institutes proceedings in the Council for the Indies to protect his interests in New Spain; beginning of litigation over right to conquer Cíbola country.

March 20. Mendoza at Jacona receives from Zaldívar the report of the Chichilticalli exploration.

March 28. Reception of the army at Culiacán on Easter Sunday.

April. The army is entertained by the citizens of Culiacán. Coronado writes to Mendoza, giving an account of what has happened (this letter has been lost).

April 17. Mendoza writes from Jacona to the king, relaying report of Melchor Díaz.

April 22. Coronado departs from Culiacán for Cíbola with about seventy horsemen and twenty-five or thirty foot soldiers.

May. The army starts from Culiacán and marches toward the Sonora River village of Corazones.

May 9. Alarcón sails from Acapulco with two ships to coöperate with Coronado.

May 25. The fiscal of the Council for the Indies reports that in his judgment none of the claimants has the right to explore Cíbola, thus giving Mendoza a free hand as the king's representative in New Spain.

May 26. Coronado and his flying squadron reach Corazones in the Ures basin of the Sonora River.

June 11. Charles V writes letter (which has been lost) to Coronado, which reaches him at Tiguex before April 20, 1541.

June 23. Coronado crosses the Gila and enters the wilderness south of Cíbola.

June 25. Cortés presents his "Memorial upon Injuries" before the Council for the Indies.

July 7. Coronado reaches Cíbola and captures the first town, Hawikuh, which he calls Granada.

July 11. The Indians of Hawikuh retire to their stronghold on Corn Mountain.

July 15. Pedro de Tovar leaves Cíbola to explore Tusayán, or Hopi.

July 19. The Council for the Indies issues an order to Mendoza not to hinder Cortés in his explorations of the South Sea.

July 19. Coronado goes to Mátsaki and returns the same day.

July–August. The army builds the town of San Gerónimo in the Ures basin, but the site is soon moved upstream. Maldonado leads a scouting party to the Gulf coast.

August. Pedro de Alvarado sails from Acajutla with a large fleet to obtain stores at Tehuántepec for voyage to Spice Islands.

August 3. Coronado writes to Mendoza. He sends Melchor Díaz with orders for the army, and Juan Gallego with despatches to Mexico. Fray Marcos accompanies Gallego.

August 25. García López de Cárdenas leaves Cíbola to explore the canyons of the Colorado River.

August 26. Alarcón enters the mouth of the Colorado River and starts upstream in two boats.

August 29. Hernando de Alvarado sets out eastward from Cíbola for the discovery of Tiguex, Cicuyé, and the buffalo plains.

September. Díaz and Gallego reach San Gerónimo about the middle of the month, and the army starts for Cíbola. Before the end of the month Díaz starts from San Gerónimo with twenty-five men to march northwest toward the crossing of the Colorado. Diego de Alcaraz is left in command at San Gerónimo, now situated in the "Señora" basin.

September 7. Hernando de Alvarado reaches the upper Río Grande and discovers the villages of Tiguex.

September 14. Alarcón starts up the Colorado on his second boat expedition.

October. Alarcón leaves the mouth of the Colorado about the middle of the month on his homeward journey to New Galicia.

October–November. The army under Arellano marches to Cíbola.

November. Pedro de Alvarado's fleet vainly tries to obtain supplies at Guatulco and Acapulco, and puts in at port of Santiago.

November. Coronado marches to Tutahaco with staff and thirty men, and thence to Tiguex.

November. Early in the month Alarcón with three ships puts in at port of Santiago, where he finds fleet of Pedro de Alvarado. He delivers his report to viceregal officials and sails away to avoid clash.

November. Melchor Díaz arrives from Sonora at the banks of the Colorado River.

November 29. Mendoza and Pedro de Alvarado at Tiripitío sign a partnership contract in regard to common explorations and conquests.

December. The army under Arellano marches from Cíbola to Tiguex by way of Acoma.

December 25. Mendoza at the Pacific port of Navidad is informed by Cristóbal de Oñate, lieutenant governor of New Galicia, that trouble is brewing among the Indians.

December 30. Melchor Díaz in Lower California is injured by a lance butt.

1541

January 18. Melchor Díaz, twenty days after his injury, dies on the road from the Colorado River crossing to San Gerónimo in the Sonora basin.

February–March. The siege of Tiguex. Discovery of Quirix. Coronado visits Cicuyé.

April 10. Defeat of the Spaniards at the *peñol* of Mixton opens the Mixton War in New Galicia.

April 20. Coronado at Tiguex writes a letter (which has been lost) to the king, sending it south with Pedro de Tovar, who is ordered to take charge at San Gerónimo.

April 23. Coronado starts with all his force from Tiguex to march to Cicuyé and the buffalo plains, to investigate the stories of The Turk.

May. De Soto reaches the Mississippi River near Chickasaw Bluffs.

May 26. A council of war is held by the army in the ravines of the upper Brazos River of Texas. Coronado and thirty horsemen depart a day or so later to discover Quivira by riding due north.

May 31. Mendoza writes instructions to be followed by Alarcón on a second voyage to the Colorado River (an expedition which never set out).

May or *June.* Tovar moves town of San Gerónimo from Sonora basin upstream to its third site, the valley of Suya, "forty leagues farther toward Cíbola."

June. The army under Arellano leaves the ravines about the middle of the month and strikes out to the west on the return to Tiguex.

June. De Soto crosses the Mississippi River.

June 12. Pedro de Alvarado with two hundred men reaches Guadalajara to aid in fighting the Mixton War.

June 24. Pedro de Alvarado is fatally injured at the battle of Nochistlán in Zacatecas, dying a week or so later at Guadalajara.

June 29. Coronado with thirty horsemen crosses the Arkansas River near Ford, Kansas, on his way to Quivira.

July. The army under Arellano returns to Tiguex from the buffalo plains by way of the Pecos River, after a journey of twenty-five days.

August. Coronado, after spending about twenty-five days exploring Quivira, leaves for Tiguex by way of the Cimarrón River trail.

August. Barrionuevo explores the Jemez River pueblos and the Río Grande towns as far north as Taos. Another captain descends the Río Grande to the Jornada del Muerto.

September. Coronado returns from Quivira to Cicuyé and Tiguex.

September 8. Francisco de Bolaños sails from Navidad with several ships to explore the west side of Lower California, and returns in the spring of 1542.

September 28. The Indians of New Galicia attack the town of Guadalajara in force, but are beaten off.

October 6. Mendoza writes to the historian Oviedo in Spain, stating that Coronado had reached a distance of nine hundred leagues from Mexico and had not found any gold or silver, but had heard that farther on were many golden vessels, pearls, and great cities and houses, and a country with very abundant food, especially cattle.

October 20. Coronado at Tiguex writes to the king describing his discoveries in Quivira.

November. Cárdenas starts to return to Mexico with some other invalids of the army. He finds the village at Suya in ruins and hastily returns to Tiguex.

December. Coronado falls from his horse and is seriously injured. The news that Cárdenas brings on his return from Sonora is a severe shock that causes the general to return to his bed.

December. The town of Mixton is surrendered to Mendoza during holiday week, after a three-week siege, and the revolt in New Galicia is crushed.

1542

March. De Soto descends the Arkansas River after spending the winter about thirty miles east of the Oklahoma-Arkansas boundary.

April 1. Army under Coronado abandons Tiguex and starts on the long retreat to Mexico, leaving Fray Juan de la Cruz at Tiguex, Fray Luis de Escalona at Cicuyé, and Fray Juan de Padilla with several companions to Christianize Quivira.

April 17. De Soto reaches the mouth of the Red River, where he dies on May 21.

June 24. Coronado with army leaves Culiacán on return to Mexico.

June 27. Cabrillo starts from port of Navidad on his voyage up the California coast.

September 28. Discovery of Alta California by sea; landing of Cabrillo at Bay of San Diego.

October 6. Narrative of Cabeza de Vaca is published at Zamora, Spain.

October 13. Coronado attends a meeting of the *cabildo* in Mexico City after an absence of precisely three years.

November 1. Ruy López de Villalobos sails on voyage to Philippines.

November 25 (?). Fray Juan de la Cruz killed at Tiguex. Fray Luis probably killed about this time at Cicuyé. Fray Juan de Padilla, after living in Quivira for some time, is killed by the Kansa tribe either in 1542 or 1544. The companions of Padilla make their way to Pánuco, reaching there before 1552.

1543

January 3. Death of Cabrillo on San Miguel Island off California coast.

March 1. Ferrelo in command of Cabrillo expedition reaches latitude of about forty-two degrees off California coast near Oregon line, farthest northern point attained on the voyage.

April 14. Ferrelo with two ships returns to port of Navidad.

September 7. Lorenzo de Tejada is appointed to conduct *residencia* on Coronado's administration of New Galicia by *cédula* signed by Prince Philip at Valladolid.

September 10. The survivors of the De Soto expedition reach the mouth of the Pánuco River.

1544

Sebastian Cabot publishes his map of the New World.

August 8. Hearings in *residencia* of Coronado are opened at Guadalajara by Lorenzo de Tejada.

September 17. Tejada finds Coronado guilty of various charges, deprives him of office, fines him six hundred gold pesos, and holds him under technical arrest.

1547

January 18. Coronado testifies publicly in *visita* reviewing official acts of Mendoza as viceroy.

December 2. Death of Cortés at Seville at age of sixty-three.

1552

First publication of Gómara's *Historia de las Indias*.

1554

October or *November.* Death of Coronado in New Spain at age of forty-four.

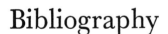

Bibliography

TITLES marked with an asterisk are contemporary documents of first importance in any study of the Coronado expedition.

"Winship," frequently found in the Notes and the Bibliography, refers to the memoir in the *Fourteenth Annual Report of the Bureau of Ethnology*, which, although long out of print, is still the most available English translation of the more important Coronado documents, including the narrative of Castañeda. Dr. Winship's work has been used as the basis of many of my own translations throughout the book.

The most important modern research students of the Coronado expedition, aside from Winship, are Aiton, Adolph F. Bandelier (who, however, must be read with some caution, as many of his conclusions have been revised by later workers), Hodge, and Sauer. To Dr. Aiton thanks are due for permission to examine two of his papers in advance of publication; and Dr. Hodge kindly consented to the use of a base map prepared under his direction. No attempt has been made to include herein more than the few most pertinent studies in the vast field of archaeology and anthropology dealing with the Indians of Mexico and the Southwest.

It was customary for Spanish exploring parties in the New World in the sixteenth century to appoint an official chronicler with the duty of recording a complete account of all events and acts, as well as distances covered and other geographical facts regarding the country traversed and the manners and customs of its inhabitants. If any such official marched with Coronado, however, no fragment of his labors has survived. Beyond a few letters and official hearings, all that anyone knows regarding the incidents of the great journey was derived from some half-dozen accounts left by men who took part in these exploits.

Most of the eyewitness records are brief and of limited scope. Viceroy

Mendoza wrote to the king on April 17, 1540, quoting in full the report of Melchor Díaz regarding his northward scouting trip to Chichilti-calli. Coronado wrote to Mendoza on August 3 of the same year from the newly subdued "first city" of Cíbola, relating the incidents of the journey thither and the first encounters with the natives. Another valuable document is the letter written by Coronado to the emperor on October 20, 1541, after his return from the quest of Quivira. Two anonymous accounts, the "Traslado de las nuevas" and the "Relación del suceso," were written by members of the army who have never been identified. The "Relación postrera de Sívola" was apparently written in 1541 from the Indian villages of New Mexico by one of the Franciscan friars with the expedition. There also exists a brief "Account of What Hernando de Alvarado and Fray Juan de Padilla Discovered Going in Search of the South Sea." More important than these brief anonymous records is the factual account of Captain Juan Jaramillo, an account, like that of Castañeda, put down some years after the event. The final and fullest eyewitness record of the expedition is the narrative of Pedro de Castañeda de Nájera, which gives a lean but explicit story of the expedition from start to finish.

The style of Pedro de Castañeda's narrative is terse, pertinent, and robust. Although he did not claim to be either a polished man of letters or a skilled geographer, he had a sincere respect for truth, and recorded scrupulously, if bluntly, all the facts he was able to gather concerning the new lands upon which white men had never before gazed; and his campaigner's eye for the country enabled him to state distances and describe terrain in such a way that recent researchers are able to identify without great hesitation most of the landmarks of Coronado's route. His allusions are sound, he had a good historical sense of the important, and his chronicle stands out above most of the early narratives of Spanish discovery. "Although not in a polished style," he says in the modest Proem to his chronicle, "I write that which happened—that which I heard, felt, saw, and lived."

The original manuscript of the narrative, written by Castañeda or his hired scrivener, has never been found. All that exists is a single handwritten copy made by some unknown clerk in Seville in 1596. This manuscript, as may be seen by examining it in the treasure room of the New York Public Library, where it now reposes, is corrupt, full of copying errors, and in places quite incoherent.

The narrative was composed by Castañeda in the town of San Miguel de Culiacán, where he had settled on his return from the pueblos; and there, twenty years after his return, he set down his recollections, dedicating the work to an unnamed noble patron.

Of Castañeda himself, almost nothing is known. He was a native of the little town of Nájera in Logroño, a northern province of old Spain. He may have been related to the Alonso de Castañeda mentioned by A. F. and Fanny Bandelier (I, 35) who had served with Nuño de Guzmán in the conquest of the "terrible Chichimecs" and later settled at Compostela. In 1554 Pedro's wife, María de Acosta, and her four sons and four daughters filed a petition against the treasury of New Spain for remuneration of services rendered by him to the Crown (Pacheco, XIV, 206).

After their return from Quivira, a number of Coronado's veterans settled, as Castañeda did, on the frontier to earn a harsh living by homesteading small allotments. Many times they yearned to go again to the north and see the good land that they might have made their own. "Since they came back from the country which they conquered and then abandoned," Castañeda wrote in his Proem, "time has given them a chance to understand the direction and location in which they were, and the borders of the good country they had in their hands, and their hearts weep for having lost so favorable an opportunity" (Winship, p. 472).

It is my belief that Castañeda's yearning to explore the north again was satisfied by a last adventure that fits all the canons of romance. In 1565, only a year or so after the aging soldier put down his memories of Cíbola and the way thither, there arrived in Culiacán the exploring party of Francisco de Ibarra, governor and captain general of the newly formed interior province of New Biscay. Again Pedro de Castañeda enlisted under an exploring young governor, and took the northward road, to find his last resting place in a freshly discovered pueblo in an unexplored corner of Mexico's frontier.

Tucked away in the narrative of Antonio Ruiz, a member of the Ibarra party (Sauer, *Road to Cíbola*, p. 55), there is found what one may consider to be the epitaph of Pedro de Castañeda de Nájera: "In a village called Paquimy [Paquimé, an abandoned pueblo identified with the well-known Casas Grandes in northwestern Chihuahua] it happened that a soldier named Pedro de Nájara went to look for a horse that he had tethered in a thicket to browse, and when he reached him, going in company with two or three others, he gave the horse a slap on the rump, and as the horse was startled, it knocked him dead upon the ground, an unfortunate occurrence that caused the governor great grief. They buried him as secretly as possible so that the Indians would not find the body."

Three later sources of information on the Coronado expedition are of high importance. Gómara in his *Historia general de las Indias,* published in 1552, has a few valuable pages on the subject. Baltazar de Obregón, born in Mexico City in 1544, made a voyage to California with Antonio de Luna in 1563, and in 1565–1566 accompanied Francisco de Ibarra on his *entrada* in northwestern Mexico. Obregón may have spoken with men who served under Coronado; but the history that he wrote in 1584, containing occasional references to Coronado, is often confused and verbose, and must be taken with a grain of salt. The most important noncontemporary account of the expedition is given by Mota Padilla, who wrote in 1742; he apparently had access to papers left by Don Pedro de Tovar in Culiacán (see Day, "Mota Padilla"). Mention of Coronado by Villagrá in his versified *Historia de la Nueva México*, published in 1610, is brief and altogether untrustworthy.

Actos de cabildo del ayuntamiento de Mexico. See Orozco.

AITON, ARTHUR SCOTT. *Antonio de Mendoza, First Viceroy of New Spain.* Durham, N.C., 1927.

*———. "Coronado's Commission as Captain-General," *Hispanic American Historical Review*, XX (February, 1940), 83–87.

*———. "Coronado's First Report on the Government of New Galicia," *ibid.*, XIX (August, 1939), 306–313.

*———. "Coronado's Muster Roll," *American Historical Review*, XLIV (April, 1939), 556–570.

———. "The Later Career of Coronado," *ibid.*, XXX (January, 1925), 298–304.

*AITON, ARTHUR SCOTT, and REY, AGAPITO. "Coronado's Testimony in the Viceroy Mendoza's *Residencia*," *New Mexico Historical Review*, XII (July, 1937), 288–329.

*ALARCÓN, HERNANDO. "De lo que hizo por la mar Hernando de Alarcón, que con dos nauios andaua por la costa por orden del visorrey don Antonio de Mendoça." *In* HERRERA, dec. 6, lib. 9, cap. 13.

———. "Relación del armada del Marqués del Valle, capitaneada de Francisco de Ulloa ... y de la que el virey de Nueva España envió con un Alarcón." In *Colección España*, IV, 218–219.

*———. "Relatione della navigatione & scoperta che fece il capitano Fernando Alarcone per ordine dello illustrissimo signor Don Antonio di Mendozza vice re della Nuoua Spagna." *In* RAMUSIO, III, 363–370 (ed. 1556). French trans. in TERNAUX, IX, 299–348; English trans. in HAKLUYT, III, 425–439 (ed. 1600); IX, 115–168 (ed. 1914).

*ALVARADO, HERNANDO DE. "Relación de lo que Hernando de Alvarado y Fray Joan de Padilla descubrieron en demanda de la Mar del Sur, agosto de 1540." *In* PACHECO, III, 511–513; also SMITH, *Colección*, I, 65–66. English trans. in WINSHIP, pp. 594–595.

ALVARADO, PEDRO DE. "Asiento y capitulaciones, entre el virey de Nueva España, D. Antonio de Mendoza, y el adelantado, D. Pedro de Alvarado, para la prosecución del descubrimiento de tierra nueva, hecho por Fr. Marcos de Niza, Pueblo de Tiripitio de la Nueva España, 29 noviembre, 1540." *In* PACHECO, III, 351–362; *ibid.,* XVI, 342–355.

ARTEAGA Y S., ARMANDO. "Fray Marcos de Niza y el descubrimiento de Nueva Mexico," *Hispanic American Historical Review,* XII (November, 1932), 481–488.

"Autos del Marqués del Valle, Pánfilo de Narváez ... 1526." *In* PACHECO, XVI, 67–87.

BALDWIN, PERCY M. "Fray Marcos de Niza's *Relación*," *New Mexico Historical Review,* I (April, 1926), 193–223.

BANCROFT, HUBERT HOWE. *Arizona and New Mexico.* San Francisco, 1889.

————. *North Mexican States and Texas.* 2 vols. San Francisco, 1886.

BANDELIER, ADOLPH F. *Contributions to the History of the Southwestern Portion of the United States. Papers of the Archaeological Institute of America,* American Series V. Cambridge, Mass., 1890.

————. *The Delight Makers.* New York, 1890.

————. "The Discovery of New Mexico by Fray Marcos of Nizza," *New Mexico Historical Review,* IV (January, 1929), 28–44 (reprinted from *Magazine of Western History*).

————. *Documentary History of the Rio Grande Pueblos. Papers of the School of American Archaeology,* No. 13. Santa Fe, N.M., 1910 (reprinted in *New Mexico Historical Review,* V, 38–66, 154–185, 240–262, 333–385).

————. "Documentary History of the Zuñi Tribe," *Journal of American Ethnology and Archaeology,* III (1892), 1–115.

————. *Final Report of Investigations among the Indians of the Southwestern United States.* 2 vols. *Papers of the Archaeological Institute of America,* American Series III and IV. Cambridge, Mass., 1890, 1892.

————. "Fray Juan de Padilla, the First Catholic Missionary and Martyr in Eastern Kansas," *American Catholic Quarterly Review,* XV (No. 59, 1890), 551–565.

————. *The Gilded Man.* New York, 1893.

————. *Historical Introduction to Studies among the Sedentary Indians of New Mexico. Papers of the Archaeological Institute of America,* American Series I, pp. 1–33. Boston, 1881.

————. *A Visit to the Aboriginal Ruins in the Valley of the Rio Pecos. Ibid.,* American Series I, Part 2, pp. 37–133. Boston, 1881.

BANDELIER, A. F., and BANDELIER, FANNY. *Historical Documents relating to New Mexico* (ed. by CHARLES D. HACKETT), Vol. I. *Bulletin No. 330,* Carnegie Institution. Washington, 1923.

BARRA, LUIS L. DE LA. "The Coronado Genealogy." *In* JONES, pp. 188–200.

BASKET, J. N. "A Study of the Route of Coronado between the Rio Grande and Missouri Rivers," *Kansas State Historical Society Collections*, XII (1912), 219–252.

BEALS, RALPH L. *The Acaxee, a Mountain Tribe of Durango and Sinaloa. Ibero-Americana*, No. 6. Berkeley, Calif., 1933.

BENAVENTE, TORIBIO DE. *See* MOTOLINIA.

BENAVIDES, ALONSO DE. "Memorial." *In Land of Sunshine* (1900–1901), XIII, 277–290, 345–358, 435–444; XIV, 39–52, 137–148, 227–232. Translated by MRS. EDWARD E. AYER, annotated by F. W. HODGE, edited by CHARLES F. LUMMIS.

BÉTHENCOURT, FRANCISCO FERNANDO DE. *Historia genealógica y heráldica*. 10 vols. Madrid, 1897–1920. For Coronado, see IX, 500.

BLANCO-FOMBONA, R. *El conquistador español del siglo XVI*. Madrid, 1922.

BLAKE, W. P. "The *Chalchihuitl* of the Ancient Mexicans," *American Journal of Science* (2d ser.), XXV (1858), 227–232.

BOLTON, HERBERT EUGENE. *The Spanish Borderlands. Chronicles of America*, Vol. XXIII. New Haven, Conn., 1921.

―――― (ed.). *Spanish Exploration in the Southwest, 1542–1706. Original Documents of Early American History*, Vol. XVII. New York, 1916.

BROWER, J. V. *Harahey. Memoirs of Explorations in the Basin of the Mississippi*, Vol. II. St. Paul, Minn., 1899.

――――. *Quivira. Ibid.*, Vol. I. St. Paul, Minn., 1898.

CABEZA DE VACA, ALVAR NÚÑEZ. "La relación que dió Aluar Núñez Cabeça de Vaca de lo acaescido en las Indias en la armada donde yua por gouernador Pãphilo de Narvaez." Zamora, 6 octubre, 1542; reprinted, Valladolid, 1555. Italian trans. in RAMUSIO, III, 310–330 (ed. 1556); French trans. in TERNAUX, Vol. VII; paraphrased from Ramusio into English in PURCHAS, Part 2, Book 8, chap. 1, pp. 437–521 (ed. 1906); for English trans., see SMITH, *Narrative*.

CABRILLO, JUAN RODRÍGUEZ. "Relación, o diario, de la navegación que hizo Juan Rodríguez Cabrillo con dos navíos, al descubrimiento del paso del Mar del Sur al norte. ..." *In* SMITH, *Colección*, pp. 173–189; also PACHECO, XIV, 165–191. English trans. in WAGNER, *Spanish Voyages*, pp. 79–93. *See also* HERRERA.

*CASTAÑEDA, PEDRO DE. "Relación de la jornada de Cíbola conpuesta por Pedro de Castañeda de Naçera donde se trata de todos aquellas pobladas y ritos, y costumbres, la cual fue el año de 1540." *In* WINSHIP, pp. 414–469; English trans., pp. 470–546. French trans. in TERNAUX, IX, 1–246.

Castro y Bravo, Federico de. *Las naos españoles en la carrera de las Indias*. Madrid, 1927.

"Códice de leyes y ordenanzas nueuamente hechas por su Magestad para la gouernación de las Yndias y buen tratamiento y conseruación de los Yndios, etc. [September 24, 1571]." *In* Pacheco, XVI, 376–460.

Colección de documentos inéditos para la historia de España (ed. by Martín Fernández Navarrete *et al.*). 113 vols. Madrid, 1842–1895. Cited as *Colección España*.

Colección de documentos inéditos para la historia de Mexico. See García and García Icazbalceta.

Colección de documentos inéditos relativos al descubrimiento, conquista, y colonización de las posesiones españolas en América y Oceania. See Pacheco.

Córdova y Bocanegra, Francisco Pacheco de. *Petition, 1618*. Coronado was his maternal grandfather; see pp. 217–219.

*Coronado, Francisco Vásquez. "Carta de Francisco Vázquez Coronado al emperador, dándole cuenta de la espedición a la provincia de Quivira, y de la inexactitud de lo referido a Fr. Marcos de Niza, acerca de aquel pais, desta provincia de Tiguex, 20 octubre, 1541." *In* Pacheco, III, 363–369; also XIII, 261–268. French trans. in Ternaux, IX, 355–363; English trans. in Winship, pp. 580–583.

*———. "Commission as Captain-General." Archivo General de Indias, Justicia, 48-3-3/30. *In* Aiton, "Coronado's Commission."

*———. "Copia delle lettere di Francesco Vazquez di Coronado, gouernatore della Nuoua Galitia, al Signor Antonio de Mendozza, vicere della Nuoua Spagna, date in San Michiel di Culnacan, alli otto di marzo, 1539." *In* Ramusio, III, 354 (ed. 1556). English trans. in Hakluyt, III, 363–364 (ed. 1600); French trans. in Ternaux, IX, 352–354.

———. "Grant of *encomienda*, November 29, 1549." Archivo General de Indias, Consejo, 87-6-2, officio y parte 21.

*———. "Letter to the King, Guadalajara, December 15, 1538." Archivo General de Indias, Estado, 66-5-14. Excerpt in Aiton, "Coronado's First Report."

*———. "Letter to the King, Compostela, July 15, 1539." Excerpt in Sauer, "Discovery of New Mexico Reconsidered," p. 278.

*———. "Probanza del virrey, testigo de Francisco Vazquez de Coronado [Mexico, January 18, 1547]." Archivo General de Indias, Justicia, 48-1-9/31.

*———. "Relatione che mandò Francesco Vazquez di Coronado, capitano generale della gente che fu mandata in nome di Sua Maesta al paese nouamente scoperto, quel che successe nel viaggio dalli ventidua d'aprile di questo anno 1540, che parti da Culiacan per in-

nanzi, & di quel che trouò nel paese doue andaua.—Dalla prouincia di Ceuola & da questa città di Granata il terzo di agosto, 1540." *In* RAMUSIO, III, 359–363 (ed. 1556). English trans. in HAKLUYT, III, 370–380 (ed. 1600); WINSHIP, pp. 552–563.

*———. "Residencia que el lic'do. Lorenzo de Tejada oydor de la Audiencia Real de la Nueva España tomo a Francisco Vasquez de Coronado, gobernador que fue de la Nueva Galicia." Archivo General de Indias, Justicia, 48-3-3/30.

*———. "Svmario di lettere del Capitano Francesco Vazquez di Coronado, scritte ad vn secretario del illustriss. Don Antonio di Mendozza, vicere della Nuoua Spagna, date a Culnacan, 1539, alli otto di marzo." *In* RAMUSIO, III, 354 (ed. 1556). English trans. in HAKLUYT, III, 363 (ed. 1600); French trans. in TERNAUX, IX, 349–351.

CORTÉS, FERNANDO. *Letters* (ed. and trans. by F. A. MacNUTT). 2 vols. New York, 1908.

———. "Memorial que dió al rey el Marqués del Valle en Madrid a 25 de junio de 1540, sobre agravios ..." *In Colección España,* IV, 209–217.

———. "Memorial sobre que no se le embarace el descubrimiento de la Mar del Sur, 4 de setiembre." *Ibid.,* pp. 201–208.

CUEVAS, MARIANO (ed.). *Documentos inéditos del siglo XVI para la historia de Mexico.* Mexico, 1914.

——— (ed.). *See* OBREGÓN.

CURTIS, E. S. *The North American Indian.* 20 vols. Cambridge, Mass., 1907–1930. Vols. II, XII, XVI, and XVII refer to the Coronado country. This series, with accompanying portfolios, contains some of the finest photographs of Indians ever made.

CURTIS, F. S., JR. "Spanish Arms and Armor in the Southwest," *New Mexico Historical Review,* II (April, 1927), 103–133.

CUSHING, FRANK HAMILTON. "Outlines of Zuñi Creation Myths," *Thirteenth Annual Report, Bureau of Ethnology, 1891–1892,* pp. 321–447. Washington, 1896.

———. *Zuñi Breadstuff.* New York, 1920.

———. *Zuñi Folk Tales.* New York, 1901.

DAVENPORT, HARBERT, and WELLS, JOSEPH K. "The First Europeans in Texas," *Southwestern Historical Quarterly,* XXII (October, 1918), 111–142; XXII (January, 1919), 205–259.

DAVIS, WILLIAM WATTS HART. *The Spanish Conquest of New Mexico.* Doylestown, Penn., 1869.

DAY, A. GROVE. "Gómara on the Coronado Expedition," *Southwestern Historical Quarterly,* XLIII (January, 1940), 348–355.

———. "Mota Padilla on the Coronado Expedition," *Hispanic American Historical Review,* XX (February, 1940), 88–110.

Bibliography 389

DELLENBAUGH, F. S. *The Romance of the Colorado River.* New York, 1902.

———. *The True Route of Coronado's March. Bulletin of American Geographical Society,* December, 1897.

"Demarcación y división de las Indias." *In* PACHECO, XV, 409–539.

DE SOTO, HERNANDO. *See* SOTO.

DÍAZ DEL CASTILLO, BERNAL. *Historia verdadera de la conqvista de la Nueva España.* Madrid, 1632; reprinted, 1632, 1795, 1837, 1854. Also in VEDIA, XXVI, 1–317. English trans. by A. P. MAUDSLAY, 5 vols., Hakluyt Society, London, 1916.

Documentos inéditos del siglo XVI para la historia de Mexico. See CUEVAS.

Documentos inéditos para la historia de México. See GARCÍA and GARCÍA ICAZBALCETA.

DONOGHUE, DAVID. "The Route of Coronado in Texas." *New Mexico Historical Review,* IV (January, 1929), 77–90 (reprinted from *Southwestern Historical Quarterly,* XXXII, 181–193).

"Expediente sobre el ofrecimiento que hace Francisco Díaz de Vargas, de ir al Nuevo Mexico, y refiere la historia de este documento, 1584." *In* PACHECO, XV, 126–146 (title misplaced to p. 151). Coronado is referred to on pp. 128, 131, 144, 145.

FEWKES, J. WALTER. "A Few Summer Ceremonials at the Tusayan Pueblos." *Journal of American Ethnology and Archaeology,* II (1892), 1–159.

———. "Reconnaissance of Ruins in or near the Zuñi Reservation." *ibid.,* I (1891), 95–132. With map and plan.

"Fragmento de la visita hecha a Don Antonio de Mendoza." *In* GARCÍA ICAZBALCETA, *Colección,* II, 72–140. For replies to this *interrogatorio,* see AITON and REY.

GARCÍA, GENARO, and PEREYRA, CARLOS. *Colección de documentos inéditos para la historia de México.* 35 vols. Mexico, 1905–1911.

GARCÍA CARRAFFA, ALBERTO Y A. *Enciclopedia heráldica y genealógica hispano-americana.* Madrid, 1919—. For Coronado, see Vol. XXVII.

GARCÍA ICAZBALCETA, JOAQUÍN (ed.). *Bibliografía Mexicana del siglo XVI.* Mexico, 1886.

——— (ed.). *Colección de documentos inéditos para la historia de México.* 2 vols. Mexico, 1858, 1866.

Gentleman of Elvas. See SMITH, *Narrative;* also ROBERTSON.

*GÓMARA, FRANCISCO LÓPEZ DE. *Primera y segvnda parte de la historia general de las Indias cõ todo el descubrimiento, y cosas notables que han acaescido dende que se ganaron hasta el año de 1551; con la conquista de Mexico y de la Nueua España.* Medina del Campo, 1553 (1552). *In* VEDIA, XXII, 155–294. "There were at least fifteen editions of Gómara's three works printed during the years 1552 to 1555. Before the end of the century translations into French and Italian had been reprinted a score of times. ... For Coronado, see cap. 212–215 of the Historia de las Indias. Chapters 214 and 215 are translated in Hakluyt, vol. 3, pp. 380–382 (ed. 1600), or vol. 3, pp. 454 ff. (ed. 1810)."—Winship. *See also* translation in DAY, "Gómara."

GUZMÁN, NUÑO BELTRÁN DE. "Carta al emperador [Chiametla, January 16, 1531]." *In* PACHECO, XIII, 408–413.

HACKETT, CHARLES D. "Delimitations of Political Jurisdictions in Spanish North America to 1535," *Hispanic American Historical Review*, I (February, 1918), 40–69.

——— (ed.). *Historical Documents relating to New Mexico. See* A. F. and FANNY BANDELIER.

HAKLUYT, RICHARD. *The principal navigations, voyages, traffics, and discoveries of the English nation.* Many editions (published first in 1598–1600).

HAMMOND, GEORGE P. (ed.). *See* OBREGÓN.

HARRINGTON, J. P. "The Ethnogeography of the Tewa Indians," *Twenty-ninth Annual Report, Bureau of Ethnology, 1907–1908*, pp. 29–619. Washington, 1916.

HAYNES, HENRY WILLIAMSON. "Early Explorations in New Mexico." *In* WINSOR, II, 473–503.

HERRERA Y TORDESILLAS, ANTONIO DE. *Historia general de los hechos de los castellanos en las islas y tierra firme del mar oceano.* Madrid, 1601–1615. The best reprinted edition is that published by Barcia, 4 vols., Madrid, 1730. French translation of three decades of Herrera published between 1659 and 1671; English translation of same three decades by Captain John Stevens, London, 1725–1726, and reissued, with arrangement altered, in 1740. For Coronado, see Vol. III, dec. 6, lib. 5, cap. 9; and dec. 6, lib. 9, cap. 11–15.

HEWETT, EDGAR L. *Ancient Life in the American Southwest.* Indianapolis, 1930.

———. *Antiquities of the Jemez Plateau, New Mexico. Bulletin of Bureau of Ethnology*, No. 32. Washington, 1906.

HODGE, FREDERICK WEBB. "Coronado's March to Quivira." *In* BROWER, *Harahey*.

———. "The First Discovered City of Cíbola," *American Anthropologist*, VIII (April, 1895), 142–152.

——— (ed.). *Handbook of the American Indians North of Mexico.* 2 vols. *Bulletin of Bureau of Ethnology*, No. 30. Washington, 1907.

———. *History of Hawikuh, N.M., One of the So-Called Cities of Cíbola.* Los Angeles, 1937.

HODGE, FREDERICK WEBB. "The Six Cities of Cíbola," *New Mexico Historical Review*, I (October, 1926), 478–488.

HODGE, FREDERICK WEBB, and LEWIS, T. HAYS (eds.). *Spanish Explorers in the Southern United States, 1528–1543. Original Narratives of Early American History*, Vol. II. New York, 1907. Contains annotated editions of Winship translation of Castañeda and of Smith translations of Cabeza de Vaca and De Soto.

HULL, D. "Castaño de Sosa's Expedition to New Mexico in 1590," *Old Santa Fe Magazine*, III (October, 1916), 307–332.

*ICAZA, FRANCISCO A. DE. *Diccionario autobiográfico de conquistadores y pobladores de Nueva España*. 2 vols. Madrid, 1923.

ICAZBALCETA. *See* GARCÍA ICAZBALCETA.

*"Información del virrey de Nueva España, D. Antonio de Mendoza, de la gente que va a poblar la Nueva Galicia con Francisco Vazquez Coronado, gobernador de ella [Compostela, February 21–26, 1540]." *In* PACHECO, XIV, 373–384. English trans. (abridged) in WINSHIP, pp. 596–598.

IVES, LIEUTENANT JOSEPH C. *Report upon the Colorado River of the West*. Senate Doc., 36th Congress, 1st Session, Washington, 1861.

IVES, RONALD L. "Melchior Díaz—The Forgotten Explorer," *Hispanic American Historical Review*, XVI (February, 1936), 86–90. *See also* SAUER, "Communication."

*JARAMILLO, JUAN. "Relación hecha por el capitan Juan Jaramillo, de la jornada que había hecho a la tierra nueva en Nueva España y al descubrimiento de Cibola, yendo por general Francisco Vazquez Coronado." *In* PACHECO, XIV, 304–317; SMITH, *Colección*, pp. 154–163. French trans. in TERNAUX, IX, 364–382; English trans. in WINSHIP, pp. 584–593.

JONES, PAUL A. *Coronado and Quivira*. Wichita, Kans., 1937.

KELLY, JOHN EOGHAN. *Pedro de Alvarado, Conquistador*. Princeton, N.J., 1932.

KIDDER, A. V. *The Artifacts of Pecos*. New Haven, Conn., 1932.

———. *An Introduction to the Study of Southwestern Archaeology with a Preliminary Account of the Excavations at Pecos*. New Haven, Conn., 1924.

——— "Prehistoric Cultures of the San Juan Drainage," *Proceedings of the Nineteenth International Congress of Americanists*, pp. 108–113. Washington, 1917.

KROEBER, A. L. *Native Culture of the Southwest*. Berkeley, Calif., 1928.

———. *The Seri. Southwest Museum Papers*, No. 6. Los Angeles, 1931.

LINDSAY, M. G. "Coronado, Searcher for the Seven Cities of Cibola," *Pan-American Magazine*, XLIII (October, 1930), 262–267.

LOWERY, WOODBURY. *Spanish Settlements within the Present Limits of the United States, 1513–1561*. New York, 1901.

LUMMIS, CHARLES F. *The Land of Poco Tiempo*. New York, 1893.

———. *Mesa, Cañon, and Pueblo*. New York, 1920.

———. *The Spanish Pioneers*. Chicago, 1893.

LUXÁN, DIEGO PÉREZ DE. *The Expedition Made into New Mexico by Antonio de Espejo in 1582–1583*. Trans. by GEORGE P. HAMMOND and AGAPITO REY. *Quivira Society Publications*, Vol. I. Los Angeles, 1929.

MACNUTT, F. A. (ed. and trans.). *See* CORTÉS.

MANJE (MANGE), JUAN MATHEO. *Luz de tierra incógnita en la América septentrional y diario de las exploraciones en Sonora*. Mexico, 1926.

———. "Historia de la Pimería Alta." *In* GARCÍA, GENARO (ser. 4), I, 226–402. (Same as Manje's *Luz de tierra incógnita*, lib. 2.)

*MARCOS DE NIZA. "Relación del descubrimiento de las siete ciudades." *In* PACHECO, III, 329–351. Italian trans. in RAMUSIO, III, 356–359 (ed. 1556); French trans. in TERNAUX, IX, 256–284; English trans. in HAKLUYT, III, 366–373 (ed. 1600), and in BALDWIN, pp. 201–221.

MCGEE, W. J. "The Seri Indians," *Seventeenth Annual Report, Bureau of Ethnology, 1895–1896*, Part I, pp. 9–344. Washington, 1898.

MECHAM, J. LLOYD. *Francisco de Ibarra and Nueva Vizcaya*. Durham, N.C., 1927.

———. "The Northern Expansion of New Spain, 1522–1822: A Selected Descriptive Bibliographical List," *Hispanic American Historical Review*, VII (May, 1927), 233–276.

MENDIETA, GERÓNIMO DE. *Historia eclesiástica Indiana, obra escrita a fines del siglo XVI ... la publica por primera vez Joaquín García Icazbalceta*. 2 vols. Mexico, 1870.

MENDOZA, ANTONIO DE. "Asiento y capitulaciones, etc." *See* ALVARADO, PEDRO DE.

———. "Carta a la emperatriz, participando que vienen a España Cabeza de Vaca y Francisco Dorantes, que se escaparon de la armada de Pánfilo de Navaez, a hacer relación de lo que en ella sucedió [Mexico, February 11, 1537]." *In* PACHECO, XIV, 235–236.

———. "Carta al emperador [December 10, 1537]." *In* PACHECO, II, 206.

*———. "Carta del virey don Antonio de Mendoza al emperador [Jacona, April 17, 1540]." *In* PACHECO, II, 356–362. English trans. in WINSHIP, pp. 547–551; French trans. in TERNAUX, IX, 290–298.

*———. "Coronado's Commission as Captain-General." *See* AITON.

*———. "Instrucción de don Antonio de Mendoza, visorey de Nueva España (al Fray Marcos de Niza)." *In* PACHECO, III, 325–329. French

trans. in TERNAUX, IX, 249–255; English trans. in BANDELIER, *Contributions*, pp. 109–112.

————. "Instrucción que debía observar el capitán Hernando de Alarcón [May 31, 1541]." *In* SMITH, *Colección*, pp. 1–6.

————. "Letter to Fernández de Oviedo, October 6, 1541." *In* OVIEDO, III, 539–540.

*————. "Lettere scritte dal illvstrissimo signor don Antonio di Mendozza, vice re della Nuoua Spagna, alla maesta dell' Imperadore. Delli cauallieri quali con lor gran danno si sono affaticati per scoprire il capo della terra ferma della Nuoua Spagna verso tramontana, il gionger del Vazquez con fra Marco à San Michiel di Culnacan con commissione à quelli regenti di assicurare & non far piu schiaui gli Indiani." *In* RAMUSIO, III, 355 (ed. 1556). French trans. in TERNAUX, IX, 285–290; English trans. in HAKLUYT, III, 364–365 (ed. 1600). (Letter, undated, sent to the king enclosing report of Marcos de Niza.)

————. "Probanza del virrey, etc." *See* CORONADO.

MINDELEFF, VICTOR. "A Study of Pueblo Architecture: Tusayan and Cibola," *Eighth Annual Report, Bureau of Ethnology, 1886–1887*, pp. 1–228. Washington, 1891.

MOONEY, JAMES. "Quivira and the Wichitas," *Harpers Magazine*, June, 1899, pp. 126–136.

MORGAN, LEWIS HENRY. "The Seven Cities of Cibola," *North American Review*, CVIII (April, 1869), 457–498.

*MOTA PADILLA, MATÍAS DE LA. *Historia de la conquista de la provincia de Nueva-Galicia, escrita en 1742. Boletín de la Sociedad Mexicana de Geografía y Estadística*, Mexico, 1870. Issued separately with "Noticias Biográficas" by JOAQUIN GARCÍA ICAZBALCETA, Mexico, March 12, 1872. For Coronado expedition, see annotated translation in DAY, "Mota Padilla."

MOTOLINIA, TORIBIO DE BENAVENTE, O. *Memoriales* (ed. by LUIS GARCÍA PIMENTEL). Mexico, 1903.

————. "Historia de los indios de la Nueva España." *In Colección España*, LIII, 297–574; also in GARCÍA ICAZBALCETA, *Colección*, I, 1–249.

NAVARRETE, MARTÍN FERNÁNDEZ (ed.). *See Colección España.*

NÚÑEZ, ALVAR. *See* CABEZA DE VACA.

*OBREGÓN, BALTAZAR DE. *Historia de los descubrimientos antiguos y modernos de la Nueva España* (ed. by MARIANO CUEVAS). Mexico, 1924 (written in 1584). English trans. by G. P. HAMMOND and AGAPITO REY under title of *Obregon's History of Sixteenth-Century Exploration in Western America* (Los Angeles, 1928).

"Ordenanzas de su Majestad para los nuevos descubrimientos, con-
quistas y pacificaciones [July 13, 1573]." *In* PACHECO, XVI, 142–187.

*OROZCO Y BERRA, MANUEL (ed.). *Actos de cabildo del ayuntamiento
de Mexico.* Mexico, 1859.

OVIEDO Y VALDÉS, GONZALO FERNÁNDEZ DE. *La historia general de las
Indias.* Seville, 1535; reprinted, Salamanca, 1547, and Madrid, 1851–
1855 (last is definitive edition).

PACHECO, JOAQUÍN F., CÁRDENAS, FRANCISCO DE, and MENDOZA, LUIS
TORRES DE (eds.). *Colección de documentos inéditos relativos al
descubrimiento, conquista, y colonización de las posesiones españolas en América y Oceanía* ... 42 vols. (index for Vols. I–XXXII in
Vol. XXXIII). Madrid, 1864–1884. Cited as PACHECO.

PASO Y TRONCOSO, FRANCISCO DEL. *See* TEJADA, "Carta al rey del licenciado Tejada."

PERALTA. *See* SUÁREZ DE PERALTA.

"Proceso del Marqués del Valle y Nuño de Guzmán y los adelantados Soto y Alvarado, sobre el descubrimiento de la tierra nueva,
en Madrid, 3 marzo, 1540; 10 junio, 1541." *In* PACHECO, XV,
300–408.

PURCHAS, SAMUEL. *Purchas his pilgrimage, or relations of the world
and the religions observed and places discouered* ... Many editions. Part 2, Book 8, chap. 3, deals with Coronado.

RAMUSIO, GIOVANNI BATTISTA. *Terzo volume delle navigationi et viaggi.*
Pp. 310–370. Venice, 1556. Various later editions, of which the most
complete is that of 1606 in 3 vols.

*"Relación del suceso de la jornada que Francisco Vazquez hizo en el
descubrimiento de Cibola, año de 1531 [1541]." *In* PACHECO, XIV,
318–329; also SMITH, *Colección,* pp. 147–154. English trans. in WIN-
SHIP, pp. 572–579.

*"Relación postrera de Sívola." *In* WINSHIP, with English trans., pp.
566–571.

REMÓN, ALONSO. *Vida y muerte del siervo de Dios Don Fernando de
Córdova y Bocanegra.* Madrid, 1617.

"Requerimiento que se hizo a los indios de Nueva Galicia." *In*
PACHECO, III, 369–377.

RICHEY, W. E. "Early Spanish Explorations and Indian Implements
in Kansas," *Transactions of Kansas State Historical Society,* VIII
(1903–1904), 152–168.

———. "The Real Quivira," *ibid.,* VI (1896–1900), 477–485.

ROBERTSON, JAMES A. (trans.). *True Relation of the Hardships Suffered by Governor Hernando de Soto ... by a Gentleman of Elvas.
Publications of the Florida State Historical Society,* No. 22, 2 vols.,
1932–1933.

Rudo ensayo. See SMITH.

RUIZ, ANTONIO. "'Testimony from Historia del Archivo General de México, vol. 316". *In* SAUER, *Road to Cíbola*, p. 55.

SAUER, CARL. *Aboriginal Population of Northwestern Mexico. Ibero-Americana*, No. 10. Berkeley, Calif., 1935.

———. "Communication," *Hispanic American Historical Review*, XVII (February, 1937), 148–150.

———. "Discovery of New Mexico Reconsidered," *New Mexico Historical Review*, XII (July, 1937), 270–287.

———. *The Distribution of Aboriginal Tribes and Languages in Northwestern Mexico. Ibero-Americana*, No. 5. Berkeley, Calif., 1934.

———. *The Road to Cíbola. Ibid.*, No. 3. Berkeley, Calif., 1932.

SAUER, CARL, and BRAND, DONALD. *Aztatlán. Ibero-Americana*, No. 1. Berkeley, Calif., 1932.

SEDGWICK, MRS. WM. T. *Acoma, the Sky City*. Cambridge, Mass., 1926.

"Segunda relación anónima de la jornada de Nuño de Guzmán." *In* GARCÍA ICAZBALCETA, *Colección*, II, 296–306.

SHEA, JOHN GILMARY. "Ancient Florida." *In* WINSOR, II, 231–298.

SIMPSON, JAMES HERVEY. "Coronado's March in Search of the 'Seven Cities of Cibola', and Discussion of Their Probable Location," *Report of Smithsonian Institution for 1869*, pp. 309–340.

SMITH, (THOMAS) BUCKINGHAM. *Colección de varios documentos para la historia de la Florida y tierras adyacentes*, Vol. I (1516–1794). London (Madrid), 1857. Only one vol. published. Cited as SMITH, *Colección*.

——— (trans.). *Narrative of the Expedition of Hernando de Soto, by the Gentleman of Elvas. In* HODGE AND LEWIS, pp. 133–272.

——— (trans.). *Narrative of Alvar Núñez Cabeza de Vaca*. Washington, 1851; New York, 1871. Reprinted in HODGE AND LEWIS, pp. 12–126.

——— (ed.). *Rudo ensayo, tentativa de una prebencional descripción geográphica de la provincia de Sonora ... compilada así de noticias adquiridas por el colector en sus viajes por casi toda ella, como suministradas por los padres misioneros y practicos de la tierra*. San Augustín de la Florida, 1863 (written in 1761–1762). English trans. by EUSEBIO GUITÉRAS, *Records of the American Catholic Historical Society* (Philadelphia, June, 1894).

SOTO, HERNANDO DE. "Asiento y capitulación hechos por el capitán Hernando de Soto con el emperador Carlos V para la conquista y población de la provincia de la Florida, y encomienda de la gobernación de la isla de Cuba, Valladolid, 20 abril, 1537." *In* PACHECO, XV, 354–363; also in SMITH, *Colección*, pp. 140–146.

Soto, Hernando de. *Narrative of the Expedition of Hernando de Soto, by the Gentleman of Elvas.* See Smith; also Robertson.

Stevens, Captain John (trans.). *See* Herrera.

Stevenson, (Mrs.) M. C. "The Sia," *Eleventh Annual Report, Bureau of Ethnology, 1889–1890,* pp. 9–157. Washington, 1894.

———. "The Zuñi Indians, Their Mythology, Esoteric Fraternities and Ceremonies," *Twenty-third Annual Report, Bureau of Ethnology, 1901–1902,* pp. 1–608. Washington, 1904.

Suárez de Peralta, Joan. *Tratado del descubrimiento de las Yndias y su conquista, y los ritos ... de los yndios; y de los virreyes y gobernadores ... y del prinçipio que tuvo Françisco Draque para ser declarado enemigo* (ed. by Justo Zaragoza). Madrid, 1878 (written in last third of sixteenth century).

"Sumario de las Yndias tocante a la geografía." *In* Pacheco, XV, 461.

Taylor, Paul S. "Spanish Seamen in the New World during the Colonial Period," *Hispanic American Historical Review,* V (November, 1922), 631–661.

*Tejada, Lorenzo de. "Carta al rey del licenciado Tejada oidor de la Audiencia de México haciendo relación de todo lo que había proveído en la visita hecha a la Nueva Galicia, para tomar residencia al gobernador Francisco Vázquez Coronado, y a los capitanes, oficiales y justicias de dicha provincia.—De México, a 11 de marzo de 1545." *In Epistolario de Nueva España,* IV, 183–190. Mexico City, 1939. Ed. by Francisco del Paso y Troncoso.

*———. "Residencia, etc." *See* Coronado.

Tello, Antonio. "Fragmentos de una historia de la Nueva Galicia." *In* García Icazbalceta, *Colección,* II, 343–438.

———. *Libro segundo de la crónica miscelanea, en que se trata de la conquista espiritual y temporal de la santa provincia de Xalisco.* Guadalajara, 1891 (written in 1653).

Ternaux-Compans, Henri. *Voyages, relations et mémoires originaux pour servir à l'histoire de la découverte de l'Amérique publiés pour la première fois, en français.* 20 vols. Paris, 1837–1841. Vol. IX contains the Coronado documents. Cited as Ternaux.

"Testimonio dado en Mexico sobre el descubrimiento de doscientas leguas adelante de las minas de Santa Bárbola, gobernación de Diego de Ibarra." *In* Pacheco, XV, 80–150.

Thomas, A. B. *After Coronado: Spanish Exploration Northeast of New Mexico, 1696–1727.* Norman, Okla., 1935.

Thomas, C., and Swanton, J. R. *Indian Languages of Mexico and Central America. Bulletin of Bureau of Ethnology,* No. 44. Washington, 1911.

Bibliography

TORQUEMADA, JUAN DE. *Los veynte i vn libros rituales y monarchia yndiana, con el origen y guerras de los Yndios Occidentales. Compvesto por Fray Ivan de Torquemada, ministro prouincial de la orden de S. Françisco en Mexico, en la Nueba España.* Seville, 1615; reprinted by Barcia, Madrid, 3 vols., 1723 (definitive edition). Book 5, chap. 2, has a short account of Coronado and Alarcón.

*"Traslado de las nuevas y noticias que dieron sobre el descobrimiento de una cibdad, que llamaron de Cibola, situada en la tierra nueva, año de 1531 [1541]." *In* PACHECO, XIX, 529–532. English trans. in WINSHIP, pp. 564–565.

TWITCHELL, RALPH E. *Leading Facts of New Mexican History.* 2 vols. Cedar Rapids, Iowa, 1911.

ULLOA, FRANCISCO DE. "A relation of the discouery, which in the name of God the fleete of the right noble Fernando Cortez Marques of the Valley, made with three ships . . . of which fleet was captaine the right worshipfull knight Francis de Vlloa borne in the citie of Merida." *In* HAKLUYT, III, 397–424 (ed. 1600). Trans. from RAMUSIO, III, 339–354 (ed. 1556).

———. "Relación del armada, etc." *See* ALARCÓN.

VEDIA, ENRIQUE DE (ed.). *Historiadores primitivos de Indias.* 2 vols. (Vols. XXII and XXVI of *Biblioteca de Autores Españoles*). Madrid, 1852, 1862.

VELASCO, JUAN. *Histoire de royaume de Quito. In* TERNAUX, Vols. XVIII and XIX.

VETANCURT, AUGUSTÍN DE. *Menologio francescano de los varones más señalados.* Mexico, 1871.

———. *Teatro mexicano: descripción breve de los sucesos exemplares, históricos, políticos, militares, y religiosos del nuevo mundo.* Mexico, 1698 (2 vols.); Mexico, 1870–1871 (4 vols.).

VILLAGRÁ, GASPAR PÉREZ DE. *Historia de la Nueva México.* Alcala, 1610. Facsimile edition with prose trans. by GILBERTO ESPINOSA and notes by F. W. HODGE. Quivira Society, Los Angeles, 1933. Cantos 3 and 4 deal with Coronado.

WAGNER, HENRY R. *Cartography of the Northwest Coast of America to the Year 1800.* Berkeley, Calif., 1938.

———. "Fray Marcos de Niza," *New Mexico Historical Review,* IX (April, 1934), 184–227.

———. "A Fray Marcos de Niza Note," *ibid.,* IX (July, 1934), 336–337.

———. *The Spanish Southwest, 1542–1794: An Annotated Bibliography.* 2 vols. *Quivira Society Publications,* No. 7. Albuquerque, N.M., 1937.

———. *Spanish Voyages to the Northwest Coast of America.* San Francisco, 1929.

WHIPPLE, LIEUTENANT A. W., and IVES, LIEUTENANT J. C. *Report of Explorations for a Railway Route*. Senate Ex. Doc. No. 78, 33d Congress, 2d Session. Washington, 1856.

WINSHIP, GEORGE PARKER. "The Coronado Expedition, 1540–1542," *Fourteenth Annual Report, Bureau of Ethnology, 1892–1893*, Part I, pp. 329–613. Washington, 1896. Cited as WINSHIP.

———. *The Journey of Coronado*. Trail Makers Series, New York, 1904.

——— (trans.). *The Journey of Francisco Vazquez de Coronado, 1540–1542*. Limited edition containing translations of Castañeda and other chronicles, with introduction and notes by F. W. HODGE. San Francisco, 1932.

———. "Why Coronado Went to New Mexico in 1540," *Annual Report of the American Historical Association, 1894*. Washington, 1895.

WINSOR, JUSTIN (ed.). *Narrative and Critical History of America*. 8 vols. Boston and New York, 1889.

ZUMÁRRAGA, JUAN DE. "Letter of April 4, 1537," to an unknown correspondent in Spain. *In* CUEVAS, p. 83.

———. "Letter of April 17, 1540." *In* CUEVAS, p. 103.

Index

Index 405

Index

Index

Index

416 Index

Discoveries of the

CORONADO EXPEDITION

1540–1542

- – – – – – Route of army led by Francisco Vásquez Coronado

- ●–●–●–● Route of Melchor Díaz, 1540

- +++++ Routes of Pedro de Tovar to Tusayán and García López de Cárdenas to the Grand Canyon, 1540

- ■–■–·–■ Route of fleet of Hernando Alarcón, 1540

- **I, II, III** Successive sites of Villa de San Gerónimo on the Río Sonora

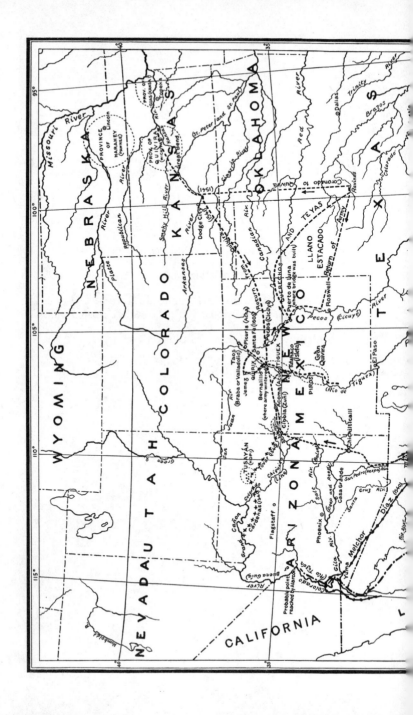

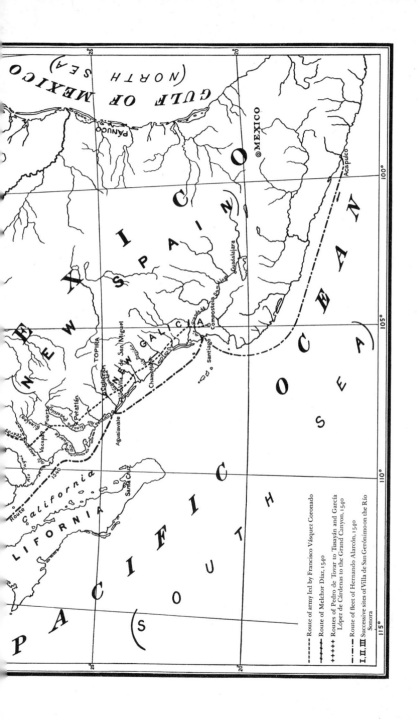

Legend:

- - - - - Route of army led by Francisco Vásquez Coronado
—•—•— Route of Melchor Díaz, 1540
+ + + + + Routes of Pedro de Tóvar to Tusayán and García López de Cárdenas to the Grand Canyon, 1540
—••—••— Route of fleet of Hernando Alarcón, 1540
I, II, III Successive sites of Villa de San Gerónimo on the Río Sonora